# Unknowing Fanaticism

## Reformation Literatures
## of Self-Annihilation

Ross Lerner

FORDHAM UNIVERSITY PRESS

*New York 2019*

Fordham University Press gratefully acknowledges financial assistance and support provided for the publication of this book by the Louis and Hermione Brown Humanities Support Fund, Occidental College.

Fordham University Press has no responsibility for the persistence or accuracy of URLs for external or third-party Internet websites referred to in this publication and does not guarantee that any content on such websites is, or will remain, accurate or appropriate.

Fordham University Press also publishes its books in a variety of electronic formats. Some content that appears in print may not be available in electronic books.

Visit us online at www.fordhampress.com.

Library of Congress Cataloging-in-Publication Data available online at https://catalog.loc.gov.

Printed in the United States of America

21  20  19    5  4  3  2  1
First edition

# CONTENTS

# Receiving Divine Action:
# Fanaticism and Form in the Reformation

Still,
I've stood, a soldier listening for the word,
Attack, a prophet praying any ember be spoken
Through me in this desert full of fugitives.
Now, I have a voice. Entered, I am lit.

—JERICHO BROWN, "The Burning Bush"

If acts of religious fanaticism suggest a certain immediacy, supposedly having a direct origin in God's will, they nonetheless circulate mediately, often as story or song. I begin with one such story, paraphrased from verse. Imagine a holy warrior who undertakes a spectacular act of religious violence, what turns out to be a suicide mission in an apocalyptic confrontation. Whether he knew in advance that the battle would cost him his life is unclear. Yet in order to underwrite his mission for holiness and lay the groundwork for a new sacred nation, this soldier of God tries and fails to destroy his enemy, dying twice in his attempt. Miraculously, he is resurrected after each death. Killed but made new by divine force, he destroys his enemy in the end.

Returning from his mission, this resurrected and triumphant warrior meets another fighter for truth and his teacher, both of whom are beginning a related mission. The teacher of the second warrior recounts how the suicide attacker's sacrificial violence has made him famous throughout the cosmos. You have achieved something absolutely glorious, the instructor says. The warrior retorts: I did not do anything. The achievement and the glory are not mine—both are God's alone. God made me into an empty organ of his might and acted through me, and that is the only reason our enemy was destroyed. Annihilated, I became an instrument for God's divine violence.

This might sound like a parable taught at what in mainstream Western media are often called terrorist training camps, far afield from the canon of European Renaissance literature. In fact, this story is my simplified description of an episode from Edmund Spenser's *The Faerie Queene* (1590, 1596), one that unfolds across the eleventh canto of the poem's first book and the beginning of its second book. Redcrosse, the knight of holiness, is the one who dies twice and is miraculously reborn in an apocalyptic battle with a dragon, living on as Saint George, patron saint of England. It is the Palmer, guide to Guyon, the knight of temperance, who has to deal with Redcrosse's claim to divine possession. The Palmer struggles to know what to do with Redcrosse's correction, which suggests that even the knight of holiness could not achieve victory as a willing agent. Readers struggle with this moment, too, and typically sidestep its refusal to resolve which version of history the poem authorizes: the Palmer's narrative of heroic achievement and willful action or Redcrosse's chronicle of self-annihilation and divine instrumentality. How do we know whether Redcrosse became what he calls "the organ of [God's] might" (2.1.33)?[1] How can Redcrosse narrate his transformation to us if he claims to have been a passive vessel at the moment the dragon was defeated? How can Spenser compose his allegorical poem in such a way that makes Redcrosse's self-annihilating violence into a didactic lesson about holiness and the sacred foundations of the English nation?

This book will attend to the poetic and political problems that fanaticism inspires, with a particular emphasis on how moments such as this one—in which poems meditate on the vexed relationship between divine violence and human agency—participate in or resist Reformation polemics about religious fanaticism. In order to frame this book's larger question about the relationship between fanaticism and form, Chapter 1 will offer an extended analysis of the disagreement about Redcrosse's status as an organ in *The Faerie Queene* and the tremors it sends through the poem's larger allegorical design. Though Spenser's poem is uniquely inclined to present scenes in which characters find themselves unable to interpret a problem that the poem itself created, this scene is not exceptional. Depictions of religious violence and uncertain witness such as this one proliferate in Renaissance poetry, but we have only developed confused ideas about the difficulty such scenes pose to verse-making and reading, not to mention to politics and ethics.

This is in part because dominant perceptions of religious fanaticism today tend to be as polemical and reductive as they were in the early modern period. We live in a world in which Reformation condemnations of fanaticism, usually meant to justify state violence, live on in systemic strategies of racialized neocolonial brutality that rely on terms such as "terrorist" and "fundamentalist" to vindicate war, indefinite detention, torture, murder, dispossession, and economic immiseration—in short, to make many lives, especially in the so-called Greater Middle East, "ungrievable."[2] Scholarship has not been innocent in this regard. Contemporary scholars within and beyond literary studies tend to share with early modern philosophers and theologians a reductive sense of fanaticism as the incarnation of religion devoid of reason, the antitype of modernity.[3] Influenced by a long history of polemics against fanaticism, these scholars typically seek to disenchant or to condemn the fanatics' claims that they do God's will or that God works through them, whether in fictional or nonfictional accounts of fanatical violence. Yet doing so misreads the complex ways in which early modern religious forms interacted with and shaped the emergence of modernity. Rejecting the simplified binary of fanatical religion and rational politics, this book demonstrates that fanaticism was integral to how modern politics and poetics developed. Poets such as Edmund Spenser, John Donne, and John Milton recognized in fanatics' claims to divine agency an epistemological and representational crisis—an incapacity to know and depict the true origins of sacred violence. Yet this crisis was a productive one. It led these writers to experiment with poetic techniques that would allow them to address fanaticism's tendency to unsettle the boundaries between human will and divine agency and between individual and collective bodies.

Because "fanaticism" is a mobile term that has been produced through a history of polemic, it is difficult to use it with precision, both in the Reformation and today. Much of this Introduction attempts to offer a historically textured description of fanaticism as the concept took shape in the Reformation, but an initial definition may be useful. Throughout the Reformation, "fanaticism" evoked the idea of individuals who, through a process of mystical self-annihilation, became vessels filled with God's violent action, negating "the distinction," to recall Ralph Cudworth's phrase, "betwixt God and the creature."[4] (From Luther's early fascination with negative theology to George Herbert's poetic meditations on what Stanley Fish calls "letting go" of self, there are theologies and literatures of self-annihilation that have no direct relationship to violence in the world; these are not the focus of this book.)[5] Several figures will emerge over the course of this book to give form to fanaticism's unmaking, but Spenser's figure remains especially compelling: fanatics are "organ[s]" of divine might who undergo a self-loss so total that they can become purely passive instruments of God. Renaissance English readers would have regularly come across references to nonmusical organs; the figure gained popularity throughout the late sixteenth and seventeenth centuries in England, especially in Calvinist writings. Calvin himself referred to prophets as "organs" (*organa*, *organes*) of the Spirit,[6] and related terms (such as versions of the words "instrument" and "vessel") can be found throughout his work. A look ahead to John Owen, the seventeenth-century English Calvinist, helps underscore the significance of the organ in theological writing of the long Reformation period, since he articulates it with particular clarity. Owen claims that prophets do not work by way of "any Skill or Ability residing in them, but they were meerly *Organs* of the Holy Ghost which he moved at his Pleasure."[7]

The Renaissance English poets who focus most on fanaticism—Spenser, Donne, and Milton—almost always represented fanatics as men.[8] For this reason I use "he" to refer to the fanatic in the singular. There has been much excellent work done on women and religious ecstasy, prophecy, and martyrdom in sixteenth- and seventeenth-century Europe, if not on fanaticism as defined by self-annihilation and violence.[9] I have avoided explaining why Reformation fanatics tend to be represented as men with recourse to claims about male fantasies of passivity associated with femininity (though this informs my analyses, especially of Milton's representation of Samson), since such claims would bypass the central epistemological and aesthetic dilemma on which I am focused by offering a psychic explanation of a phenomenon that is claimed to induce the emptying of individuals' psyches.[10]

In trying to understand how fanaticism involved something like an organ of divine might, clarifying its difference from what later came to be referred to as enthusiasm is instructive. (Such instruction has philological limitations, though: "fanaticism" and "enthusiasm" were regularly used as synonyms in the sixteenth and seventeenth centuries.) In an extremely subtle study, Jordy Rosenberg defines eighteenth-century enthusiasm "as the passionate experience of unmediated communion with God, and as the capacity of individual subjects to know and understand divine order."[11] Fanaticism departs from this definition by calling into question almost all of its key terms. Whether or not such a state of divine inspiration is possible or desirable, whether it can be known by the organs or by those who witness their actions, whether what fanatics experience (or fail to experience) or achieve (or fail to achieve) is representable and under-standable, whether organs are still individual subjects or deindividualized members of a larger assemblage, whether experience and mediation or their absence apply to persons who have been annihilated in order to be-come holy instruments: these are questions that the poems I analyze in this book think about with great complexity and no small amount of am-bivalence. Central to my argument is the overarching claim that this po-etic thinking emerges not only in the works' conflicted representations of fanatical individuals and communities but also immanently at the level of form (a term I define at some length later).

Over the course of this book, I interlace two entangled approaches to fanaticism in the long Reformation: the targeting of it as an extreme po-litical threat and the engagement with it as a deep epistemological and poetic problem. In the first, thinkers as disparate as Martin Luther and Thomas Hobbes (central to this Introduction and Chapter 3, respectively) positioned themselves against fanaticism to pathologize rebellion and abet theological and political control. In the second, which arose alongside and often in response to the first, poets investigated the link between fanatical self-annihilation—the process by which one could become a vessel for di-vine violence—and the practices of writing poetry. Considering these di-verse thinkers together, we see that religious fanaticism was central to the evolving relationships between religion, state, and poetic form during the Reformation.

The interaction between these two uses of fanaticism—as a political foil and as a tool for asking fundamental questions about agency and authority—shaped its meanings. The poets of fanaticism voiced the epistemological question underlying the demonization of fanatics: how can one know if a fanatical act is undertaken with human or divine will? Reactive dismissals of fanaticism as madness or demagoguery proliferated across theology, philosophy, and politics. Even thinkers such as René Descartes who were critical of fanaticism not primarily because it threatened state sovereignty but because they worried that it was ultimately rooted in hatred (of self and others) tended to view the zeal associated with fanaticism as a deluded presumption of intimacy with God.[12] Yet Spenser, Donne, and Milton remained haunted by the epistemological mystery of individuals who an-nihilate themselves to become instruments of divine violence. This book contends that fanaticism's violence became inseparable from intractable questions of modernity: skepticism (how we can know anything about the passions and actions of others and ourselves), causation (how we can know whether and how divine agency functions within the world), and power (how we can know what shapes who we are and how we behave). These were questions that made possible some of the most creative experiments with verse in the late sixteenth and seventeenth centuries.

Because scholars have too often leaned on narratives of secularization to explain European culture's supposed transition from a benightedly religious Middle Ages to the increasingly disenchanted early modern period, fanaticism has been relegated to a fringe phenomenon in early modern scholarship. Even scholars resistant to narratives of secularism, who emphasize the codevelopment of religious and secular forms of life in early modern Europe, have trouble accounting for the forces of self-annihilation and divine immanence that fanaticism seems to summon.[13] With important exceptions, scholarship has tended to take dismissive, muddled stances toward fanaticism, interpreting it as the embodiment of unreason or a symptom of a personal or social pathology.[14] Yet by aligning fanaticism with irrational conviction, we elide the subtler phenomenon of self-loss and divine inspiration at its heart. The fanatics' claims that God works through them, if they are not entirely dismissed as mad or demagogic, are taken as the object of study within a historiographical idiom that, as Dipesh Chakrabarty has shown, depends upon the disenchantment of proclamations of divine agency in the world.[15] By overlooking fanaticism's role as a prime mover for politics and poetics in the period and by focusing on the dangers religious violence poses to the legitimacy of states while effacing the violence and domination that are required to make and maintain those states, scholars of early modernity miss the crucial epistemological, ethical, and aesthetic problems that fanaticism raises. In this respect, my work is influenced by important interventions in postcolonial studies, such as the work of Ranajit Guha, which have disputed precisely this tendency to view religious violence—particularly the religious violence of peasants—in isolation from state and colonial orders of domination and discipline.[16] Refusing to discount the fanatics' claims to be vessels of divine violence and resisting teleological narratives that posit the overcoming of past religious modes, this book attends to the alternative lifeworlds, the forgotten early modernities, that made fanaticism such an urgent possibility and problem.

Fanaticism took the problem of election—how to know if anyone, oneself included, was chosen by God—and focused it intensely on a burning moment of inspired, self-immolating violence. But this intense focus could become diffuse, too, because poetic and political accounts of fanaticism struggled not only with its singularity but also its multiplicity, the capacity for divine inspiration to spread contagiously and give shape to paradoxi-

cally self-annihilating collectivities. While the modern state was con-
solidating itself in opposition to threats to its legitimacy such as religious
fanaticism in the early modern period, the poets I examine tarried with
the possibility that fanatical bodies might trouble and transform how
their poems know, represent, and teach. Spenser, Donne, and Milton
were thus forced to renovate the poetic forms they inherited, asking,
respectively, how an allegory, a sonnet, or a tragedy could represent—or
fail to represent—fanaticism's puzzle of self-loss and inspiration, singular
election and communal rebellion. Arguing that many technical innovations in poetry were mediated by the historical and cognitive problems
that religious fanaticism provoked, this book therefore focuses on how
Spenserian allegory formally addresses problems of divine possession and
our ability to recognize it as it is manifested in individual organs and collective swarms, how a Donne sonnet becomes a unique space for testing
the limits of seemingly exemplary violent self-annihilation, and how Miltonic tragedy confronts us with what it means to bear witness to acts of
religious martyrdom and mass violence. Fanaticism—as both context
and concept—transforms our understanding of how the most canonical
Renaissance authors represented divinely inspired action and passion in
poetic forms and struggled with their own skepticism about a religious
phenomenon that threatened both sovereignty and the subjects it shaped.

This book seeks to expose how fanaticism has been framed—in more
than one of that term's senses. Fanaticism is the frame through which I
analyze a series of Reformation problems surrounding religion and violence, singularity and community, epistemology and aesthetics, statehood
and domination. But I also mean "frame" in the sense of "being set up." The
figure of the fanatic comes to take the blame, to be criminalized, for a series of problems that the birth of the early modern state tried to suppress
or scapegoat. If there is something ultimately unknowable or illegible about
fanatics, how can states founded on and sustained by what Max Weber
refers to as "legitimations of domination" contain the threat that there
are forces that will forever surpass, interrupt, or dispute its legitimacy and
its violence?[17] Walter Benjamin's meditations on divine violence in "Zur
Kritik der Gewalt" ("Critique of Violence") bear on this question directly.
How does the violence meant to institute and preserve law—to bind citizens to law—work to maintain itself in the face of divine violence that
destroys law and unbinds citizens from the structures that make them
legible and obedient?[18] Perhaps the anarchic and unknowable features of
divine violence explain why Thomas Hobbes, the greatest theorist of
state sovereignty and obedience, and the focus of Chapter 3, could ask

8 *Introduction: Receiving Divine Action*

rhetorically in the wake of the English Civil War, "What can be more pernicious to peace, than the revelations that were by these *fanatics* pretended?"[19] In an effort to secure the state's authority over life and death, to systematize the state's claim to have "the monopoly of legitimate physical violence,"[20] thinkers from Luther to Hobbes invented the fanatic not as a possible vessel of divine violence but as a madman or demagogue, a "stock character" of asocial antimodernity who is impervious to reason and determined to use his own deluded or deluding claims to God-given power as an instrument for, at best, self-aggrandizement or, at worst, the obliteration of the distinction between the City of God and the City of Man.[21]

An example will render concrete the two entangled positions this book studies: fanaticism as a frame through which to construe and control a particular kind of religious phenomenon with extreme political consequences, on the one hand, and fanaticism as a limit-experience drawing into the open vexed epistemological and ethical questions that poets explore through the form and content of verse.[22] Contrast an exemplary sentence from John Locke's 1689 philosophical critique of enthusiasm in *An Essay Concerning Human Understanding*—"God when he makes the Prophet does not unmake the Man"[23]—with two lines from John Donne's 1633 poetic exploration of zeal in one of his *Holy Sonnets*, "Batter my hart":

> That I may rise, and stand, orethrow me; and bend
> Your force to breake, blow, burne, and make me new.[24]

One asserts the absence and, implicitly, the impossibility of divine self-emptying; the other implies not only its possibility but its urgent necessity.

Locke's sentence describes prophecy's relation to religious enthusiasm, and it cordons off the event of being made into a prophet from the unmaking of a person.[25] God decidedly *makes* a prophet, one who receives and communicates divine will, and this is opposed to *unmaking* (transforming through self-annihilation) a person. Transformed by divine power, a prophet remains a person with the faculty to reason and thus to evaluate whether the voice that moves through him is divinely authenticated. In Locke's text, anyone who claims to have been emptied of self in the event of becoming a prophet is merely an enthusiast, one who has convinced himself or others of divine revelation or compulsion but who is in fact a madman or a charlatan—a victim or a perpetrator of "ungrounded Fancies."[26] One can only come to know that one has experienced God's internal testimony by reason: "But if they know it [divine Light] to be a Truth, they must know it to be so either by its own self-evidence to natural Reason; or by the rational Proofs that make it out to be so."[27] Locke suggests that anyone who alleges such self-unmaking should be questioned, disciplined, and controlled. And he participated in a larger Restoration skepticism toward enthusiasm. As Sharon Achinstein has shown, "the enemies of enthusiasm claimed that this mode of immediate compulsion was dangerous not only because of its rhetorical power . . . but also, and more importantly, because those who used it appeared to make unverifiable, and unstoppable, claims for their own private authority."[28] Locke wants to ensure that enthusiasts cannot claim that their actions are products of divine "possession,"[29] of "the Hand of GOD moving them from within."[30] For the philosopher who defines consciousness as "the perception of what passes in a Man's own mind,"[31] and who emphasizes the proprietary ownership of whatever passes through the mind, it is impossible for God's light or hand to be present in—let alone overtake and compel—a person without that person being able to evaluate the origin of the attendant perception with reason. Locke's entire theory of personal identity is grounded on the idea of consciousness as self-ownership,[32] a model in which divine revelation could never usurp reason's authority. For Locke, "*Reason* is natural *Revelation*," and reason is impossible without consciousness. Revelation could never unmake the man.[33]

Locke's double negation ("does not unmake the Man") could not be further from the proposal poetically tested in "Batter my hart": the indwelling of God requires the unmaking of self; God must "orethrow me" to "make me new." To be made "new," to "stand" as a vessel of divine will, the sinful self must be annihilated. Another poem from Donne's *Holy Sonnets* elaborates explicitly—and considers formally—this kind of zealous self-annihilation:

> I ame a litle World, made cunningly
>> Of Elements and an Angelique Spright,
>> But blacke Sin hath betrayd to endles night
> My Worlds both parts, and Oh both parts must dy.
> You, which beyond that heauen, which was most high
>> Haue found new Sphears, and of new Lands can wright
>> Powre new Seas in myne eyes, that so I might
> Drowne my World, with my weeping ernestly.
> Or washe it: if it must be drown'd no more:
>> But Oh it must be burn'd; alas the fyer

Of Lust and Envy haue burnt it heretofore
  And made it fouler; Let those flames retyre,
And burne me O God with a fiery Zeale
Of thee,' and thy house, which doth in eating heale.

Typically read as a prayer for grace, this sonnet depicts the speaker demanding that divine fire unmake the self and reconstitute it as an instrument of zeal. Throughout the poem, the speaker claims that the self as
"World," both its elements and its "Angelique Spright, . . . must dy." The
method of dying is twofold: the self must be drowned, in a witty, techno-
logically enhanced echo of the Genesis flood narrative, in order to be
washed clean, and if drowning does not work, then it must be burned.
Personal apocalypse is key to the capacity for "healing." What takes the
place of the sin-betrayed self? "A fiery Zeale / Of thee": the speaker asks to
be burned with a zeal *for* God that is also *of* God, to have the difference
between God and self overcome. Zeal burns and unmakes the self so that it
can be healed—made new in and as God's presence. The poem articulates
a state, or at least a desire for the achievement of such a state, in which zeal
itself at once cannibalizes and constitutes the being that remains after the
self has been annihilated. Yet the poem's refusal to disclose whether such
a zealous life can be attained or what exactly it would look like, even as it
suggests that only God's consuming presence will allow it to appear, is part
of what makes it so formally innovative. This sonnet is not only the representation or expression of an attitude toward the divine but is itself a devotional act, a practical enactment of supplication that at once unfolds and
forestalls what it seeks: the immolation of the sinful self that enables the
poem to be written.[34] The question of whether the willful activity of com-
posing a poem can call forth such zeal or whether the poem itself prevents
the arrival of zeal is one that the poem poses thematically but also formally. There is a tension, then, between the poem's consideration of zeal as
an experience that the activity of writing in some manner can *cause* and
zeal as an experience of passive possession. I discuss the problem of fanaticism and form in Donne's *Holy Sonnets* at greater length in Chapter 2, but
for now attending to one element of the problem that zeal poses at the level
of form will demonstrate how Donne experiments with technique in order
to think through the epistemological challenge of fanaticism.

    The poem begins with the first quatrain's description of the speaker's
current state: betrayed and corrupted by sin. The sonnet then reveals its
own struggle to represent the solution to this betrayal. It wanders through
the extravagant but inadequate conceit of self-drowning in the second

quatrain (a conceit that has more sustained efficacy elsewhere in Donne's poetry) before it turns to the "fiery Zeale," which is counterpoised to "the fyer / Of Lust and Envy," that might destroy the self in the third quatrain. A problem, followed by two possible solutions. Structurally, Donne's sonnet thus delays the invocation of self-annihilation by God's fire—indeed, the volta takes place a line after the end of the octave, in line 10—restraining our arrival at a figure or solution that, insofar as it posits the fiery consumption of the speaker, would spell the end of the poet's voice, his capacity to perform willfully any devotional act, including the crafting of a poem. The philosopher Giorgio Agamben's comment on poetic endings may help to illuminate Donne's deferral: Agamben draws an analogy between poems and the *katechon* (delayer or restrainer) in Paul's Second Epistle to the Thessalonians (2:7). The *katechon* "slows and delays the advent of the Messiah," and similarly, the poem delays its own completion, since its end "would destroy the poetic machine by hurling it into silence."[35] Poems try to keep themselves ongoing. Something similar but more formally specific—because structurally enacted—happens in Donne's sonnet, which delays the resolution of the theological problems that it poses. The sonnet is thus a conflicted artifact, an act of devotion that, as poem, resists through its organization of lines the theological resolution that might make its composition irrelevant. The poem is not doctrine; the sonnet only allows us to imagine what might emerge beyond its closing couplet, what kind of being would exist after this zeal immolates the self. And indeed, I claim in Chapter 2 that one of Donne's greatest innovations in the *Holy Sonnets* is to worry over poetry's potentially constitutive incapacity, at once productive and disabling, to enact the self-annihilation required for zeal and martyrdom alike. The performance of inability in poetic form makes the *Holy Sonnets* uniquely paradoxical acts of devotion, exercises in failure and impossible action, insistent on their capacity for wondrous devotional articulation and yet convinced of their incapacity even to begin the acts they set out to perform: "Yet grace, if thou repent thou canst not lacke. / But who shall giue thee that grace to begin?"[36] Yet the figure of the fanatic—of a self emptied of self and paradoxically defined by its own unmaking, driven by a fiery zeal that is not its own but God's—emerges in the concluding couplet of "I ame a litle World" as a possibility toward which Donne gestures.[37] Zeal posited but postponed beyond the end of the poem: this is how the sonnet, through its structuring of lines and images, thinks about whether it can play any role in creating the condition for zealous inhabitation.

The fundamental divide between Locke and Donne on the topic of annihilatory unmaking, which cannot be explained entirely with reference to their historical, generic, or methodological differences, brings into focus a number of problems that are central to this book. On the one hand, Locke's prophet, held together through the double negative of "not unmade," always maintains the capacity to reason about his experience of the divine word and to present a reasoned account to the public. Reason evaluates any internal sense in order to determine and authenticate whether it is of divine origin. Failure to use reason to examine the origins of revelation equals enthusiasm, which "takes away both Reason and Revelation" and leaves behind only tautology: "*It is a Revelation, because they firmly believe it*, and *they believe it, because it is a Revelation.*"[38] A person possesses the capacity to reason and reflect, to determine his experience of the divine, even when made into a prophet, and not to use that reason properly is to prove that the revelation is false. By contrast, Donne's *Holy Sonnets* raise the possibility that God can be present within the self only if the self is immolated by zeal. Reason is only one more faculty that sin has corrupted, as in lines 7 and 8 of "Batter my hart": "Reason your viceroy in me, me should defend, / But is captiv'd and proves weake or vntrew." Despite being some sort of deputy of God that inhabits the speaker, reason here is not, contra Locke, a mode of divine revelation that can reflect precisely on all that passes through the mind. Whether it is "captiv'd" or just generally "weake" and "vntrew," reason, along with the rest of the self, has to be unmade so that God's presence can inspire the speaker.

That faith induces a conviction that is not bound by the protocols of reason is a position held often in the Reformation. From Calvin to Milton, Reformed thinkers argued that faith works according to a "secret testimony" that creates greater certitude than rational proof ever could.[39] Locke, of course, is deeply committed to disenchanting such claims to secret testimony. This is why he demands that all revelation can be examined by reason, which authenticates the origins of sensations. By contrast, fanaticism doubles down on the possibility of a divine secret testimony, making conviction even more inscrutable. More than suggesting that divine testimony could create unshakable faith in a believer, fanaticism bears within it the possibility that divine testimony is present as something unknowable to reason, and unknowable because the subject who could know has been annihilated, the difference between him and the divine eliminated. In Donne's language, the self's Elements and Angelique Spright must die in order for the person to become an instrument of God, a fanatic. That is not to say that reason is opposed to zeal in a simple antithesis in Donne's sonnet, but that the former threatens to lead the speaker away from the divine word rather than allow him to know or authenticate it. Only by being overthrown and immolated, emptied of self and the very capacity to know, can one be inhabited by the presence of God. Unmaking and unknowing are prerequisite for the zeal that consumes the true believer and drives what remains to act as an instrument of the divine.

This difference between Donne and Locke is irreconcilable. Donne's self-consuming zeal cannot appear as anything other than enthusiasm from the perspective of Locke. Not unlike Paul's worry over those who speak in tongues in 1 Corinthians 14, in Locke's analysis the fanatic threatens to become illegible to a community that demands publicly determinate communication. This illegibility raises the questions that we will see emerge in all the works studied in this book. Are fanatics those who convince themselves or others that they have experienced divine inspiration, madmen or demagogues? As Locke puts the question, "How shall any one distinguish between the delusions of Satan, and the inspirations of the Holy Ghost?"[40] Or are fanatics divinely inspired instruments? How do they know? How do witnesses? And how are readers of these figures, as they are represented in the literature of the Reformation, to tell the difference? Renaissance literature persistently explores how one becomes a fanatic and how fanatical action should be interpreted. And as we will see as we move into other poetic, philosophical, and theological treatments of fanaticism, writers worry intensely over not only the individual psychological and ethical problems of inspiration but also its collective dimension—how it can be contagious, spreading to others like a virus as it gives shape to fanatical communities no longer bound by reason or law. The fanatic's withdrawal, through annihilation, from traditional forms of given political and social community, along with the possibility of the new formation of fanatical communities, provokes a breakdown of received structures for aesthetic representation and knowledge.

*Unknowing Fanaticism* reflects on these questions as they emerge in poems by Edmund Spenser, John Donne, and John Milton. It is not a project that attempts to look at how Protestant thinkers sought to answer these questions but rather an inquiry into how literary authors influenced by the Reformation and the violence that proliferated through this era of massive political and religious transition confronted the possibility that such questions were not definitively answerable. Less an analysis of the "science of the soul" of the fanatic than a meditation on the failure of systematic attempts to determine the cause of fanaticism, this project asks how the epistemological questions surrounding fanaticism gave rise to profound aesthetic experimentation even while they tended, in philosophy, politics, and theology, to abet strategies of reactive social control.[41]

It is perhaps not surprising to observe that religious violence and its organs proliferate across literary texts composed in a period often thought of as punctuated by so-called wars of religion,[42] but it remains the case that a systematic study of the relationship between religious fanaticism and literature in the early modern period has not yet been undertaken. This may be in part because we have been so invested, and understandably so, with the powerful work done to establish and analyze the new self-consciousness about the human individual in the Renaissance. Many of the most famous studies of the Renaissance, from Jakob Burkhardt's to Stephen Greenblatt's, have claimed that despite the religious violence that proliferated throughout the sixteenth and seventeenth centuries, a new sense of individualized self-consciousness, an ability to manipulate and present the self no longer as dependent on God, began to take center stage.[43] The fanatic presents an unsettling idea of character. It is not sufficient to claim that a fanatic is a character who is defined by his individual will's bondage to God's greater will (as the Lutheran argument would have it);[44] by his execution of unwilled, involuntary action whose origin resides in God;[45] or by some desire to experience the pleasure of self-shattering.[46] Rather, a fanatic only comes into the scene when character—self—has itself been annihilated. The fanatic's will is not only coerced or causally determined but emptied, overtaken, and inspired as an instrument of inscrutable divine force. Fanaticism may—and this is one of the reasons it has been either reviled or dismissed—present something of an affront to this renewed self-consciousness of individuality. In an age when new opportunities for fashioning individual identity were being imagined, fanaticism evoked the possibility that identity might for some be emptied and that such self-emptying could be both coveted and illegible. It is that potential loss of self in Redcrosse's victory against the dragon, in Donne's figuration of zeal, and Milton's depiction of Samson's final act of violence that seems to allow divine action to move through a being whose identity can no longer be accurately represented as an individual self-consciousness. This paradox—that the new emphasis on the character of the fanatic must, by necessity, focus on a characterless character, a self-annihilating vessel for a divine force—may be why fanaticism is often seen as atavistic: not because it is some medieval remnant in a secularizing age but because it focuses our attention on a figure possessed by a divine force that any idea of individualized human being cannot account for.

Much has been written about the discourse of the passions in the early modern world,[47] and one might say that fanaticism is the limit-experience of the passions in the ancient, nonpejorative sense of *passio* that Erich Auerbach traces:[48] a seizure of the self, a throwing of the self into a radically empty passivity, but with the possibility that such self-annihilation, pushing the self out of itself so that the divine can gather within, may result in violent action such as rebellion or martyrdom. In attempting to address the epistemological and ethical opacity of fanaticism, Spenser, Donne, and Milton were moved to innovate and create radically new forms of allegorical, lyric, and tragic verse. At the same time, my analyses of Luther and Locke (in this Introduction) and Hobbes (in Chapter 3) provide case studies of what these poets of fanaticism were resisting: polemics that targeted fanatics as enemies of the state—and by extension, enemies of all reasonable humans—and that foreclosed rather than dwelled within the questions opened up by fanaticism.

Spenser, Donne, and Hobbes are especially concerned with the relationship between the self-emptying of the individual fanatic and the formation of fanatical collectives, and the link between the individual and collective strains can be addressed by clarifying my terminology. Why "fanatic"? I focus primarily on religious fanaticism rather than religious enthusiasm for a series of reasons that I explain later, but it will become clear that the distinction between the two, as terms of abuse, only occasionally holds. For the most part, those who use these terms and their cognates in the Reformation mean to disparage someone as irrational and disobedient. Sometimes the terms are used to define one another, as in the writings of Friedrich Spanheim, a theology professor and Calvinist in Leiden in the first half of the seventeenth century whose works connecting the fanaticism of the early sixteenth-century German Peasants' Revolt with the radical religious movements of the English Civil War were translated into English almost immediately:

> By enthusiasts we mean fanatical men, who either feign or presume to have God's breath and inspiration, and whether by diabolical, melancholic, or voluntary illusions, deceive themselves and others that such inspiration should be assigned to divine revelation.[49]

For Spanheim, "fanatic" is simply another name for "enthusiast." Both figures "feign or presume to have God's breath and inspiration." The emphasis on deception is typical; fanatics must be either deceiving themselves or knowingly deceiving others.

The terms have quite different etymologies, of course. "Enthusiasm" derives from the Greek *entheos*, the state of being possessed by a god; it entered Latin as *enthusiasmus*. A literal touchstone is Plato's *Ion*, in which Socrates describes the rhapsode in the following manner:

> It's a divine power that moves you, as a "Magnetic" stone moves iron rings. . . . This stone not only pulls those rings, if they're iron, it also puts power *in* the rings, so that they in turn can do just what the stone does—pull other rings—so that there's sometimes a very long chain of iron pieces and rings hanging from one another. And the power in all of them depends on this stone. In the same way, the Muse makes some people inspired [entheous] herself, and then through those who are inspired a chain of other enthusiasts is suspended. You know, none of the epic poets, if they're good, are masters of their subject; they are inspired, possessed, and that is how they utter all those beautiful poems. . . . A poet is an airy thing, winged and holy, and he is not able to make poetry until he becomes inspired and goes out of his mind [ekphrōn] and his intellect [nous] is no longer in him. . . . One poet is attached to one Muse, another to another (we say he is "possessed" [katechetai], and that's near enough for he is *held* [echetai]).[50]

Often glossed in the Renaissance as *furor poeticus* thanks to the subtitle (*De furore poetico*) that Marsilio Ficino gave to his commentary on the *Ion*, enthusiasm is described by Socrates in this passage as the divine possession that constitutes the rhapsode's performance, in opposition to a technique or skill. A simile structures the exposition: enthusiasm is like a magnetic stone encircled by iron rings. The magnetic stone not only overtakes the movement of the ring closest to it, but it also communicates its power to subsequent rings, each of which then bears the force of the original magnetic stone. Likewise, a Muse inspires an individual rhapsode—the god possesses the person, emptying him of his mind and rendering him *ekphrōn*—and that enthusiast communicates that possessive force to others, spectators to the song, who are emptied and inspired thereby as well.

There are two primary features of enthusiasm in its Ionic mode: a divine possession that empties the rhapsode of self so that the god can act through him and a communication of the state of being "held" beyond the initial event of inspiration, spreading out in a magnet-like force that possesses all who are present within a given radius.[51] This is enthusiasm as an intense singularity—the rhapsode held by the god so that the poet's words can move through him—and as a contagious movement—the force spreading from ring to ring, bringing all into a collective inspiration.

Though there was significant debate over the possibility of poetic enthusiasm in the Renaissance from Ficino through Milton, the term came to mean something different than it had for Socrates in a culture that wrestled with the relationship between antiquity and Christianity. By the time of Spanheim and Locke, enthusiasm did not primarily denote claims of divine possession but rather the boasting of "*divine inspirations, extasies*, and *secret communication with God*, obtruding their Prophesies for the word of God, and preferring them before the written Word."[52] "Enthusiasm" signifies here the conviction that one has had a direct experience of the divine word revealed—an experience that is typically dismissed as a symptom of delusion or madness. As the first half of the seventeenth century unfolded, enthusiasm came to be seen as a disease; this line of thinking culminated in the publication of both Meric Casaubon's *Treatise Concerning Enthusiasm* in 1655 and Henry More's *Enthusiasmus Trimphatus* in 1656.[53] Yet despite the repeated diagnosis of the enthusiast as a melancholic or mad individual, cut off from communal conversation or reasonable discourse, divine possession and inspiration, as with Plato's rhapsode, still threatened to pull others into the orbit of its power.

Most directly derived from the Latin *fanum* (temple), "fanaticism" as a term of abuse has a particular historical association, emerging directly from a set of Reformation disputes. This is not to say that "fanaticism" did not exist as a term of abuse before the Reformation,[54] but, as scholars such as Dominique Colas and Alberto Toscano have shown, it is only in the Reformation, in particular in the wake of the Anabaptist uprisings in Germany in the 1520s, that fanaticism came to be so widely associated with a particular kind of sacred fury.[55] It is with the figurehead of the Peasants' Revolt in Germany, Thomas Müntzer, and with Martin Luther and Philipp Melanchthon's polemics against him and the peasant rebels with whom he organized, that the modern sense of "fanaticism" was born. What characterized the "*archfanaticus*," at least in the eyes of his enemies, was a total refusal, justified through divine inspiration, to accept state authority, private property, or church hierarchy as legitimate.[56] The term Luther used to designate Müntzer and the peasant rebels as fanatics was *Schwärmer* in German. *Schwärmer* refers to a group of swarming animals, but as Colas reveals through his research on the Reformation linguistic history of "fanaticism," *Schwärmer* is the German term for what Luther and Melanchthon refer to as *fanaticus* or *phanaticus* in their Latin writings. Colas

confirms that *Schwärmer* was rendered as "fanatic," "phanatic," or "phanatik" in the earliest English translations of the German polemics against
the peasants, too, even though it was later translated as other terms, including "enthusiasm."[57]

The Peasants' Revolt in Germany became a primal scene for early modern fanaticism, especially in England. "England's Warning by Germany's
Woe": the title of Spanheim's 1646 denunciation of the fanatics and enthusiasts in the peasants' uprisings of the 1520s explicitly connects these
events with sectarian revolts in England during the English Civil War.
Anabaptism's association with the German Peasants' Revolt led many in
England in the second half of the sixteenth century and into the seventeenth to see in Anabaptism the recipe for religious revolt characterized
by what they took to be unreason and extremism. What the multiple
etymologies and translations of fanaticism reveal is that fanaticism presents, like Ionic enthusiasm, a complex composition of singularity and multiplicity, of singular divine possession and collective swarming. Müntzer
became the exemplar for England to fear, positioned as a threat at the very
inception of the Reformation, insofar as he claimed to be God's instrument, moved to act in violent ways against state and church establishments
and, at the same time, to bring others into his inspired uprising.

Most of the recent genealogical studies of fanaticism begin with the polemic between Luther and his former follower-turned-antagonist,
Müntzer. And the work of establishing the origins and shifting meanings
of the word and the theological and philosophical force of the dispute about
it has been extremely valuable.[58] But these studies have not analyzed, except in passing, what is most peculiar about Müntzer's so-called fanaticism.
Both Colas and Toscano emphasize that fanaticism appears as a figure for
willed extremism or intense commitment. Both thinkers take Friedrich
Engels's attempt to claim the Anabaptist peasant rebels as the original com-
munists (who were, in Engels's estimation, deluded by their religious beliefs)[59] as an invitation to trace such so-called fanaticism forward through
time. The two take starkly different but intriguingly overlapping positions. Colas positions Müntzer as the originator of a fanaticism that leads
to "fanatical Marxism," which rejects, in Colas's anticommunist reading,
political representation and seeks to bring about a "joyous Apocalypse
that will witness the famous 'withering of the state.'"[60] Although a much
more sympathetic and subtle reader of Marx and the histories of com-
munism, Toscano similarly conflates the religious fanaticism of Müntzer
and the peasant rebels with later examples of "unconditional and passionate subjective convictions that determine a radically transformative and

unequivocally antagonistic stance against existing society."[61] Taking his cue from Alain Badiou's reading of Saint Paul, which brackets Paul's message of faith in order to recover Paul as a model for militancy, Toscano takes the fanatic as a paradigm for his study of passionate zeal and willed commitment more broadly.[62]

My work on fanaticism resists both tendencies. Insisting that a unique phenomenon appears if we zoom in rather than out, I look at religious fanaticism in the Reformation and consider how poetry encounters its particularity. I track a history of thinking about fanaticism that both Colas and Toscano overlook—fanaticism as a phenomenon ambiguously emerging between passivity and activity, annihilating self-sacrifice and radical action. This mode of studying fanaticism is necessary for understanding the epistemological and aesthetic questions, fundamental to the poetic works I explore, that arise for literature when fanaticism is not taken as equivalent to a secular political phenomenon.

What is the nature of fanaticism in Müntzer? Scholars have shown that Luther finds *Schwärmer* dangerous for a host of reasons that led him to call for extreme violence against them: The fanatics wished to overthrow the secular realm, which, as it began to take the shape of the modern state, Luther believed was irreducibly necessary. They maintained that Luther's distinction between inner freedom and faith and outward obedience to state authority, famously articulated in the 1520 *Von der Freiheit eines Christenmenschen*, was false and reactionary. They questioned the value of Luther's grounding of Reform on the foundation of the written word, *sola scriptura*, if it foreclosed the possibility of God speaking to individuals in the present, and instead produced what Niklaus Largier calls "inspired, mystical reading practices" through which new kinds of community and devotion were shaped. They appropriated elements of the German mystical tradition that were dear to Luther but to radically different and more politicized ends. They believed that God inspired them to rebel violently. They opposed Luther's continued investment in the sacraments of infant baptism and the Eucharistic presence of Christ. And they believed that they, as God's instruments, could usher in the kingdom of God, which would produce a utopia of nonhierarchical and universal salvation in the present.[63] For all these reasons did Luther consider Müntzer and the peasant rebels to be *Schwärmer*, fanatics who, overtaken by Satan, needed to be exposed as madmen or liars and killed by the state's military force.[64]

Yet what tends to be overlooked by scholars' emphasis on Müntzer's ferocious counterattacks against Luther, his certainty that he was inspired by divine revelation, and his commitment to communization (*omnia sunt communia*, the phrase supposedly extracted from him through torture before his execution) is the particular emphasis on enthusiastic possession that defines Müntzer's fanaticism.[65] Influenced by the late medieval mysticism of Meister Eckhart and his disciples, Johannes Tauler in particular, Müntzer at his most theologically dense moments claims, in fact, that he is not the agent of the violent acts that he and the peasants undertake against church and state. For Müntzer, it is God's indwelling action that acts through the person who has emptied himself.[66] He describes the process in his famous sermon to the German princes, an extended interpretation of the second chapter of the Book of Daniel: "Sol nw der mensch des worts gewar werden und das er sein empfintlich sey, so muß ym Gott nemen seyne fleischlichen luste, und wenn die bewegung von Gott kumpt ins hertz, das er töthen wil alle wollust des fleisches, das er yhm do stadt gebe, das er seine wirckung bekummen mag" (If a person would now become aware of the word and receptive to it, God must remove all his fleshly desires, and if the movement from God comes into his heart, so that he wants to kill all the desires of the flesh, he gives way to him, so that he may receive his action).[67]

This mystical language of self-annihilation was both beloved and popularized in the early sixteenth century by Luther himself. Steven Ozment has shown how much Luther gravitated to this strand in German mysticism; Luther edited a manuscript that he titled *Theologia Deutsch*, a collection of mystical writings that Luther may have believed were authored by Tauler. In quoting an exemplary passage from the *Theologia Deutsch*, Ozment comments: "'The created will must flow into the eternal will, there dissolve itself and come to nought, so that only the eternal will remains to will, to want, and to be.' Of such notions were born both saintly reformers and heretical fanatics."[68] Luther wanted self-annihilation to be a mystical aesthetics of the interior, a personal and private ascension to God; Müntzer took it as a collective call for transformation, political and public. In contrast to the unbelievers such as Luther, who cannot fully empty themselves ("sie kunnen und wollen nit leherwerden," they can and will not become empty, Müntzer writes in the extended version of *Das Prager Manifest*),[69] Müntzer specifies that mystical annihilation of the self is necessary for faithful action in the world. When the believer is receptive ("empfintlich") to the word of God, God's movement ("bewegung") can enter—or reveal its presence within—the heart of the believer. In that enthusiastic emergence, God violently negates the self and the distinction between the person and the divine dissolves. Hence in the instant of self-annihilation, there

is no self that can have or know what Toscano has called "passionate subjective convictions."[70] Artfully captured by the clause "das er yhm do stadt
gebe" (he gives way to him), in which the pronouns ("er"/"yhm") make it
impossible to distinguish grammatically between the human and divine (a
pronominal conflation we will see again in Chapter 1), God moves into
the place ("stadt") of the self, and that internal movement kills the self.[71]
God is not transcendent in this moment; the divine is entirely immanent,
but in such a way that erases the distinction between "er" and "yhm," God
and self. The divine comes into the believer and he loses himself in the
receiving of divine action. As with Donne's zeal, the believer must be unmade in order to become new, an instrument of divine action. For in this
process of self-loss and divinization, God, immanent in the person, is the
agent—it is God's action ("wirckung") that the believer receives ("bekummen mag"). The believer does not will to fulfill God's will, for he has
been freed from his own will; God's will works in and through him. The
self, annihilated, becomes an organ for divine action. In Müntzer's case,
that action includes violent revolt against the state. And divine action may
not end there, moving through one person and into the world; indeed, it
may catch on and spread, as it did with the peasants with whom Müntzer
rebelled, creating a swarm that is defined at once by collective self-loss and
violent action.

Reformation theories of self-annihilation such as Müntzer's can be
traced back not only to medieval mysticism like Eckhart's but also to the
most canonical Christology (as Eckhart and his followers were themselves
well aware). Saint Paul's description of the incarnation in the Letter to the
Philippians is the primary proof text:

> Let the same mind be in you that was in Christ Jesus [Touto phroneite
> en hymin ho kai en Christō Iēsou] who, though he was in the form of
> God [en morphē Theou], did not regard equality with God as some-
> thing to be exploited, but emptied himself [heauton ekenōsen], taking
> the form of a slave, being born in human likeness. And being found in
> human form, he humbled himself and became obedient to the point of
> death—even death on a cross.[72]

*Kenosis* is thus originally a term for the self-emptying specific to Christ,
who abandoned his divinity in order to take human form and then to die
on the cross. Yet Paul's description indicates that *kenosis* is not an action
that is exclusively Christ's: "Let the same mind be in you that was in Christ
Jesus." *Kenosis* is to be imitated or transferred—what was in Christ ("en
Christō Iēsou") should be in you ("en hymin")—though Paul does not

specify what self-emptying should look like for those who follow Christ. (It is worth noting that although Paul is clear that Christ's *kenosis* should be imitated or transferred to believers, divine inspiration, at least in the example of glossolalia at Corinth, worried him considerably, as mentioned earlier, not least because inspired individuals become illegible to their community: "For those who speak in a tongue [ho lalōn glōssē] do not speak to other people but to God; for nobody understands them, since they are speaking mysteries in the Spirit."[73] Such illegibility will be precisely what the poets of fanaticism focus on.) Though Müntzer is not as invested in the intricate theological debates that exist in the traditions of kenotic mysticism on which he drew,[74] his innovations are influential. First, he believed that such a process of self-emptying for a human believer was the prerequisite for divine inspiration and that "receiving divine action" would itself lead to the transformation of the world, through violence if necessary. Second, though he argues that each individual believer must experience this self-loss for himself, a community of believers can take shape to perform the acts required to allow more individuals to experience the movement of God into their hearts. This community, not unlike the ring of Ionic enthusiasts, is defined by the fact that it is collectively lost to itself. It is God's action that moves through the community and into the world.

Whether individuals choose to participate in a fanatical "swarm" or are emptied of self and possessed is a problem that several of the poems I examine and that Hobbes's philosophical works, too, address at great length. The fanatical swarm multiplies the political and epistemological problems that Ian Munro has located in the early modern crowd's threat to social order and hierarchy: "The urban crowd is invisible and ungraspable until reaching a certain level of intensity, gathering and scattering and gathering again."[75] Crowds' illegibility is exacerbated when they take shape, or at least claim to take shape, through a collective process of self-annihilation and inspiration. For this reason, and as I will show at greater length in the chapters that follow, fanaticism is at the heart of Renaissance debates about the power or threat of the multitude, about exemplarity and imitation, and about agency, determinism, and the passions.

When I speak of fanaticism in this book, I mean to evoke the kind of self-annihilating inspiration that Müntzer claims to have undergone. (I bracket for now the question of how one knows and writes of what cannot have been experienced.) Despite the differentiation between fanaticism and the discourse of enthusiasm that becomes increasingly important in the wake of the seventeenth century, there are reasons to see how Reformation fanaticism and Ionic enthusiasm as I have defined them meet in

Müntzer, not least because the mystical tradition on which he draws is almost as deeply influenced by modes of Neoplatonic thought as it is by Pauline *kenosis*. In contrast to what Colas and Toscano have argued, I propose that fanaticism cannot be the formal equivalent of passionate conviction unless we dismiss the specificity of Müntzer's professions or fold them into an idiom that disenchants his claim to be a self-emptying vessel for God's action. Refusing to disenchant Müntzer allows us to revise the claim that martyrs who commit acts of violence are committed to what Talal Asad, in his study of suicide bombing, describes as "the limitless pursuit of freedom, the illusion of an uncoerced interiority that can withstand the force of institutional disciplines," or to performing actions that are "exemplary" works that all Christians are enjoined to follow.[76] There is no self to be convinced of its righteousness or freedom in Müntzer's paradigm, no self that seeks to fashion itself as evangelical exemplar for a community. (There is more to say about the tension between fanaticism and *imitatio Christi* in the chapters that follow.) It is God who acts in and through the self and thus tears that self away from its prior community, even if such self-annihilation may be the entrance to a new kind of community, too. When the self is emptied, God can move it to a violent act that may end, as it did for Müntzer, in martyrdom, another version of self-loss. When Luther claims that the Holy Spirit does not act in the secular world and that Müntzer's claims are thus categorically false, or when he asserts that Müntzer, if he were honestly inspired by God, "would first allow himself to be tested and judged, in humility"[77] (a biblically inflected version of Locke's demand that enthusiasts submit to observation and have their reason examined), he attempts to deny in advance the possibility that God might be actually working through Müntzer. Luther's refusal of that possibility turns out to be literally murderous; he calls on the state to eradicate Müntzer and all his followers. This strategy—to demand that fanatics give an account of themselves to a state that seeks to criminalize and, often, to kill them—takes various forms from Luther to Hobbes and Locke. It is not a strategy confined to the past.

If we resist dismissing Müntzer as a false prophet or madman, without ignoring that his inspiration remains illegible, we can imagine his claim of self-annihilation and inspiration as an intensification of a theological problem that raised epistemological and ethical worries more broadly, a problem that produced some of the period's most complex poetic thinking about the representability of divinity and agency. After all, the language of self-annihilation circulated widely in the sixteenth and seventeenth centuries, across confessional divides. Debora Shuger has demonstrated

that even Lancelot Andrewes—certainly no proponent of peasant revolt
or communization—asserts that the self, at least in its good works, is
"inspired" by Christ as a kind of "principium motûs." Andrewes's theory
of in-operation reveals his belief in divine inhabitation clearly:

> All our well-wrought works, of them, we say not only, *sine Me nihil
> potestis facere*, we can do none of them without Him; but further, we
> say with the prophet, *domine, omnia opera nostra operatus es in nobis*. In
> them He doth not only co-operate with us from without, but even
> from within; as I may say, in-operate them in us.[78]

In language that will be relevant for how Spenser's Redcrosse is "wrought"
by God into an organ of divine might, Andrewes's God is the in-operator
that undertakes every well-wrought work. Christ is, as Shuger puts it, "the
natural source of all activity."[79] For Andrewes here, the line between
Christ's divine agency and human agency is blurry; though he is not satisfied with a claim of "co-operation," which would propose that the divine
will works along with or supports human will from the outside, "in-
operation" also does not negate "co-operation" ("He doth not *only* cooperate with us"). In a way that is exemplary for much of Andrewes's
thinking about will, God can inhabit the self, be the source of all human
works, and yet not annihilate the human will that can cooperate with it.
Müntzer's position is less equivocal. It proposes not that humans cooperate with God, or have him inoperate in them, but that true believers have
God annihilate them, turning them into vessels for his action. Müntzer's
position, that self-annihilation should spread to form collectives that can
rise up to overthrow the current state of the world and found a new way of
being that accords with God's will, may be an extreme position, but the
violence of Luther's dismissal of it is its own kind of extremism, dressed
up as common sense. Luther purposefully distracts us from seeing the
complex problems that self-annihilation posed for many different kinds of
writers and thinkers throughout Reformation Europe.

It is my claim in this book that Spenser, Donne, and Milton find themselves unsatisfied with the polemical disavowal and policing of claims such
as Müntzer's. Commanding fanatics to account for their relationship to
God and then imprisoning, exiling, or killing them when they could not
or would not provide a satisfactory account did not resolve the fundamental problems that fanaticism posed. I do not wish to draw a direct connection between Müntzer and the representations of fanaticism in the literary or
theological works of these authors, though the idea of an Anabaptist threat
is often very visible in Nashe, Spenser, Jonson, and Hobbes. Nor do I pro-

pose that these poets are especially invested in traditions of mysticism, though Donne obviously was, if ambivalently.[80] My claim is rather that these poets were haunted by the model of fanaticism that Müntzer introduced to the Reformation, a model based upon the annihilation of the self, divine inspiration, and the communicative or mimetic possibilities of both. They recognized in the epistemological question that Müntzerian fanaticism raised—how can one know if a fanatical act is undertaken with one's own will or with God's?—a provocation to innovate poetic forms to address the possibility that this question might, in certain instances, remain unanswerable. Indeed, the ethical and the poetic are intervolved for these poets, not least because their verse thinks immanently about whether poetry is itself a product of inspiration (the poet as God's instrument), or whether the willful labor of poetic making bars authors from a true experience of self-annihilation.[81] Spenser, Donne, and Milton dwelled with the uncertainties raised by fanaticism and, understanding that fanatics might prove to be limit cases for what their didactic and representational projects could do, they transformed the poetic materials available to them to explore with enormous complexity the nearly inexplicable problems that fanatical organs and communities brought into view.

There is a long tradition of studying radical religion and its relationship to literature in the early modern period. Yet since the indefinite entrenchment of the so-called war on terror at the start of the twenty-first century, early modern studies has taken a renewed interest in the relationship between religion and the arts of the period, in religious violence, and in the tension between political and religious authority. The turn to political theology in English Renaissance studies, most visible in the essential work of critics such as Julia Reinhard Lupton, Victoria Kahn, and Graham Hammill, has produced a renewed conviction that the literary works of the period were deeply engaged with the evolving relationship between religion and the state, whether conceiving of the state as itself a secularized version of a religious concept or taking it as reoccupying a site of legitimacy that religion could no longer maintain.[82] My project's contribution to the field of political theology lies in a swerve away from the focus on sovereignty, law, and citizenship at the moment in Renaissance Europe when the state produced itself as the institution claiming a monopoly over force and obedience. Though Lupton, in particular, has been attentive to the ways in which a focus on political theology allows critics to examine the procedures by which literary characters are represented in moments of exception as "dying into citizenship,"[83] scholars of political theology have not studied religious fanaticism and its threat to the forms of sovereignty that were developing in the early modern world. Even in Lupton's masterful account of the early modern saint, her emphasis, like that of the liberalism she wishes to enhance, remains on individual choice. She defines her saint as someone who "*elects* to join the City of God at the expense of the City of Men."[84] Self-election is antithetical to the instrumentalization that the fanatic purportedly undergoes when annihilated and rendered a vessel of God's will. My work reveals a literary reckoning with the capacity of an individual or community to become, through self-annihilation, organs of divine violence. Fanatics undergo—or at least claim to undergo—a self-unmaking transformation that cannot be circumscribed by the protocols of either citizenship or sainthood, even if it shares a family resemblance with the potential for radical singularity that Lupton locates in the latter. They do not just go beyond a particular legal order but lose themselves entirely to become instruments of God that evacuate will and interrupt the order of the world.

Furthermore, studies in political theology have tended to divorce themselves from an emphasis on the formal analysis of literary texts. This is not to say that these scholars do not perform "close readings" of literature— they do, often masterfully—but rather that these close readings tend to presuppose that political theological problems are poured into literary forms from the outside rather than being immanent within those forms. A recent call to resuscitate formalism to reconsider the interaction of martyrdom and literature in the period renders form too broad a category for my purposes; there, "form" comes to mean "the textual production of martyrdom" in general rather than referring to local formal details in texts.[85] I hope, by contrast, to take some of the central questions of political theology and show how, in fact, they create occasions for reflections on and experimentations with the poetic forms in which such questions are posed. Because fanaticism raises problems of will and causation, of who or what makes a given action possible and realizable, it is intrinsically a matter of form, the way in which elements are assembled.

"Form" can sometimes be a rather formless term in literary studies, remaining too broad to allow for precision or remaining undefined altogether.[86] Anahid Nersessian and Jonathan Kramnick have proposed that "formalism need not, indeed cannot provide a single definition of form because form is an entity known by occasion, through encounters with its subsidiary phenomena,"[87] and for that reason I want to be precise about what I take "form" to mean for the purposes of studying poets' encounters with fanaticism. In this book, "form" denotes technique in the sense that Theodor Adorno articulated it: "Technik ist nicht Abundanz der Mittel sondern das aufgespeicherte Vermögen, dem sich anzumessen, was objektiv die Sache von sich aus verlangt" (Technique [in art] is not an abundance of means but rather the accumulated capacity to be objectively suited to what the thing itself demands).[88] When Adorno speaks of technique, he means something very specific—not all of the various means by which something might be represented in an artwork but rather the concrete manner in which an artwork attempts to think about its object through features of its composition. For poetry, this would include line, rhyme, assonance, syntactic and metrical segmentation, and genre, to name a few. As Simon Jarvis has put it, technique is "the way in which art thinks and the way in which the work of art most intimately registers historical experience, . . . the point at which the voices of the many living and dead that are the poet's repertoire or material are selected from, cut into, distorted, twisted, and precipitated into this or that composition—where their natural-historical antagonisms are exposed, concealed, exacerbated, or fudged."[89] A formalism that focuses on technique, then, would explicate how specific texts are composed in ways that are mediated by inherited material pasts (the technical labors "preserv'd and stor'd up" in poems, to adapt Milton's phrase from *Areopagitica*),[90] by the possibilities and pressures of the moments of composition, and by the specificity of the poetic object. Thus the kind of attention to form that this book cultivates is what Anthony Reed has called a "situated formalism," one that claims that poetic technique crystallizes and complicates social antagonisms and thereby "holds open a place for the unthought, for what is unassimilable to the prevailing regime of power"—or what Colleen Rosenfeld, following Philip Sidney, refers to in her recent study of Renaissance figures of speech as "what may be," new possibilities for imaginative relation to texts and worlds.[91] We cannot understand how Spenser's *The Faerie Queene* thinks about fanaticism without taking into account how its formal innovations in allegorical composition at local moments (to name only one technical register relevant to the intricacy of a given line or stanza) are the means through which it strains to do this thinking. Yet if fanaticism figures the possibility of a person or a collective that is emptied of will and transformed into an instrument of God's violence, then I will need to put pressure as well on the idea of literary form as willed technique, since several of the poets about whom I write announce their own instrumental relationship to God. Fanaticism annihilates form as willed technique, but it also gives shape to new forms as poets uncover ways to know it, or experience it, in verse.

In order to articulate what is unique about my approach, it is necessary to differentiate my claim about form and fanaticism from the argument of one recent critical study that emphasizes the formal literary implications of early modern religious violence. Feisal Mohamed's *Milton and the Post-Secular Present: Ethics, Politics, Terrorism*, a sophisticated expansion of his post–September 11, 2001, exchange with John Carey over whether Milton's *Samson Agonistes* is a celebration of religious terrorism,[92] elaborates his argument that "at his triumph, Milton's Samson is much less a human subject than he is a vessel of God's wrath, which wrath is an irruption of the divine into our world."[93] Mohamed draws a clear connection between Samson and contemporary suicide bombers in order to dispute Milton scholars' tendency to embrace Milton's republican politics without acknowledging the place in his thought for the justification of divinely inspired violence. At the same time, Mohamed attempts, at least in his first chapter, to reveal how Milton's representation of such divinely inspired violence reverberates formally in his poetry. Glossing the "rousing motions" that lead Samson to his final act of suicidal mass killing as unambiguously divine, Mohamed links moments of what he calls "plain style" in *Paradise Lost* and Samson's violence: "If there is an equivalent to Samson's rousing motions in *Paradise Lost*, it is those moments where plain-spoken truth distances us from the aesthetic response invited by the poem's richly expressed passages."[94] Indeed, Mohamed eloquently interprets moments in Milton's verse, such as Abdiel's rejection of Satan, where zeal for the divine creates an expression of "unadorned truth" in which Milton simplifies syntax, regularizes meter, and momentarily abandons his multilingual wordplay.[95] All of Mohamed's claims contribute to an effort to persuade the reader that "perhaps more than any other poet, John Milton makes us keenly aware of the limits of an emphasis on ambiguity," and thus to show the reader once and for all that Milton was fully convinced of Samson's divinely inspired violence, and that our investment in finding ambiguity in *Samson Agonistes* has led us to ignore Milton's commitment to religious violence.

I am not so sure. Mohamed's argument against ambiguity allows him to decide in advance that Milton's Samson is a vessel of divine violence, and yet it is difficult, as I show in Chapter 4, to understand how any reader of the play could confidently claim that Samson's inspiration is unambiguous. Milton goes out of his way to make the question of Samson's relationship to God entirely inaccessible not only to the spectators within the play but also to those of us reading it. By denying this point, Mohamed's analysis views *Samson Agonistes* as at least in part a "conduct

manual for failed revolutionaries" imagining terrorism as their final recourse, and his important claim about form—the significance of the sim-
plification of stylistics and versification—becomes a justification for
viewing the play as uninterested in thinking through ambiguity.[96]

My study of fanaticism takes a radically different approach. I claim that
the very ambiguity that Mohamed dismisses is inescapably present in these
literary representations of religious fanaticism. And how could it not be?
As I have shown in this Introduction, religious fanaticism emerges with
the possibility that the divine could annihilate and act immanently through
a person—not only binding a person to a specific set of rituals or actions
but unmaking the person and remaking him as sacred instrument. Yet,
given such annihilation, how could a fanatic or a community of spectators
ever truly know, through reason or debate, if the person is a divine instrument or madman? This epistemological aporia provokes formal experimentation in the poets in this book. Technique—form—becomes the realm
in which the epistemological, ethical, and aesthetic ambiguity that fanaticism raises is immanently crystallized, even if fanaticism indicates a
state in which technique is absent (as Ionic enthusiasm suggests and as I
address in my chapters on Spenser and Donne). These poets rethink how
an allegory, a devotional sonnet, and a tragedy work at both the most fundamental and the most minute structural levels in order to grapple subtly
with the unknowability that fanaticism introduces in their art; their transformation of literary techniques at once registers and attempts to address
the conceptual complexity of fanaticism. To adapt a suggestion from Gillian Rose's commentary on Rosa Luxemburg's "Organizational Questions
of the Russian Social Democracy," these poets find that a "deeper submission to uncertainty leads to a more inclusive activity—to cultivation of plas-
ticity rather than culture of terror."[97] Even if there are moments when
these poets seem certain that what they are representing is divine inspiration (such as, at least momentarily, in Redcrosse's transformation into an
organ of divine might in the penultimate canto of Book I of *The Faerie
Queene*, to which I now turn), they return time and again to worry over
whether their poems can ever know such a thing with certainty. They
maintain a fidelity to the potentially unknowable that fanaticism involves.
Their fidelity shapes how they think fanaticism in verse.

# CHAPTER I

# Allegorical Fanaticism: Spenser's Organs

Dieu comme objet d'amour est la lumière et l'âme humaine
est l'œil, un organe de vision. Elle est l'organe du je. Mais quand
le je s'est effacé, sans que l'organe ait perdu sa vertu, l'âme
devient organe de la vision de Dieu.

—SIMONE WEIL, *Cahier* 7

In *The Faerie Queene*, uncertainty about divine inspiration accrues with
particular urgency around the equivocal poetic figures the poem uses to
represent religious fanaticism. This chapter examines two of those
figures—the metaphor of the "organ" of divine might and the simile of the
"swarm" of flies—and their significance for the poem's thinking about divine violence and rebellious collectivities, about the allegorical techniques
it uses to construct didactic exemplars of virtues, and about local poetic
details that strain against the poem's larger allegorical design. Spenser's
transformation of Redcrosse into an "organ" of divine might at the end of
Book I provokes a series of productively destabilizing questions with which
the poem will ever after wrestle, echoing first across the protagonists of
Books II and III, and then returning most threateningly, and with the greatest political and poetic consequences, in Book V's likening of a fanatical
collectivity to a "swarm" of flies.

Spenser's engagement with fanaticism asked in different ways whether fanatics were willful agents or divinely inspired instruments, and whether
fanatics themselves or witnesses to their violence (both firsthand witnesses
and those readers who encountered representations of such action in verse)

could tell the difference. To explore the significance of fanaticism in *The Faerie Queene*, I begin with a reading of Redcrosse's transformation at the end of Book I and the interpretive dilemma that arises around its reception early in Book II. Next I examine moments in the poem that recapitulate the problem of the "organ" where we least expect it, in episodes in which both holiness and Book I's epistemological bewilderment seem to have been left behind: Guyon's "rigour pittilesse" at the end of Book II and the divine directing of Britomart's action at the start of Book III. The poem grows increasingly more worried about its capacity to distinguish between true instruments of the divine and false prophets, and this anxiety is at its acutest in the egalitarian Giant episode of Book V, where the poem works ambivalently to expel fanaticism's collective antinomian threat. The final section of this chapter reveals the importance of fanaticism to discourses of the rebellious multitude, and Spenser's meditation on fanatical "swarms" suggests a direct connection to the legacy of Müntzer. Throughout this chapter, I emphasize that Spenser thinks about the relationship between agency and instrumentality in the fanatic's violent act *in* and *as* allegory, allegory understood to encompass verse techniques for producing personifications to teach by "ensample."[1] Indeed, the representation of fanaticism in the poem's first book suggests that allegory in its purest form may no longer be allegory and may itself become fanatical: the emptying out of a character and incarnation of divine will. The poem's allegorical techniques attempt but productively fail to give readers the tools to authenticate the origins of fanaticism. At the end of this chapter, I suggest some similarities between this productive epistemological failure to let us know the difference between inspiration and delusion within *The Faerie Queene* and Spenser's depiction of the process of poetic creation itself.

"THE LEGENDE OF THE KNIGHT OF THE RED CROSSE/ OR/ OF HOLINESSE." This is how the first page of Book I of *The Faerie Queene* describes its contents.[2] This *"OR"* raises a question about whether the book will primarily be about Redcrosse as a character or about holiness as the book's central virtue. The usual way of answering the question, no doubt influenced by Spenser's own suggestions in the "Letter to Raleigh," is to say that the book's aim is to "fashion" Redcrosse the erring character into an exemplar, a personification of holiness.[3] In the analysis that follows, I claim that the opposite is the case: Redcrosse does not simply become "fashioned" into "holiness," but in fact that holiness unfashions him as a character.[4]

In his third attempt to fulfill his mission and destroy the dragon that holds Una's parents captive, Redcrosse seems finally to become the personification of holiness that we expect. Yet in that moment of triumph the poem elides his agency:

> And in his first encounter, gaping wyde,
>> He thought attonce him to haue swallowd quight,
>> And rusht vpon him with outragious pryde;
>> Who him rencountring fierce, as hauke in flight,
>> Perforce rebutted backe. The weapon bright
>> Taking aduantage of his open iaw,
>> Ran through his mouth with so importune might,
>> That deepe emperst his darksom hollow maw,
> And back retyred, his life blood forth with all did draw.
>
> (1.11.53)

The pronomial ambiguity in this stanza is significant: the "he" and "his" that refer to Redcrosse and the dragon become especially difficult to track in the stanza's first four and a half lines.[5] In the second sentence, beginning with the stanza's only enjambment, Redcrosse disappears as a grammatical subject entirely, supplanted by his weapon: "The weapon bright/Taking aduantage of his open iaw,/Ran through." Redcrosse's weapon goes unnamed. But whether it is a sword or a lance, the iconographic tradition of the sword of the spirit is still literally at hand; his weapon is, paradoxically, a medium for unmediated divine violence.[6] The rhyming of "bright" and "might" further underscores that the force seems to emerge directly from the sword rather than from Redcrosse. This is perhaps the most difficult allegorical crux at the end of Book I, a book that has been especially concerned, from the first stanza, with the problem of how to know who or what something is: Redcrosse suddenly made new by God, finally fashioned into a personification of the virtue of holiness in the book's penultimate canto, is at the same time unmade as subject and agent.[7] The "importune might" of God becomes manifest in the world of the allegory through him by erasing him and thus we know that Redcrosse has become the personification of holiness only insofar as we lose him as a subject of knowledge and action. This canto ends with an alexandrine that elides the difference between God and Redcrosse: "Then God she [Una] praysd, and thankt her faithfull knight,/That had atchievde so great a conquest by *his* might" (1.11.55, my emphasis). In this context, the pronomial ambiguity here is intriguingly similar to Müntzer's description of mystical annihilation and inspiration: "das er yhm do stadt gebe, das er seine wirckung bekummen mag" (he gives way to him, so that he may receive his action).[8]

As is common in *The Faerie Queene*, characters gather to interpret a particularly difficult moment. At the beginning of Book II, Redcrosse hands off the baton to Guyon, but Guyon's sidekick, the Palmer, takes a moment to gloss the end of Book I:

> Ioy may you haue, and euerlasting fame,
>> Of late most hard atchieu'ment by you donne,
>> For which enrolled is your glorious name
>> In heauenly Regesters aboue the Sunne,
>> Where you a Saint with Saints your seat haue wonne:
>> But wretched we, where ye haue left your marke,
>> Must now anew begin, like race to ronne;
>> God guide thee, *Guyon*, well to end thy warke,
> And to the wished hauen bring thy weary barke.
>
> Palmer, him answered the *Redcrosse* knight,
>> His be the praise, that this atchieu'ment wrought,
>> Who made my hand the organ of his might;
>> More then goodwill to me attribute nought:
>> For all I did, I did but as I ought.

(2.1.32–33)

Glossing the defeat of the dragon as a product of Redcrosse's own *doing*, the Palmer seems suggestively unaware of the role God's grace plays in Book I.[9] But Redcrosse imputes the act to God. In his transformation into holiness, Redcrosse, or at least his synecdochic hand, becomes both a figurative and literal organ of divine might—the manifestation of God's word in the world and the executor of divine violence as his weapon, "organ" suggesting both sound and instrumentality.

Readers attentive to Spenser's theology, from A. S. P. Woodhouse to Daryll Gless, often take Redcrosse's correction as a didactic lesson about the theology of grace in which a Protestant hero corrects the mistake of a presumptively Catholic Palmer.[10] But more is at stake in this interpretative divergence than doctrinal precision, and the hierarchal structure of grace is insufficient to elucidate the supposedly indwelling presence of God in Redcrosse as his organ. Redcrosse does not primarily remind the Palmer that willed temperance is inadequate for salvation or for the violent execution of God's will. Rather, he insists that he himself was not the agent of the violence that killed the dragon. "His be the praise, that this atchieu'ment wrought" at once counters the Palmer's earlier attribution of agency to Redcrosse and renders the actual agency of the "atchieu'ment" ambiguous. "Wrought" is equivocal in its ascription of agency; it fails to disclose who actually "wrought" the "atchieu'ment." And this line also tracks in two directions syntactically. If "atchieu'ment" is a subject, then the line suggests that the "atchieu'ment" itself wrought the praise that is due to God. But if achievement is a direct object, then it is the praise (perhaps Redcrosse's own performance of praise in the past) that wrought this "atchieu'ment." The grammatical doubleness at once draws our attention to Redcrosse's desire to highlight God's achievement and makes it difficult to determine the agent of the "atchieu'ment." The next dependent clause—the next line—seems meant to clarify the situation. "Who made my hand the organ of his might" retroactively renders it unambiguous that God transmuted Redcrosse into an "organ"; God was the agent and Redcrosse's hand a passive vessel. But in the following line, Redcrosse asks to have "goodwill"—though no more than "goodwill"—"attribute[d]" to him, and this is hard to square with the sense that he undertook the "atchieu'ment" only as an "organ." What does "goodwill" look like when one is not in control of one's own will, or when the divine empties an individual's will? "Attribute," too, is more ambiguous than it first seems; if "goodwill" needs to be attributed by another, then it is not inherently present.

In his correction of the Palmer, Redcrosse provokes a series of questions about human and divine will that the poem does not resolve. In what sense does a passive organ have "goodwill," except perhaps as an external force that God supplies to it?[11] Or, in a distinction familiar from a recent philosophical discussion by Daniel Wegner, might we "attribute" to Redcrosse the experience of "goodwill"—perhaps the only mode in which his reconstituted mind, as it tries to recollect its own annihilation after the fact, can register the presence of God—without concluding that that experience implies his will as cause?[12] Or is it rather that the transformed Redcrosse cannot even properly be said to have experience, since he was annihilated so that God could inhabit him? In this sense, "goodwill" would be the affective passivity opened up at the moment Redcrosse is emptied and transformed into an organ—the very opposite of an act undertaken by his own will.

Redcrosse's response to the Palmer draws our attention to the fact that these stanzas are thinking about the ambiguity of Redcrosse's transformation precisely through the poetic techniques by which they are "wrought"— and the uses of repetition and rhyme are significant for how stanza 33 in particular develops a sonic texture to address the figure of the organ. Red-crosse's slightly pat but cryptic "For all I did, I did but as I ought" raises more questions about the agency driving the doing of this "atchieu'ment" than it answers. The repetition obscures the chain of causation that "made" Redcrosse's "hand" do God's will. The stanza's rhymes reverber-ate that concealing anadiplosis: "ought" is conjoined with the rhyme words "wrought" and "nought," making the question of duty and will all the more difficult to surmise. "Ought"—duty—is contained within both "wrought" (which refers ambiguously to the agency of this "atchieu'ment") and "nought" (which refers to Redcrosse's lack of agency). Redcrosse's achievement—the fulfillment of the "ought" for which he was "wrought"—renders his will "nought," emptied out at the very moment he is refash-ioned into the achieved personification of holiness. This is more than an exemplary instance of what the critic Gordon Teskey calls allegorical cap-ture, wherein the poem's disordered and wandering meaning is coercively corralled into a system of orderly didactic personifications.[13] In an instant, we witness—or at least this is what Redcrosse's account argues for—the totality of divine capture and immanence. Paradoxically, at the moment that the totality of sacred presence emerges in the poem, allegory evacu-ates itself of its power to regulate meaning by ordering differential personifications. Redcrosse becomes the personification of holiness inso-far as he becomes purely an instrument of divine violence, not a represen-tation of a virtue or a character who has finally done something right but an organ of God's immanence.

Andrew Escobedo has claimed that one of Spenser's greatest innova-tions in Book I is the synthesis of Redcrosse's apocalyptic and national identities in the final cantos, inscribing a moment of apocalyptic violence within a genealogy of English nationhood.[14] Yet before he is safely con-verted to Saint George, Redcrosse in the penultimate canto of Book I is reducible to neither the allegorical consolidation of holiness nor the epic ambitions of retrospective nation-founding. He seems to be, rather, an ab-solute manifestation of God's violence. But in addition to resisting the poem's attempted union of allegorical and epic ambitions, Redcrosse's fanaticism introduces into the poem an epistemological and ethical prob-lem, one that the Palmer's redescription of Redcrosse's "atchieu'ment" poses acutely. After all, the poem authorizes neither the Palmer's attempt to demystify Redcrosse's violence as willful heroism nor Redcrosse's interpre-tation of his own divine inspiration, which has its own equivocations. The reader is left to choose without definitive evidence, which exacerbates the problem with which Book I has been obsessively concerned: how to know who or what another being is and how to determine whether another person is good or evil, truthful or fraudulent. Inspiration presents a limit case for Book I's perpetual epistemological worries; unlike with Archimago or Duessa, whose fraudulence can more or less be revealed for what it is, the poem never allows readers of and in the poem—and perhaps Redcrosse himself—to know with certainty what constitutes the unmaking and remaking of Redcrosse as an organ. Whether Redcrosse became a vessel of divine violence or whether his violence was a "most hard atchieu'ment by [him] donne" remains unsettled once the knight of holiness leaves Book II.

This question is worked out through both the form and content of the verse's articulation of Redcrosse's transformation, and it leads Spenser to reflect, with increasing ambiguity as the poem unfolds, on how allegory can—or cannot—represent the violent manifestation of divine presence in the poem. It will be useful here to explain how critics often describe the kinship between allegory and daemonic possession in Spenser's poem, and to register some of the difficulties that fanaticism presents for this mode of thinking about allegory. Criticism on allegory, the Spenserian kind in particular, has long been concerned with its structural dependence on the negation of individual will. Most influentially, Angus Fletcher considered allegory as a medium in which daemonic possession and compulsion act as structural norms.[15] More recent theorists have developed the formal contours of the daemonic in allegory; Teskey's claim that allegory literalizes Neoplatonic *raptio* is a particularly sophisticated and influential elaboration.[16] But these accounts have not explicitly addressed what place there is in Spenser's allegorical poem for the absoluteness of God's indwelling presence. Fanaticism poses this question, and in doing so it reveals a radical case of Susanne Wofford's claim that "moments in which the figurative scheme of the poem must be made to have effect within the action become fictionally moments of compulsion or possession, . . . with the resulting moral and aesthetic difficulty that no means for distinguishing a divinity from a daemon can be proposed within the text."[17] What happens, then, when Redcrosse as allegorical sign becomes a pure expression—an organ—of divine violence that has an effect within the world of the poem?

Following Isabel MacCaffrey, theorists of Spenserian allegory tend to agree that the mode is "analytic" in its purest sense;[18] allegory breaks things down, seeks to order meaning in and against the disorderly genre of romance. It explains the motives of characters and illustrates why they act in certain ways by reducing them to a stable meaning. Allegory, in other words, assumes at a structural level that the fictional world it upholds is like a puzzle, in which each singularity can be represented as one interact-ing part within a whole. But the fanatic *is* the whole—not an emblem of an individual impulse in God's creation but a vessel for God's violent might. And yet as soon as the poem achieves his personification, doubt emerges about allegory's capacity to help spectators and readers tell the difference between a truly inspired knight and an insurrectionary or zealot who fraudulently claims that he enacts God's will. If the metaphor of the "or-gan" of divine might is meant to reveal Redcrosse as an instrument of sa-cred force, the guarantee of English sovereignty itself, then it also jeopardizes the allegorical distinctions that the poem depends on to pro-duce its mythopoesis of sovereignty.

For this reason, fanaticism threatens allegory in at least two ways. First, it demands that we look back to an origin, to trace the source of divine in-spiration or misdirected passion, yet it continually forces us to discover that we are barred from that origin. This is an epistemological aporia. Second, to return to the initial claim about Redcrosse's unfashioning, fanaticism unsettles the poem's didactic project. In the "Letter to Raleigh," Spenser claims that the purpose of allegory is to "fashion a gentleman or noble per-son in vertuous and gentle discipline."[19] Yet in his conversion to an "organ," Redcrosse comes to allegorize the *un*fashioning of "vertuous and gentle discipline," an annihilation of the "ensample" of holiness the poem has been haphazardly building across Book I. Redcrosse's transformation into a vessel of divine force requires that the narrative must risk losing both the personification of holiness and the national didactic lesson it is meant to teach. The poem has trouble sustaining for more than a few stanzas its con-fidence in Redcrosse's metamorphosis. Crossing the threshold between Books I and II with allegorical crisis in tow, this episode is the paradigm for a larger struggle in *The Faerie Queene*. The poem strains to weigh the differ-ence between Redcrosse's claim to be an instrument of God and a range of supposedly false assertions of it that proliferate later in the poem.

In his defeat of the dragon, Redcrosse embodies the poem's most direct and immediate manifestation of self-emptying and inspired violence. The di-vine capture that transforms Redcrosse into holiness seeks to bring to an end the epistemological problems that suffuse Book I of *The Faerie Queene*. It does so only tenuously; the Palmer's comments at the start of Book II make us question further, and the poem never resolves the disagreement definitively. Book II seems to promise an escape from Book I's epistemo-logical insecurity. That it begins with Guyon not being fooled for more than a moment by Archimago's plot to make him think Redcrosse is a rapist is a sign of its more epistemologically tempered mood. Yet the problem of fanaticism is not contained after the disagreement between the Palmer and Redcrosse at the beginning of Book II, and it is when fanaticism seems to emerge again at the end of Book II, with Guyon overtaken by a tempestuous force, that the poem finds itself again in an epistemological aporia.

Guyon's earthbound virtue is in some sense a response to the unsustainable aspirations of holiness in the first book; if fanatical holiness is an impossible object of knowledge for the poem, then temperance—a classical virtue based on the incremental reconstitution of the self through constant modulation and discipline—is easier to grasp.[20] Yet at the end of Book II, Guyon's decimation of the Bower of Bliss seems to recapitulate formally Redcrosse's self-annihilation during his final defeat of the dragon. Like Redcrosse's, Guyon's violence serves a distinctly Christian God, and a number of critics have identified it as a kind of iconoclasm.[21] Harry Berger sees Acrasia in the Bower of Bliss as both "the enemy of Christian temperance" and "an enemy of God, competing with the Divine creation."[22] In his final act of violence, and for no explicit reason, Guyon moves with a newfound force to destroy this threat to God's order:

> But all those pleasaunt bowres and Pallace braue,
>   *Guyon* broke downe, with rigour pittilesse;
>   Ne ought their goodly workmanship might saue
>   Them from the tempest of his wrathfulnesse,
>   But that their blisse he turn'd to balefulnesse:
>   Their groues he feld, their gardins did deface,
>   Their arbers spoyle, their Cabinets suppresse,
>   Their banket houses burne, their buildings race,
> And of the fayrest late, now made the fowlest place.
>
> (2.12.83)

The unfolding of this stanza occults the causality of Guyon's defacement of the Bower.[23] The single-minded nature of Guyon's "rigour pittilesse" gestures ahead to the kind of ruthless force that readers typically associate with Talus.[24] Though no "yron man," Guyon in this moment does seem to have been overtaken by an impersonal force: "the tempest of his wrathfulnesse." This may be more than an atmospheric metaphor. The tempest that envelops Guyon echoes the "roaring hideous sownd,/That all the ayre with terror filled wyde" (1.11.4) from the penultimate canto in Book I: the introductory soundtrack to Redcrosse's apocalyptic showdown with the dragon.[25] As with the representation of the annihilation of Redcrosse, this stanza thinks about Guyon's disappearance within the tempest formally. At the start of the stanza the agency of the actions, if not their motivation, is relatively clear: "*Guyon* broke downe." But the situation changes after the first quatrain. The lack of metrical stress on pronouns referring to Guyon in the stanza's fifth and sixth lines, the disappearance of subject pronouns in the final three lines of the stanza, and the jarring proliferation of caesuras in the final four lines—all of these poetic details seem to empty out Guyon as an actor, rendering him as a passive vessel for a violence that is executed through him.[26]

Critics have often noted the paradox in the narrative logic of the Bower's destruction. The final achievement of temperance is not an act of restraint or of self-discipline but of convulsive violence. It is violence as impersonal force, forgetful of all the lessons about self-tempering that Book II had ostensibly been offering.[27] In his destruction of the Bower, Guyon achieves a more culturally approved—because patriarchally identifiable—version of the self-loss with which Acrasia tempts him: he becomes a tempest. As with Redcrosse, this moment of violence functions as the achievement of allegorization—Guyon's personification of temperance seems like it should be consolidated in the completion of the main mission of Book II—but if this is the ultimate exemplification of temperance, then something is wrong with allegory's own analytic "rigour." The intensity of the violence here, the fact that its expression seems to dissolve Guyon as character, makes the final achievement of temperance resemble fanaticism, the arrival of a force that annihilates the self so that a "tempest of wrathfulnesse" can appear in the world of the poem. Unlike with Redcrosse, however, there is no implication of what force overtakes Guyon; the narrator never names it, nor does the Palmer, and Guyon never gets a chance to explain himself. No one gathers to interpret *this* achievement.

Whether the poem endorses Guyon's violence in the Bower has been a subject of much debate.[28] This debate may be irresolvable, because the poem obscures the source of Guyon's violence and makes irresolvability an issue of form, of grammar and meter. Is Guyon overtaken by the passion of fury, perhaps the Furor who earlier in the book can provoke "the *tempest* of his passion wood" (2.4.11, my emphasis), or is he an instrument of divine vengeance?[29] The poem attempts but fails to use Guyon's virtue as a resolution to the problems that achieving holiness made so palpable. Whichever reading we choose, we are left with the uncomfortable fact that this particular scene of violence imperils the logic of the allegorical process itself. If Guyon's fury is a rupture that overwhelms temperance, then the destruction of the Bower of Bliss represents the failure of the central virtue of Book II and the unmaking of its central personification. By contrast, if wrath in the Bower is the manifestation of divine retribution against Acrasia, then divine violence ruins the consolidation of Guyon's self-discipline, annihilating his will and capacity for self-control. One might attribute the poem's refusal to supply the source of Guyon's "rigour pittilesse" to what John Guillory has called Spenser's "critique of origins."[30] Yet the epistemological critique of origins in this scene gains more specific political urgency when we see it as a return of the repressed threat of fanaticism that Cantos 2–11 in Book II had implied we left behind with Redcrosse. With the allegory of temperance, in other words, the poem seems to give up its agenda of epistemological destabilization when it turns away from its most radical instance, the irresolvable disagreement about Redcrosse's achievement, only to refigure fanaticism's unknowable origins in Guyon's culminating violence.

This epistemological obscurity is solved—or at least, once again, seems to be solved—early in Book III, at the origin of Britomart's quest. Redcrosse appears to become God's vessel after undergoing a Christlike narrative of death and resurrection, but we do not see the moment of inspiration itself. I have suggested that something similar could be said for Guyon, whose "tempest of wrathfulnesse" comes on at once to sacrifice and save temperance without cause or explanation. Graciously, the poem offers us a transparent, unproblematic depiction of divine inspiration at the inception of Britomart's quest, when she sees the image of Artegall, her future husband, in Merlin's mirror:

> Most sacred fyre, that burnest mightily
> > In liuing brests, ykindled first aboue,
> > Emongst th'eternall spheres and lamping sky,
> > And thence pourd into men, which men call Loue;
> > Not that same, which doth base affections moue
> > In brutish mindes, and filthy lust inflame,
> > But that sweete fit, that doth true beautie loue,
> > And choseth vertue for his dearest Dame,
> > Whence spring all noble deedes and neuer dying fame:
>
> Well did Antiquity a God thee deeme,
> > That ouer mortall mindes hast so great might,
> > To order them, as best to thee doth seeme,
> > And all their actions to direct aright;
> > The fatall purpose of diuine foresight,

Thou doest effect in destined descents,
   Through deepe impression of thy secret might,
   And stirredst vp th'Heroes high intents,
Which the late world admyres for wondrous moniments.

But thy dredd dartes in none doe triumph more,
   Ne brauer proofe in any, of thy powre
   Shew'dst thou, then in this royall Maid of yore,
   Making her seeke an vnknowne Paramoure,
   From the worlds end, through many a bitter stowre:
   From whose two loynes thou afterwardes did rayse
   Most famous fruites of matrimoniall bowre,
   Which through the earth haue spredd their liuing prayse,
That fame in tromp of gold eternally displayes.

                                      (3.3.1–3)

At the start of this canto, we find a Neoplatonic explanation of the love for Artegall that Britomart first experiences as an "engraffed payne" that grows inside her (3.2.17).[31] Though Britomart's love seems fundamentally different from the ambiguous violence that emerges as Redcrosse and Guyon fulfill their missions, the structures of inspiration in all are suggestively similar, but with a crucial difference in Britomart's case. Britomart's love is not a willed attachment; "Loue" is the name of a force that is "ykindled" in the heavens and "thence pourd into men" to become a fire, not entirely unlike Donne's zeal. That fire leads individuals to experience a "sweete fit," an ecstasy that is the true origin of all the good done in the world but that also empties the self in order to "fit" it to a divine will.[32] This force or fire that men call Love is itself a god—or at least Spenser's narrator judges it proper that antiquity named Love a god ("Well did Antiquity a God thee deeme"). The experience of love appears to be characterized by having something divine—that fire kindled in the heavens—inhabit one's chest. That manifestation of divine fire is more than metaphor. It has a palpable "might," it "order[s]" men's minds, it "direct[s]" all their actions, and it "effect[s]" the "fatall purpose of diuine foresight." In other words, it is a fire that burns the will and the "base affections" out of someone, and as consequence of that self-annihilating "sweete fit," determines and directs their actions in the world. Divine force acts through lovers, and though the world construes their actions as "wondrous moniments" that speak to their own greatness (as the Palmer did with Redcrosse's "hard atchieu'ment"), it is divine Love itself that is acting through these human vessels.

Finally, after two books in which fanatical inspiration causes an episte-mological impasse, we see the thing itself. But, of course, not really, because this Love is different from the holiness that Redcrosse becomes in the penultimate canto of Book I; it draws more on classical mythology and Neoplatonic understandings of love than on a Christian understanding of grace, and is disconnected from any act of violence in the world. We finally witness unambiguous inspiration, but a classical god replaces a biblical one, and Love "direct[s]" Britomart toward marriage and reproductivity rather than destruction.[33] Redcrosse's transformation may be prerequisite for his indefinitely deferred marriage to Una and thus for his nationalist mission, but the divine violence that makes Redcrosse into holiness cannot be re-duced to the national or didactic narratives that the poem tells at the end of Book I. Still, the structural similarity is uncanny, for in each case we see a character in *The Faerie Queene* who becomes an instrument of a divine force.

The differences between the two, however, require us to ask why the poem gives us unambiguous access to the divine origins of Britomart's in-spiration but obscures those origins in the cases of Redcrosse and Guyon. In other words, why are we as readers assured that Britomart's inspiration is divine and yet unable to see the evidence for Redcrosse's or Guyon's inspi-ration? Redcrosse tells us after the fact that he has become an organ of God's might, but with Britomart we actually witness, through the narra-tor's mediation, the process by which Love's fire and darts "triumph" in her heart and direct her, which lends it a great deal more narrative trans-parency than Redcrosse's story has.

Addressing these questions allows us to clarify the poem's ambivalence about the divine violence that characterizes fanaticism. For the Love that usurps and directs Britomart's will, though it leaves her in potentially in-terminable grief until Merlin completes the prophecy of Britomart's future in a "suddein fitt, and halfe extatick stoure" (3.3.50) of his own, also en-sures that she pursues a path that leads her to produce with Artegall a progeny that will save the Britons. Divine inspiration supports—rather than disrupts—genealogy and allegory, both in the service of state-building. The divine, in the guise of Love, directs Britomart on a path that will lead to the future reign of "a royall Virgin" (3.3.49), an allusion to Elizabeth I as the real-world embodiment of chastity. The poem thus ap-pears less ambivalent about Britomart overtaken by Love than it does about the violence that seems to empty and inspire Redcrosse and Guyon.[34] The violence that may annihilate Redcrosse and Guyon has a more am-bivalent position within the narrative of *The Faerie Queene*. It cannot be

controlled and oriented toward the ends of political and allegorical consolidation in the ways that Britomart's can; Britomart's loss of will as
Love inhabits her is tied to a nationalist reproductive futurism directly.
The fact that Love's overtaking of Britomart raises fewer worries for the
poem may also be because of her emergence on the other side of this "fit"
as the poem's most robust character. Her relatively realist representation is not undermined by the fact that Love directs her journey through
divine inspiration.[35] The negation of her will turns out to be something
very different from the more radical self-annihilation I have associated
with Müntzer.

From Redcrosse to Guyon to Britomart, we can trace the persistence
of a problem and shifting attempts to resolve it. With Redcrosse, the poem
seems as though it is trying definitively to depict an organ of divine might,
but the exchange with the Palmer early in Book II retroactively casts a
cloud of unknowing onto the question of whose agency—God's or
Redcrosse's—achieved the death of the dragon. Guyon's case is at once
more equivocal and more straightforward; we are never even tempted to
think we know what the tempest is that overtakes him, whether a divine
force or an intemperate passion. Britomart is inspired—we are sure of
that—but we can only perceive her inhabitation insofar as the poem's iconography shifts from biblical to classical. The first three books do not allow us to solve the problem of fanatical inspiration. At the moment we see
divine will replace a character's will, the god is relegated to a safer (because
knowable) divinity from classical mythology.

The interpretive difficulty that fanaticism creates here is deeper than
the usual epistemological problems that critics have ably charted over the
first three books of *The Faerie Queene*. The inability to know is constitutive of the witness of fanaticism, and this unknowability makes it impossible to mobilize fanaticism (unlike Britomart's knowable inspiration) in
direct political ways. Fanaticism demands that we look back to the source
of inspiration to determine whether it is genuine or false, but this backward glance only reveals a deeper obscurity. The presence of divine inspiration is always in question. Spenser's allegory does not seem able to
penetrate its mystery without adding further complications: shifting to a
classical register, or turning a transparently possessed being into the
poem's richest character.

What about when the poem focuses not on a singular inspired "organ" but
rather on fanaticism as a collective problem? So far I have demonstrated
how Spenser brought to light fanaticism's epistemological aporia with

uncanny complexity; his manner of doing so through the form and content of his poem would prove extremely influential for Renaissance poetics. The final section of this chapter maps the poem's most significant strategy for addressing its own skepticism about its capacity to confirm fanaticism's origins and effects, and to delineate between a genuine instrument of God and a demagogue or madman, in the context of a collective rebellion. This political crisis casts the poem's deepening doubt in a new light and discloses an especially reactionary solution to the epistemological obscurity of fanaticism. The fifth book of *The Faerie Queene*, the book of justice, suggests that one way to recognize a false fanatic is simply to make a judgment based on his politics. Part of a "pattern of overreaction" that Jeff Dolven has shown to structure the poem,[36] Artegall and Talus's encounter with the egalitarian Giant and his rebellious multitude in the second canto of Book V reveals the poem's self-reflexively panicked effort to expel the very questions raised initially by Redcrosse's instrumental unfashioning.

Theorists writing in the shadow of Étienne Balibar have argued that much of early modern European political philosophy was shaped, constitutively, by a fear of the masses.[37] This section implicitly poses a related question: What role does a fear of the masses, and in particular fear of a fanatical multitude, play in the development of Spenser's allegorical verse? In Book V, the knight of justice, Artegall, and his iron man, Talus, are on a mission to rescue the lady Eirena (referring to the Gaelic name for Ireland) from the Catholic tyrant Grantorto. They come across the Giant and his crew early in their quest, when their desire to act as murderous police—in this case, riot police—distracts them from the larger mission. At first, Artegall and Talus merely wonder at the sheer size of the gathering: "for neuer there the like resort they knew" (5.2.29). Artegall engages in a debate with the Giant about economic and cosmological redistribution while the multitude listen, and Talus ends the dispute abruptly when he kills the Giant without any warning. When the rascal rout rises up in protest of Talus's execution of the Giant, the episode becomes an opportunity for the poem to reflect on the relationship between allegory, justice, and punishment, and the difficulty—perhaps the impossibility—of aligning them all. The poem's reflection centers on the mobile, amorphous figure of the "swarm," which, as it comes into being in the political and cosmological project that the Giant and his crew articulate, threatens both allegory and justice as Artegall imagines them.

The word "swarm" does not yet appear in the narrator's first account of the Giant and his crew, but its figural implications of contagious collectivity are already active:

For why, he sayd they all vnequall were,
    And had encroched vppon others share,
    Like as the sea (which plaine he shewed there)
    Had worne the earth, so did the fire the aire,
    So all the rest did others parts empaire.
    And so were realmes and nations run awry.
    All which he vndertooke for to repaire,
    In sort as they were formed aunciently;
And all things would reduce vnto equality.

Therefore the vulgar did about him flocke,
    And cluster thicke vnto his leasings vaine,
    Like foolish flies about an hony crocke,
    In hope by him great benefite to gaine,
    And vncontrolled freedome to obtaine.
    All which when *Artegall* did see, and heare,
    How he mis-led the simple peoples traine,
    In sdeignfull wize he drew vnto him neare,
And thus vnto him spake, without regard or feare.

                                (5.2.32–33)

These stanzas echo a discourse associated in Spenser's moment with Thomas Müntzer and the Anabaptist revolt in Germany of the 1520s, but transposed onto a colonial Irish context in which claims for ancient commonness are equally urgent.[38] The Giant critiques a world in which political and economic human inequality, so structurally entrenched, appear like natural forces. The Giant's project means to return the elements of the world to a state of prelapsarian grace, "as they were formed aunciently." In this context, the project of leveling and repair sounds less like a primitivist fantasy than an anticolonial and antistatist tactic. The alexandrine sums up the Giant's work, presupposing that the original divine creation formed a world in which "all things" were equal. Through a collective leveling, the Giant and his multitude can "repaire" or "reduce" all things so that they return to that original state.

    The next stanza works to undo this vision of redemptive revolution. It recasts the Giant's vision as demagoguery attractive only to the dipterous and self-aggrandizing "vulgar." The narrator's exposure of opportunism as the real motive of the Giant and his followers is meant to demystify their claim to intimate knowledge of divine creation along with their call to return to its original "equality." The simile ("Like foolish flies about an hony crocke") suggests a worry, though: the possibility that the crowd follows the Giant not only for purposes of self-aggrandizement but also because they suffer from an instinctual attraction to his ideas. His rhetoric is sweet and sticky, drawing people in like flies looking for honeyed sustenance. This fanatical community seems to form in the words that congeal them all together. The Giant's words and ideas seem to be contagious—the multitude sticks to the honey of his speech. In their "cluster thicke," the people here create a new multiplicity, a momentary assemblage, a communal swarm. This is, after all, one of the great fears fanaticism provokes from Martin Luther onward: it causes people to be drawn to ideas and language that make them not only disobedient but also illegible to political and religious authority alike. Luther's original term for the fanaticism of the Anabaptist rebels whom he denounced was *Schwärmerei*, an indistinguishable swarming of flies.[39] But there is an unsettling ambiguity here, a difficulty in determining whether the danger inherent in this mass of people preexists the Giant's honeyed words or whether it is the honeyed words that make them so dangerous. The fact that the vulgar are rendered "like" flies underscores the narrator's self-conscious uncertainty about whether the vulgar are always like flies. Are they inherently fly-like, endogenously able to cluster together and foment rebellion at any moment, forever longing for "vncontrolled freedome"? Or do they require a single instrumental leader to stir the honeyed pot, his rebellious words catching them like a contagion they can never really resist?

The Giant and his flies wish to level not only the hierarchal structure of economic inequality but also the allegory of justice intervolved with it. Artegall recognizes this in his accounts of the binding together of allegory and cosmos in the name of heavenly justice:

> "Such heauenly iustice doth among them raine,
>   That euery one doe know their certaine bound,
>   In which they doe these many yeares remaine,
>   And mongst them al no change hath yet beene found,
>   But if thou now shouldst weigh them new in pound,
>   We are not sure they would so long remaine:
>   All change is perillous, and all chaunce vnsound.
>   Therefore leaue off to weigh them all againe,
> Till we may be assur'd they shall their course retaine."

(5.2.36)

Artegall's perspective could not be more dissonant with that espoused by the narrator in the proem to Book V, for whom "all things else in time are chaunged quight. / Ne wonder; for the heauens reuolution / Is wandred farre

from, where it first was pight" (Proem, 4). By contrast, Artegall's "heauenly
iustice" consists of everyone always knowing his place within the whole,
his "certaine bound"—implying both limitation and bondage. In this
way, heavenly justice resembles an overwrought allegory, a hyperboli-
cally ossified example of what Fletcher calls allegory's inclination toward
the imposition of topocosmic unity, in which "euery one" has a proper
place, "remain[ing]" fixed in time, space, and meaning.[40] Overreacting
to the Giant's projected leveling, Artegall claims, "All change is perillous,
and all chaunce vnsound." Heavenly justice is absolute stasis, a perpetual
"retain[ing]" of the "certaine bound" of things as they are and are meant
to be—allegory at its most totalitarian, a cosmic naturalization of the state
in which every single being is bound to its place, and legible precisely
because it remains there.

Such ordering of everyone's proper places, the cosmological hierarchy
that binds them, and the allegorical structure by which heavenly justice
can be read in political and environmental stasis—all require the Giant and
his multitude's conversion or containment. The Giant is hardly convinced:

> "Therefore I will throw downe these mountaines hie,
>   And make them leuell with the lowly plaine:
>   These towring rocks, which reach vnto the skie,
>   I will thrust downe into the deepest maine,
>   And as they were, them equalize againe.
>   Tyrants that make men subiect to their law,
>   I will suppresse, that they no more may raine;
>   And Lordings curbe, that commons ouer-aw;
> And all the wealth of rich men to the poore will draw."

(5.2.38)

These leveling actions do not only threaten to redistribute wealth and
property. The project to "equalize againe" also hopes to undo utterly Artegall's static allegory of heavenly justice, and to return the "commons" to
a state of original divine creation. Unlike Fletcher, I do not see the Giant
as trying to convince the masses that "he (not God) can give them a New
Jerusalem of their own."[41] Despite the absence of the rhetoric of self-
annihilation and inspiration, the Giant implicitly sees the project of re-
equalization as divinely inspired, a "repairing" of divine order. Both the
Giant and Artegall, then, claim to be instruments in a divine plan, one a
manager of the unchanging bounds of heavenly justice, and the other a
leveling medium for the return to an originary divine creation held in
common.

This disagreement between two agents of divine order should recall, albeit with diminished intensity, Redcrosse's transformation into an organ of divine might. Artegall echoes Redcrosse's language explicitly when he claims that divine agency determines justice:

> "What euer thing is done, by him is donne,
>> Ne any may his mighty will withstand;
>> Ne any may his soueraine power shonne,
>> Ne loose that he hath bound with stedfast band."

(5.2.42)

Artegall's "certaine bound" cannot be undone because it is God's "mighty will." Whereas Redcrosse averred that he momentarily became God's vessel, Artegall suggests that every action is reducible to God's agency. The Giant never contradicts Artegall's claim of God's sovereign agency. Instead, he disputes the claim that God's will supports Artegall's hierarchal order and conception of justice. While Artegall's erasure of will yields an allegorical world of hierarchal, eternal stasis, the Giant implies that his will has been dissolved into the divine command to reduce the earth to its original state of shared plenitude.

As the episode turns momentarily comic, with the marvelous weighing of words, Artegall seems to have the upper hand in the argument with the Giant, but plenty of critics have shown that the poem resists any easy elevation of Artegall's vision of justice above the Giant's.[42] The poem declines to declare a winner in this argument. Here, we have two visions of divine agency pitched in irremediable disagreement. Artegall's encounter with the Giant introduces into *The Faerie Queene* the possibility that there can be two conflicting prophetic visions, both of which posit God as the author of all of actions.

The Giant echoes the slogan that was supposedly uttered by Anabaptist agitator and peasant organizer Müntzer at his execution in 1525, which itself echoed across the long Reformation: *omnia sunt communia*.[43] From the German Peasants' Revolt of the 1520s through the English Civil War of the mid-seventeenth century, fanatics like the Giant make the claim that God can annihilate and inspire individuals, leading them to undertake a revolution in the world's social and political organization.[44] Artegall's and the Giant's prophetic claims—one to divine order, one to divine equalization—cannot really be argued out. They meet in the form of what Jean-François Lyotard has described as a *différend*, a conflict "that cannot be equitably resolved for lack of a rule of judgment applicable to both arguments."[45] Both parties posit but cannot present the divine will that could adjudicate their claims. Neither readers of the poem nor witnesses to this scene, including the crowd soon to be overthrown by Talus, can know which vision of the world God has authorized and who is truly an instrument of God.

Talus realizes the problem that this *différend* introduces both to the narrative and to allegorical design itself. This is why, without a word, he approaches the Giant and "shouldered him from off the higher ground,/And down the rock him throwing, in the sea him dround" (5.2.49). The demands of allegory and of Artegall's vision of heavenly justice require the violent expulsion of the egalitarian Giant's threat. The only leveling allowed to—or rather inflicted on—the Giant is that his "high aspyring" is "humbled" with a correspondingly "huge ruine" (5.2.50). He is leveled into a broken sign of equalization's aspiration.[46]

Although the poem violently expels the Giant in order for the allegory of justice to move forward, the description of the Giant's punishment offers some resistance to the allegorical tableau that such violence tries to create:

> Like as ship, whom cruell tempest driues
>     Vpon a rocke with horrible dismay,
>     Her shattered ribs in thousand peeces riues,
>     And spoyling all her geares and goodly ray,
>     Does make her selfe misfortunes piteous pray.
>
> (5.2.50)

The narrator almost seems to pity the ruin: the tempest is "cruell" (and perhaps as excessive and unexplained as Guyon's tempestuous destruction of the Bower). He tries to attenuate this touch of compassion by depicting the ship as having, somehow, made "her selfe" into "misfortunes piteous pray." But the simile's assignment of agency to the inanimate ship does not entirely "shatter" the sense that the Giant did not deserve this punishment, not any more than a ship could ever deserve being so "spoyl[ed]." The detail of the "shattered ribs" of the ship seems to signal a misfire in the allegory, too. The simile involutes: the Giant's body is *like* a ship but the ship is also *like* a body. The ribs of the ship are also the ribs of a broken body. The simile collapses the allegorical and the literal, registering formally a trace of the struggle to convert this brutalized body into the legible allegorical sign of "high aspyring."

Thus, the Giant's fanaticism introduces a series of theological, epistemological, and political problems that destabilize the correlation between allegorical stability and judicial order, and that the stanzas I have explored register through complex poetic techniques. These problems extend to the instruments of justice, too. The poem's response to the *différend* that arises between Artegall and the Giant is an ambivalent unleashing of Talus's mechanical violence. Talus finds the Giant "lewdly minded" ("whom when so lewdly minded *Talus* found" [5.2.49]), and that seems to justify his violent outburst, but Spenser's syntax leads us, momentarily, to apply "lewdly minded" to Talus as well, suggesting that the iron man may have caught his contagious fanatical vulgarity. This syntactic ambiguity registers the potential of fanaticism to spread not only to the swarm surrounding the Giant but also to the machinery of justice. If Talus himself can appear "lewdly minded," if only for an instant before readers iron out the reference, then the poem seems worried about whether his actions in fact secure heavenly justice and allegorical hierarchy.

It is Talus's violence against the cluster of people who witness his execution of the Giant that embodies this worry most acutely.

> That when the people, which had there about
>     Long wayted, saw his sudden desolation,
>     They gan to gather in tumultuous rout,
>     And mutining, to stirre vp ciuill faction,
>     For certaine losse of so great expectation.
>     For well they hoped to haue got great good,
>     And wondrous riches by his innouation.
>     Therefore resoluing to reuenge his blood,
> They rose in armes, and all in battell order stood.
>
> Which lawlesse multitude him comming too
>     In warlike wise, when *Artegall* did vew,
>     He much was troubled, ne wist what to doo.
>     For loth he was his noble hands t'embrew
>     In the base blood of such a rascall crew;
>     And otherwise, if that he should retire,
>     He fear'd least they with shame would him pursew.
>     Therefore he *Talus* to him sent, t'inquire
> The cause of their array, and truce for to desire.
>
> But soone as they him nigh approching spide,
>     They gan with all their weapons him assay,
>     And rudely stroke at him on euery side:
>     Yet nought they could him hurt, ne ought dismay.
>     But when at them he with his flaile gan lay,

> He like a swarme of flyes them ouerthrew;
> Ne any of them durst come in his way,
> But here and there before his presence flew,
> And hid themselues in holes and bushes from his vew.

$$(5.2.51–53)$$

These stanzas represent this uprising as at once concerted and chaotic. Initially, there is the depiction of a gathering "tumultuous rout." The gathering makes them sound like an organized group—they "all in battell order stood"—but "tumult" and "rout" give the sense of disorganization and fragmentation, as though their coming together were already a kind of brokenness. This tension—the rout as its own totality and as a series of fragments—frames the narrator's imputation of a split motivation for the rout: first, that they rebel in mourning ("for certaine losse of so great expectation"); and second, that they do so for revenge ("resoluing to reuenge his blood"). Meanwhile, Artegall, concerned about the possibility of his noble hands getting dirty with base blood, sends Talus to "t'inquire/The cause of their array." The poem's layered indecision about the group's motivation prepares the reader to experience this rebellious force as a fragmented and opaque totality, one then materialized in the image of the swarm of flies.

The swarm is significant in part because it evokes Luther's fanatics, *Schwärmer*, those Anabaptist peasants who revolted to pursue a communist utopia. As I discussed in the Introduction, Luther claimed that these fanatics could not be reasoned with, and that they could not be punished and folded back into the civic order—they were, as Spenser's narrator says, a lawless multitude, and constitutively so.[47] But what is curious about the episode in Spenser is that Talus does not, and perhaps even cannot, kill them. So if Luther's swarms, his *Schwärmer*, were too animalistic to deserve any fate other than death, why do Spenser's flies survive, and what are the consequences of their dispersal?

Of course, Talus overthrows the rout like a swarm of flies, which implies that they are relatively powerless. It is important that becoming like flies is not their allegorical punishment for being so frenzied, disorganized, collective, vulgar—they are already like flies, and Talus only needs to scatter them. That seems to be the end. Artegall and Talus do not feel threatened enough by the rout to have to kill them all; they simply leave. (Their response is less murderous than Luther recommended it should be.) But the flying away and hiding of the flies is more ambiguous than it might at first seem, precisely because they escape and unsettle Artegall's image of heavenly justice as a world-order of ossified and legible allegory. Swarms are constitutively resistant to that model of hypertrophied allegorical order. As Peter Fenves has argued, members of a swarm are impossible to distinguish from one another; they cannot "even be called *members* of the swarm" because "instead of belonging to a stable collective according to which they would be recognized and named, each one is a temporary participant in an act of swarming or *Schwärmerei*."[48] The poem forecloses the possibility of understanding the motivations, let alone of rebinding the significance and political place of each fragmentary being in the uprising by turning them into a swarm of flies.

The swarm's illegibility and capacity for fugitive evasion continues even after its dissolution. Consider how the flies fly away:

> He like a swarme of flyes them ouerthrew;
> Ne any of them durst come in his way,
> But here and there before his presence flew,
> And hid themselues in holes and bushes from his vew.

There is an equivocation between lines six and seven. "Ouerthrew" echoes the punishment of the Giant, whom Talus had "throw[n]" down into the sea ("And down the rock him throwing, in the sea him dround" [5.2.49]). But what does overthrowing a swarm look like? "Ne any of them durst come in his way" suggests total evasion, especially when compared with Talus's palpable "shoulder[ing]" of the Giant. This is extended by "But here and there before his presence flew," with the temporal and spatial meaning of "before" making it seem like their flight is always one step ahead of Talus. Though the poem inclines toward eliding the difference between dispersal and defeat, the fact that these flies have hidden themselves from Talus's view suggests just how irrepressible they are as a swarming multitude, how they resist incorporation into allegory and withdraw from the poem's efforts to control and contain them, to render them legible and meaningful. Talus, and the narrator, importantly, lose track of them. Talus has overthrown their current assemblage, but they have, for now, escaped the territorial bounds of justice and allegory. The Giant himself is hugely ruined, but his multitude has hidden itself away, resisting justice's lesson. Instead of becoming divinely and politically bound to their place within the poem's geography and allegory, these rebels-turned-flies simply disappear, become unknown to justice and to the readers. Their animalization is their condition of escape, which makes this simile so fundamentally different from, say, Milton's famous simile of the swarm of bees in Book I of *Paradise Lost*, in which the very act of comparing devils to a

swarm reduces their threat and "straiten[s]" them, circumscribing and plac-
ing them within what Geoffrey Hartman has called the "counterplot" of
their predestined management.[49] We do not know where Spenser's
swarm goes. "Here and there"—which is to say, potentially everywhere
and nowhere—they hide, possibly to regroup for yet another act of fanatical swarming or for something else entirely. It is crucial that we do not
know what they do in hiding.

Joseph Campana has recently argued that images of swarms in early
modern English texts "pose a threat to the idea that sovereignty was,
whether by monarch or the people, necessary."[50] I want to add to this
important insight a sense of the way this particular swarm in *The Faerie
Queene* registers how a leaderless, vertically in-flight multitude causes an
epistemological crisis that subverts both the political state and the allegorical meaning that the poem is working, however ambivalently, to construct. In this episode, Spenser's poem enacts more than what Teskey might
call the violence that shapes and sustains allegory; it reveals how allegory
and one version of its most extreme political fantasy, in Artegall's eternally
stable and bound cosmos, fails, and must fail. Though Book V becomes
increasingly committed, with varying degrees of success, to destroying collective gatherings, in the second canto of its fifth book, the poem can only
gesture toward the swarm's disappearance into the poem's underground,
hidden from view. Fanaticism spreads from the Giant to the multitude.
Once the Giant is gone and they are confronted with Talus's seemingly
unstoppable policing, the swarm leaves entirely the allegorical cosmos that
Artegall wants to build, and about which Spenser is so endlessly ambivalent. The swarm is in but not of the poem, and we could think of their
disappearance as a departure to forge a world, unseen and unknown to
us, in which a life stolen from the allegory can foster a fugitive community, one in which "vncontrolled freedome" is the condition of possibility
for the enlivening of what the Giant refers to as a new, but also ancient,
commons.[51]

When confronted with the fanatic as "organ" or "swarm," *The Faerie Queene*
tends to use allegory as an analytic tool for distinguishing between true
inspiration and false claims to divine prompting. The poem seeks to separate true instances in which characters become instruments of a divine
will that consolidates sovereignty (e.g., Redcrosse's transformation) from
false claims to inspiration or to knowledge of the divine that threaten
both the political order and the procedures of allegory itself (e.g., the
egalitarian Giant). It includes these fanatical figures in part to diagnose

and incorporate them into the lessons the allegory can offer, to coax a structure of meaning from fanaticism's threat. As with the example of Malengin later in Book V, who stands in for the threat of Irish rebels and must be lured out of the "dreadfull depth" of his unfathomable underground hiding place ("how deepe no man can tell" [5.9.6]), fanatics must be drawn out of their supposedly internal divine inspiration and shown for what they are: false prophets, dangerous demagogues, guileful seducers of a gullible rabble. Such revelation is meant to produce lessons so that characters within the poem, and readers themselves, can discriminate between false fanatics and true organs of God's will.

Yet the problems that fanaticism raises remain, sometimes hidden, sometimes on the surface of the verse's technical accomplishments, regularly resistant to allegorical discipline. Sometimes the poem is even uncertain about its ostensibly authorized instruments of God, such as Redcrosse. *The Faerie Queene*'s extraordinary representational resources either fail or refuse to offer a sure way to know how to recognize true divine inspiration. It is an important and now widely accepted claim in recent studies that romance is pitched against allegory in *The Faerie Queene*, a struggle between genres that shapes the poem and productively mars its grandest fantasies.[52] Fanaticism's capacity for unmaking is different from romance's, since it seems to emerge *like* or even *as* allegory, its seal or promise rather than its other, only then to unmoor its didactic and political projects. With fanaticism, the poem makes us linger, repeatedly, in some of the most acute—and most politically and poetically critical—failures of its own didactic project.[53] Spenser's experiments with allegory as a genre and a set of poetic techniques attempt to do justice to the complexity of the problems fanaticism raises, while calling into question the idea and the personification of justice that Book V presents.

We have seen, with Redcrosse, that the moment when the divine empties out and inhabits a character is at once the achievement of the allegory of holiness and the undoing of allegory's ability to analyze and order the world of the poem. There is good reason for the Palmer to worry about allegory's power to contain and make use of the extraordinary violence that emerges when Redcrosse seems to become an organ of holy violence. This is perhaps why the poem never allows us to rest comfortably with our certainty about his status and why fanaticism radicalizes Book I's epistemological uncertainty, which returns with Guyon's tempest of wrathfulness and is displaced in Britomart's inspired "fit." With the Giant and his comrades, we see that divine violence, and justice's fraught attempt to police it, can have difficult political consequences. The singularity that defines the transformation of

Redcrosse into an organ of divine might can spread to a multitude. Inspiration—even a supposedly false claim to it—is transmittable; it threatens to move from one body to another, to cluster them thickly together, and to create a whole new "commons," a transindividual swarm that escapes allegory and justice. The poem has trouble confirming Redcrosse's divine mission and dismissing the Giant's. The irresistible possession of perfect allegorization allows *The Faerie Queene* to reveal the content and the formal structure of fanaticism, even as the poem works to secure, through allegory, a way to demystify fanatics and distinguish them from those true organs of divine might. Spenser is one of the poets who lingers most profoundly, as he experiments with the techniques afforded him by allegorical verse, with this knowing and unknowing that shape the witness of fanaticism. His poem invites its readers to linger there, too.

In taking the impossibility of discerning the presence of divine inspiration as a provocation internal to his poetics, Spenser sets the stage for encounters with fanaticism that emerge in Donne and Milton. Before turning to Donne's exploration of the relationship between form and fanaticism in his meditations on martyrdom, though, I want to return to Spenser's own inclination to associate poetic making with self-emptying and divine inspiration. In the "Argument" that precedes the October Eclogue in *The Shepheardes Calender* (1579), annotator E. K.'s description of poetry resonates pointedly with crucial aspects of fanaticism: "Or rather no arte, but a divine gift and heavenly instinct not to bee gotten by laboure and learning, but adorned with both: and poured into the witte by a certaine ἐνθουσιασμὸς [*enthusiasmos*], and celestiall inspiration."[54] Admittedly, the orientation of the October Eclogue's enthusiasm is distinct from fanaticism; it does not have a substantial relationship to divine violence. But the likeness is worth dwelling on, since it returns us to the complex image of the rhapsode discussed briefly in my Introduction. Spenser's annotator describes poetry not as a labor, technique, or "arte" by which, as in allegory, analytic distinctions are creatively embodied in personifications that shape the author's and readers' values; instead, poetry is itself a "divine gift and heavenly instinct" that comes absolutely spontaneously. This is an even more radical claim than John Skelton gave voice to seventy years earlier in "A Replication against Certain Young Scholars Abjured of Late," in which "spyrituall instygacion/And divyne inspyracion/ . . . kyndled" a poet in such a way that the "hete of the Holy Gost" the poet's "penne dothe lede."[55] According to the October description, God does more than lead the pen. A poet does not actively *make* verse. Poetry is given to one ("pourd into") and moves through one as a "celestiall inspiration."

Within the body of the Eclogue, the shepherd and poet Cuddie claims, "The vaunted verse a vacant head demaundes, / Ne wont with crabbed care the Muses dwell."[56] Divine inspiration empties the poet, vacating his head to allow the divine gift—in this case the Muses—to dwell within him.

If *The Faerie Queene* is meant to be both didactic and inspired in this sense, as the narrator of Spenser's epic repeatedly claims, then poetic making as *enthusiasmos*, which induces the emptying out of the poet's self, potentially disrupts the lessons that allegory's analysis is meant to teach. Careful didacticism is hard to unfold with a vacant head. The enthusiastic state of poetic utterance is similar to the kind of self-annihilation we see in fanaticism—even if, again, I have taken pains to distinguish fanaticism from, for example, Locke's definition of enthusiasm. And, as has been put forth at least since Plato's *Ion*, poetry may confront its readers or auditors with a contagion or a magnetism that binds them stickily to the divine. Vaunted verse may create a thick cluster in which the divine inhabits not only the poet but the readers or auditors themselves, fashioning them into a communal assemblage, not entirely unlike the gathering we see emerge around the honeyed words of the egalitarian Giant.[57] This is a fear to which Donne and Hobbes gave voice, as we see in Chapters 2 and 3. Inspiration—even a supposedly false claim to it—is transmittable; it threatens to move from one body to another, to cluster them together, to usher a force through them that no individual can claim, and to create a whole new "commons," to use the Giant's term. If only for a moment, it threatens a contagious sharing of divine voice.[58]

In his regular invocations of inspiration throughout *The Faerie Queene*, beginning with the Proem to Book I, Spenser implicitly imagines this structure—the annihilation of the poet's will that makes space for the presence of God—as immanent to the process of "vaunted" verse-making itself, and it will equally concern Donne and Milton. How does one know whether a poet—or, by extension, the fanaticism he portrays—is truly inspired? If the poet is himself inspired, or even claims to be, then we have no standard by which to know whether the allegories the poet makes will allow us to distinguish with certainty between true inspiration and the "crabbed care" of a false performance. This is perhaps why Spenser's narrator, shortly before he relates Redcrosse's fanatical transformation in the penultimate canto of Book I, begs the "Goddesse" who inspires him to "lay that furious fitt asyde" and only "gently come into my feeble brest" (1.11.6–7). It is as though the poet wants to modulate the intensity of poetic inspiration he himself experiences—to maintain willful control over it—in order to ensure that Redcrosse's representation as an organ of God's might is didactically clear within the text. Of course, we never know if the poet gets his wish, but the origins of Redcrosse's holy violence remain unknowable in any case.

Donne discovers a different but connected question about the relationship between fanaticism and verse-making, and does so most acutely in the form of the sonnet: what if verse-making actually bars oneself, as a devotional poet, from the nonexperience of self-annihilation? What does it mean for Donne to demand in a devotional sonnet, crafted by discipline and in a state of willful self-abnegation, that God annihilate and inhabit him? This question, worked out formally in the sonnet's choreographing of line and quatrain, creates space for Donne's theoretically and historically subtle reflection on the relationship between fanaticism and martyrdom.

CHAPTER 2

# Lyric Fanaticism: Donne's Annihilation

Aber die Wahrheit kann durch ein solches Heiligen der Endlichkeit,
die bestehen bleibt, nicht hintergangen werden, denn die wahre
Heiligung müßte dasselbe vernichten.

—G. W. F. HEGEL, "Glauben und Wissen"

At the beginning of the Introduction, I offered a partial reading of Donne's "I ame a litle World," in which I argued that the poem at once proposes and defers a conceit that renders zeal identical with self-annihilation or, more precisely, self-conflagration:

> And burne me O God with a fiery Zeale
> Of thee,' and thy house, which doth in eating heale.

In the sonnet's concluding couplet, "Zeale" and "heale" are laced together with a rhyme that renders the fiery immolation of the speaker inextricable from his reconstitution as a vessel of God. That zeal is "of" God because it is the divine force that both incinerates and heals the self, unmaking the difference between the speaker and God (hence the language of eating). The poem sustains itself through ambivalence toward this zeal, though. A deep desire for that self-consuming zeal carries the sonnet from one conceit to the next, but the multiplication of conceits is also a symptom of a worry that if this zeal consumed him, then there would be no self left to write the poem. As though in response to Spenser's ambivalence to poetic inspiration, "I ame a litle World" suggests that the self needs to defer self-annihilation in order for the poem to become a completed artifact. This ambivalence runs even deeper in another Holy Sonnet, "Batter my hart," and provides a frame for Donne's prose writing about the relationship between activity and passivity in martyrdom.

In this chapter, I pose three interrelated questions about Donne and the self-emptying zeal of fanaticism. First, what is the phenomenology of self-annihilation—that is, how and why does one become nothing in order to be transformed into an organ of divine might? Second, in an extension of the analysis of "I ame a litle World," I ask how Donne involves the techniques of verse writing in his exploration of self-annihilation. Can *poiesis* bring about the self's annihilation and inspiration, or does poetic labor defer the attainment of instrumental passivity that characterizes fanaticism? I find that Donne works through both these questions in the *Holy Sonnets* as he attempts to use the formal structure of the sonnet as a space to demand and make present his own self-annihilation and to turn himself into a vessel of God's violence. My study of self-annihilation and poetic labor in "Batter my hart" provokes a third question with more obvious political stakes: is fanaticism imitable? Martyrdom is a subcategory of fanaticism throughout Donne's prose writings because it requires the same self-annihilation and instrumental passivity that I have outlined in Thomas Müntzer's reception of divine action and Spenser's "organ" of divine might. Martyrdom can—though does not always—result in a suicide attack, as with the biblical judge Samson, a case on which Donne reflects repeatedly. Donne is deeply concerned about the spread of martyrdom to a collective through mimetic contagion, especially given the waves of Catholic and Protestant martyrdom that shaped much of the second half of the sixteenth century in England and that had drastic effects on Donne's family.

The conjunction of annihilation and martyrdom allows me to reconsider Ramie Targoff's claim that annihilation is "inconceivable" in Donne's writing by analyzing how Donne's works try, and fail, to conceive of annihilation—to make it happen and to understand its origins and effects.[1] In his poetry and prose, Donne applies his theory of self-annihilation in order to develop a unique conception of martyrdom. I call this "inimitable" or "unexemplary" martyrdom—a redefinition of sacred self-immolation as utterly singular, free from labor, and impervious to the kind of mimetic transmission that can lead to individual or collective political antagonism. This is not Donne's only definition of martyrdom, positive or negative, but it is the most complex and has been least appreciated by scholars. Ultimately, I find Donne's interest in unexemplary martyrdom to be deeply ambivalent. It produces something genuinely new in early modern thought:

a unique understanding of martyrdom that emerges from a genuine poetic dilemma and strains against both humanist and Christian attachments to exemplarity. But Donne's appreciation of martyrdom's disruptive power has its limits. His concept of unexemplary martyrdom is, in part, meant decisively to separate any singular martyrdom from collective swarms of rebellion that might follow or foment it.

To address Donne's exploration of fanaticism, I first survey the semantic richness of the terms "nothing" and "annihilation" in key passages from Donne's works. Then I turn to a reading of "Batter my hart" to explore how the techniques of this sonnet ask whether we can associate annihilation and ravishment with labor and work or whether we must understand them as experiences of passivity. In the final section, I address the problem of martyrdom in Donne directly by demonstrating what true martyrdom looks like in Donne's prose composed around the time of the *Holy Sonnets* (roughly 1608–10), particularly in *Biathanatos* and *Pseudo-Martyr*: a passive martyrdom that arrives as an event but cannot be recommended as exemplary political action or transmitted as unruly contagion. I propose that Donne's critique of contemporary Catholic martyrdom is more valuable when seen not primarily as an anti-Catholic Protestant polemic (though it of course is that, too) but rather as an attempt to theorize martyrdom, not reducible to confessional division, as a product of a singular self-annihilation that Donne glosses as an "appropinquation" to divine will.

"For his art did express / A quintessence even from nothingness, / From dull privations and lean emptiness." This is how Donne, in his 1612 "A Nocturnal upon St. Lucy's Day," describes the divine power of love.[2] Love can squeeze out of nothingness, from the leanest emptiness, a quintessence. Nothingness is a threat to material beings—they might cease altogether to exist—but the threat is not absolute; some things, the speaker in this lyric asserts, can be emptied to nothing, but then reborn into a new life: "He ruined me, and I am re-begot / Of absence, darkness, death—things which are not" (17–18). The relationship between ruin and rebegetting is a central focus of Donne's concrete concerns with martyrdom and the annihilation of the will: one must be ruined—turned to nothing—in order to be reborn as a divine instrument. As metaphysical category, natural scientific phenomenon, and state toward which our decaying bodies tend, "nothingness" is recurrently present as a concept throughout Donne's oeuvre, and surveying these definitions reveals more precisely how Donne conceives of the specific mode of annihilation that can render a person an organ of God.

Nothingness and rebegetting are perhaps never so strongly on his mind as they are in what he calls the ultimate "Image of *his Humiliation*," the series of meditations and prayers that Donne wrote under the title *Devotions upon Emergent Occasions*.[3] At the center of this text, Donne's tenth Meditation turns from a moving request for a divine remedy for his illness to the articulation of a cosmology that has annihilation at its center:

> This is *Natures nest of Boxes*; The *Heavens* containe the *Earth*, the *Earth*, *Cities*, *Cities*, *Men*. And all these are *Concentrique*; the common *center* to them all, is *decay*, *ruine*; only that is *Eccentrique*, which was never made; only that place, or garment rather, which we can *imagine*, but not *demonstrate*, That light, which is the very emanation of the light of *God*, in which the *Saints* shall dwell, with which the *Saints* shall be appareld, only that bends not to this *Center*, to *Ruine*; that which was not made of *Nothing*, is not threatened with this annihilation. All other things are; even *Angels*, even our *soules;* they move upon the same *poles*, they bend to the same *Center*; and if they were not made immortall by *preservation*, their Nature could not keepe them from sinking to this *center, Annihilation*.[4]

In the Renaissance, "annihilation" could refer to a process of emptying the self in order to unite it with God.[5] But it could also indicate, as it does most immediately in this passage, material decay or ruin. Through this elaborate image of "Natures nest of Boxes," Donne develops a theory of "concentrique" circles in which decay or ruin is the center of them all and nothingness is that out of which they are made. In Donne's cosmology, the pull of the center draws all material entities back to it as they orbit; the center of ruin sucks decaying souls, angels, and bodies inward and only God's "*Eccentrique*" light remains "not threatened with this annihilation." The "Nothing" for Donne is, then, both that which being approaches as it undergoes the process of annihilation and that from which being originates. Everything but God is created within a circle from a nothing of which God is not made, and everything within that circle is driven to decay; it is *ex* and *a nihilo*, a dark echo of "The First Anniversary: An Anatomy of the World": "We seem ambitious, God's whole work t'undo;/Of nothing he made us, and we strive too,/To bring our selves to nothing back" (155–57).

In addition to the centripetal decay that it exhibits in *Devotions*, annihilation can take several other meanings for Donne. It sometimes serves as a translation for the Greek *kenosis* or the Latin *exinanio/exinanitio* in his sermons and in *Biathanatos*. As noted in the Introduction, the central biblical passage concerning *kenosis*, Philippians 2:7, informed discussions of

Christology throughout the Middle Ages and into the Reformation. In that passage, *kenosis* names the process by which Christ empties himself of his divinity in order to become incarnate in human flesh and then die as a man. *Exinanio* (to empty out) is the Vulgate translation of *kenosis*, and Donne, one of the first to use the term "exinanition" in English according to the OED, is sensitive to annihilation's relationship to Christ's own *kenosis*.[6]

Donne is certainly not the only one in the period to link the idea of annihilation as *kenotic* self-emptying with modes of nothingness both material and metaphysical. Pierre de Bérulle, a contemporary of Donne's, differentiates three kinds of *nihil* in his writings on abnegation in *Opuscules de piété* (1644): the nothingness out of which we were created; the nothingness in which we are placed because of sin; and (with reference to Philippians 2:7) the nothingness that we have to accomplish, in imitation of Christ's *kenosis*, in order to transform ourselves.[7] Annihilation for Bérulle is the solution to the fact that human beings are constituted by the nothingness of sin. Only annihilation can unmake the sinful self and reveal the immanence of the divine in the soul. In his thinking on annihilation, Bérulle was influenced by the writings of Benet of Canfield, an English mystic who converted from Anglicanism to Catholicism before joining Recusant communities in Belgium and Paris.[8] Benet of Canfield proposes that the only remedy for the nonbeing or nothingness of the human creature (in comparison with God's perfect being) is to annihilate oneself and abide firmly in one's own nothingness: "And of our owne Nothing, as hath bein shewne, examin whether yow haue duely annihilated your self."[9]

Likewise Donne, who was probably familiar with at least Benet of Canfield's text if not Bérulle's,[10] conflates the first two modes of nothingness we find in Bérulle. Bodily decline in Donne is a movement to nothingness that is bound up with the nothingness of sin, rather than a purely material decay. But a different form of annihilation offers itself as a possible solution. In *Biathanatos*, for example, Donne writes, "Christ said this now because His passion was begun, for all His conversations here were degrees of exinanition."[11] In this instance, Donne uses annihilation—exinanition—to designate an emptying of the self that mimics Christ's life and language ("conversations") as sacrifice and passion, which might be the model for escaping the nothingness of sin and bodily decay. In another context, using alchemical terminology for the purgation, breakdown, and ultimate dissolution of matter, Donne describes something like a new humility, a decline and then clearing out of the will, at the end of Meditation 20: "I am ground even to an *attenuation*, and must proceed to *evacuation*, all waies to exinanition and annihilation."[12] As Anthony Raspa has made clear in notes to his edition of *Devotions*, this passage moves from attenuation ("the first step in purgation . . . , a process for slimming a patient down of his excess humorous fats") to evacuation ("an expulsion of material from the body") to exinanition ("complete emptying of the patient's venomous humours") and then finally to annihilation ("evaporating out of existence").[13] Though Raspa has associated this vocabulary exclusively with purgation and alchemy, it seems likely, given Donne's own use of "exinanition" as a translation of *kenosis*, that Donne is also describing a process of mystical annihilation, an *annihilation* that reduces the self to nothing in order to allow for God's presence in ways that *"attenuation"* and *"evacuation"* cannot.

In addition to decay and exinanition, moreover, annihilation in Donne's sermons can also designate the destruction of a person, either his literal loss of life or his being forgotten by God. In a Lent sermon at Whitehall (in 1626 or 1627—the date is uncertain), Donne proclaims, "If God neglect you, forget, pretermit you, it is a miserable annihilation, a fearfull malediction."[14] God's "neglect" of a person leads to a kind of annihilation, and so, too, does an individual's excessive confidence in his relationship to God, preached Donne in 1615:

> First then, Prodigality is a sin, that destroys even the means of liberality.
> If a man wast so, as that he becomes unable to relieve others, by this
> wast, this is a sinful prodigality; but much more, if he wast so, as that he
> is not able to subsist, and maintain himself; and this is our case, who
> have even annihilated our selves, by our profuseness; For, it is his mercy
> that we are not consumed. It is a sin, and a viperous sin; it eats out his
> own womb. . . . It is *peccatum Biathanaton*, a sin that murders it self.[15]

In this third meaning, then, annihilation registers a forgetting by God or an improper self-dissolution. To be forgotten by God is to become nothing in sin. Prodigal sin empties out the self, but not in a positive sense; annihilation by profuseness is mere waste. Sin of this kind "eats out his own womb"; it is a self-murdering sin (*"peccatum Biathanaton"*). Annihilation can, therefore, also mean the exact opposite of *kenosis*: not emptying the self to nothing to make space for divine immanence in the soul, but rather, as Donne put it in an Easter Monday sermon in 1622, wasting the self to nothing through sin: "There is an annihilation in sin; *Homines cum peccant, nihil sunt*: Then when by sin, I depart from the Lord my God, *in whom only I live, and move, and have my being*, I am nothing."[16]

These uses illustrate how annihilation in Donne shifts semantically from a theory of matter's ruination to a vocabulary of *kenosis*, sacrifice, and destruction that blurs action and passion as a person turns to nothing.

Annihilation in Donne manifests that which we hold in common with all earthly beings, the capacity to sin and to decay into the nothing of which we are made and against which we define ourselves. But annihilation also tears us away from our human community and identity. This sundering can signal proper or improper dissolution, the transformation of self into an instrument of God's will or a wasteful destruction that bars the self from such inspiration.

"Batter my hart" is Donne's most famous exploration of the specific mode of annihilation with which this book is concerned: the self-emptying of a believer who is transformed into an instrument of holy violence. But the kind of annihilation that the poet first encounters is the slow painful decay wrought by sin and the failure to feel God's presence. When confronted with the seeming omnipresence of sin, the poet turns instead to seek another kind of annihilation—God's ravishment. By demanding that a rupturing event of God's presence annihilate him, the poet in this sonnet labors to initiate his true rebegetting as a zealous vessel of divine force:

> Batter my hart, three-person'd God, for you
> As yet but knock, breathe, shine, and seeke to mend;
> That I may rise, and stand, orethrow me; and bend
> Your force to breake, blow, burne, and make me new.
> I like an vsurp'd towne to'another dew
> Labor to'admit you, but Oh to no end.
> Reason your viceroy in me, me should defend,
> But is captiv'd and proves weake or vntrew.
> Yet dearly I love you, and would be loved faine:
> But ame bethroth'd vnto your enemy:
> Diuorce me, vnty or breake that knott agayne,
> Take me to you, emprison me, for I
> Except you enthrall me neuer shalbe free,
> Nor euer chast except you rauishe mee.

The sonnet grapples with a paradox: that the response to domination by sin is to demand martyring ravishment so extreme that the speaker would be unmade. Registering this paradox formally through an initial metrical inversion, the sonnet initiates from its first word, "batter," a dual track for the brutality invoked. "Batter" signifies not only the violence of a repeated striking. The term can also mean "paste together" or "fix," and occasionally even "exchange":[17] break me into nothing, the poet seems to say, but make this annihilation a re-collection of me in wholly new form.[18]

Making and unmaking are rhythmical propositions in the first line. An irruption within the structure of the sonnet's normative world that has not yet been established here, the metrical irregularity of "batter" registers the entanglement of the violence of annihilation with the production of a new instrumental work of God. From the first phrase, the text locates a nexus of making and unmaking, putting together and breaking apart: to unmake the sinful life bound to annihilation is to open up the possibility of a radical new life, one that perhaps only martyrdom and "rauish[ment]" might achieve.

The sonnet makes this ravishment appear to be the achievement of a particular sort of labor—a mental and physical labor, perhaps, of self-abandonment. This sonnet's particular interest in calling readers' attention to labor is apparent in the fault line between its two rhyme structures: an Italian octave (abba abba) that is followed by a Shakespearean sestet (cdcd ee).[19] This doubleness, or structural volta, calls attention to the elaborate work put into this particular act of *poiesis*, as though the sonnet is itself "batter[ed]" together. Both the sonnet's initial phrase and its overall structure thus confront us with the problem of whether ravishment itself can be achieved and experienced as an active labor of the self or must be construed as a passion of the self's undoing. Resonating with the "Eccentrique" idiom of Donne's *Devotions upon Emergent Occasions*, "Batter my hart" presents a speaker who seeks to create a self free of sin and decay and utterly "new," yet it suggests that the willful work for martyrdom may bar the speaker from the sacred violence that would annihilate and re-make him.[20]

Following the imperative to "Batter my hart," the speaker temporalizes this violent relationship to God, stating that "as yet" God has moved but to "knock, breathe, shine, and seeke to mend." The trinity of contiguous stresses on the fourth, fifth, and sixth syllables connects this line with the fourth line as the past and future, respectively; both are rhythmic batterings. In the fourth line, oriented to that future tense, the speaker demands that God "breake, blow, burne, and make me new," create a "me" who would be perpetually new and not subject to sinful decay. The sonnet registers a desire not for gradual self-reform but rather for a rupture of self so total that the self can be unmade and remade as a divine instrument, entirely freed from the material decay and spiritual devastation of the former self. These binaries of past and future modes of being ("knock"/"breake"; "breathe"/"blow"; "shine"/"burne"; "mend"/"make . . . new") seem themselves to be ontologically linked, though, despite the emphasis on rupture; "breake, blow, burne" are intensified versions of "knock, breathe, shine," rather than drastic departures in the characterization of divine action. The intensified verbs, however, mark a particular shift in divine gender from a feminized God (mending) to a masculinized one (breaking). The third line further evokes the radicalness of the speaker's demand. In order to "rise, and stand," the speaker requests that God "orethrow" him.

In "Batter my hart," we witness a wish both to be hurled into an abyss of divine decreation and to be remade in order to "rise, and stand."[21] These movements mirror Christ's *kenosis* and resurrection but in sexualized terms. While there are broader implications of the sonnet's gendered and sexualized language, which critics have ably studied, what concerns me is that the erotics of "rauish[ment]" and resurrection should not be divorced from the mystical concepts of self-annihilation and inspiration and their political consequences in fanaticism.[22] This point is especially crucial if we are to understand the relationship between "Batter my hart" and Donne's prose about martyrdom, in which the gender and sexuality of self-annihilation and inspiration are less present. Even if the historical context of martyrdom is only obliquely present in the poem, the double entendres that suffuse the first quatrain soon turn into (no-less-eroticized) metaphors of colonial and monarchical struggle, reinscribing the battered heart—a figure for interiority and its annihilation—within a sociopolitical discourse. For example, the subject of line 5, "I," is displaced from its action by an entire poetic line, a line that characterizes the speaker as "an vsurp'd towne to'another dew" whose only action is to "Labor to'admit you." The speaker, according to this figure, is a town that has been taken over and colonized by another. The speaker wishes that he could merely genuflect in self-evacuation as God breaks into his "towne" and replaces his captive "viceroy," reason, but the speaker cannot himself actively begin this process through labor.

The sonnet's ambiguous mix of gender, sexuality, politics, and theology evolves through the third quatrain, but it is in the final couplet that it seems that the speaker has finally settled on a figuration of self-annihilation and divine inspiration: "For I/Except you enthrall me neuer shall be free,/Nor euer chast except you rauishe mee." "Rauishe" evokes mystical annihilation, but it is hard not to hear "rape" here, too; Katherine Eggert has shown how ravishment at the turn of the seventeenth century retained both these meanings—sexual assault and ecstatic possession by the Holy Spirit.[23] "Rauishe" is likely from the Latin *rapere*, which, as Gordon Teskey has reminded us in a discussion of allegorical violence, "is a literal translation of *harpazein* in the Chaldean Oracles and in Proclus's commentary on the *Parmenides*, where it denotes an act of violent seizing by which beings are returned to the One."[24] Donne's sonnet articulates a longing for ravishment as a brutal but potentially effective way to empty a sinful self and fill it with God.

Yet the sonnet equally considers the possibility that the physical violence it evokes may not offer the self-annihilation and divine immanence that the speaker seeks. Violence that annihilates the self may be recuperated within a narrative of the self's return to itself. The speaker "would be loved faine" by his God, but the physical violence summoned for that purpose hints that the speaker is worried that such love is a kind of feign, an invention or falsification. This anxiety reveals a skepticism not toward sacred violence itself but rather toward the willful demand for such violence as prerequisite for indwelling divine presence. It makes us look awry at the will that would so confidently demand ravishment as a model for union with God. The sonnet thus negatively imagines a form of self-annihilation proceeding from a "prevenient violence," to borrow a phrase from Teskey,[25] that would rid the self of the will and all its labors. Annihilation of the self may be an activity, but it cannot be actively initiated. Instead, God must annihilate the self that desires self-emptying.

The speaker's demand for divine violence, in other words, seems to fail because he wills his own annihilation and does not begin with an annihilation of the will. In this beautifully disciplined poem, the speaker still tries to remain in control of his own annihilation—a problem nicely embodied by the elision of the unstressed "I" in line 9: "Yet dearly I love you, and would be loved faine." Here, and in marked contrast to the irregularly stressed "I" that begins the fifth line, the pronunciation of the "I" must, out of prosodic necessity, be elided at just the moment when the speaker describes the desired link between active and passive love ("love"/"would be loved"), willed love for God and release into divine love. As Susan Linville has put it more generally about this sonnet, here the desire for self-annihilation and the rhythm of the poem neatly coincide.[26] But the poem does not rest in this conforming of form to content. It demystifies it as a willful achievement that blocks the transformation of the poet into an vessel of God. The poem's unfolding after line 9—in particular, the contrast that develops between the bloodless emptying of the "I" through elision in line 9 and the brutality of the final projected ravishment— suggests that if the poet can suppress the pronunciation of the "I" for the sake of prosodic necessity, then perhaps the abandonment of the "I" that the poet imagines actually takes place through self-control—in this instance, through the discipline of meter—and that the capacity for such poetic skill is part of the problem. I mean this not, of course, as a criticism of the poem or of poetry. It is what the poem beautifully and disturbingly reveals to us: that poetic making itself may prepare for but ultimately marks the lack of the self-annihilation required for martyrdom.[27] This is to say, contra T. S. Eliot, that Donne's "Batter my hart" does not—and discovers that it cannot—possess "a mechanism of sensibility" that could "devour" the "experience" of fanaticism.[28] The poem unfolds a self-disabling, skeptical claim against the enthusiastic model of inspired authorship that Spenser ambivalently embraces.[29] Annihilation without labor—devotional passivity that can be neither communicated nor copied—is a state that the speaker cannot attain even if the poem gestures toward it. The sonnet's conception of unwilled annihilation seems to promise a release from the labor of poetic making itself, yet it is a lesson that Donne learns—and powerfully transmits—through his experimentation with this sonnet's form. As with the deferred figuration of zeal as fiery self-immolation in "I ame a litle World," "Batter my hart" suggests that devotional poetry may only be able to think about the passive self-annihilation required for fanaticism negatively, by enacting its own productive failure to cause the poet's own decreation.

We see in "Batter my hart" an abortive movement toward ravishing martyrdom. Donne's conceptualization of self-annihilation echoes Müntzer's theorization of divine action: to have the possibility of true self-emptying or martyrdom, one must be released from the will, must make space in the self that is passive enough to receive God. "Batter my hart" fails to be about the experience of self-annihilation; that is its greatest success, what it reveals most intimately about how one becomes or fails to become a proper martyr, a kind of fanatic. In other words, Donne's poetic labors expose what they cannot attain: a model of martyrdom devoid of labor. The ban on labor implies the impossibility of active imitation, too.

In the final section of this chapter, I show how it is precisely this idea of a martyrdom purified of both imitation and labor that underwrites Donne's complex prose meditations on martyrdom and suicide. At the end of this chapter, we will see in Donne's uneasy and reiterated reflections on Samson that his theory of martyrdom also applies directly to fanaticism's most pressing threat to the sovereign authority that Donne, at least in his *Pseudo-Martyr*, seems to be defending: divinely inspired violence against a state.

James I claimed in *Triplici nodo, triplex cuneus. Or an Apologie for the Oath of Allegiance* (1608) that anyone who did not take and abide by the 1606 Oath of Allegiance—"whereby," as he puts it, all his subjects "should make a cleare profession of their resolution, faithfully to persist in their obedience vnto mee"—was "carried away with the like fanaticall zeale that the Powder-Traitors were," referring to the Catholic rebels who attempted to assassinate him in the foiled Gunpowder Plot of 1605.[30] By using "fanaticall zeale" as a concept to encompass the affects of political dissidents, would-be assassins, and Catholics who would rather become martyrs than take an oath that Pope Paul V condemned, James linked fanaticism and martyrdom explicitly. Recapitulating claims from James's *Triplici nodo*, Donne also argues in his 1610 *Pseudo-Martyr* that Catholics should take the oath and not become martyrs. But Donne's writing on martyrdom is expansive and contradictory, in and beyond *Pseudo-Martyr*. A major part of Donne's purpose in these writings, and especially in *Biathanatos*, is to develop a charitable account of the "fanaticall zeale" involved in martyrdom. He outlines—and refuses to dismiss, as James I would wish—the concept of unexemplary martyrdom rooted in the passive annihilation of the will, one that we are in a position to understand only if we grasp the relationship between self-annihilation and ravishment that "Batter my hart" explores. In order to distinguish more clearly the kinds of martyrdom that Donne condemns and those that he finds productive, I first want to examine some comments by Donne in a sermon on conversion. Donne's theory of conversion gives us a key to understanding his thinking on martyrdom, a key already glimpsed in our reading of "Batter my hart": the homology between Christ's passion and our passivity. The conceptual importance of this connection will become more apparent, but I hope that my linking of conversion to martyrdom will seem something less than surprising from the start. After all, it was something like a conversion that saved Donne, unlike most of the rest of his family, from being remembered as a Catholic martyr, a fact to which Donne himself alludes in the Preface to the 1610 publication of *Pseudo-Martyr*.[31]

In one of his final sermons preached at St. Paul's Cathedral in 1628, a meditation on the conversion of Saint Paul, Donne takes as his proof text an isolated part of Acts 28:6: "They changed their minds, and said, that he was a God."[32] The "he" referenced here is Paul, but interestingly the proof text refers to a change (the Vulgate has "convertentes se") not so much in Paul but in those he has encountered during his shipwreck on the island of Malta on his way to be tried in Rome. (Donne initially says this is a moment of "super-canonization," in which the people who see Paul on Malta identify him as a god.) Donne's sermon will circle around and ultimately focus on the grammatical, narrative, and theological conjugation of "change." What does it mean to change one's mind, to convert to a new belief, a novel structure of piety?

Donne develops a complex affective and theological description of conversion and relates it to rapture and martyrdom. Early in the sermon, Donne describes Paul's own conversion as follows: God "gave him a Rapture, an Extasie, and in that, an appropinquation, an approximation to himselfe, and so some possession of Heaven in this life."[33] Here, we see conversion initiated by an ecstasy that has at its core what Donne calls "appropinquation"— Paul is emptied of self and, "in that," is also approximated to "himselfe," made into a kind of organ of God. But this rapturous ecstasy and attendant appropinquation, this going out of oneself to become approximated to one's true self through the indwelling of God, is the annihilation and rebegetting of Paul in this life.

As the sermon proceeds, Donne elaborates on the aftermath of conversion with a reference to Denys the Areopagite:

> As S. Denys the Areopagite expresses it, *A Deo doctus, non solùm divina discit, sed divina patitur,* (which we may well translate, or accommodate thus) He that is thoroughly taught by Christ, does not onely beleeve all that Christ says, but conformes him to all that Christ did, and is ready to suffer as Christ suffered. Truly, if it were possible to feare any defect of joy in heaven, all that could fall into my feare would be but this, that in heaven I can no longer expresse my love by suffering for my God, for my Saviour.[34]

Rapture and ecstasy lead to a conversion, and in that conversion, Paul experiences an approximation to Christ: in the wake of conversion, one's faith is defined in part by one's ability to "conform" to Christ. This approximation means to conform to all Christ did. Appropinquation is self-emptying. "Conforming" to Christ, as *imitatio Christi*, presents a paradox, since such conforming is fundamentally antimimetic if we think of imitation as an activity. Conversion is defined by passively undergoing an approximation to Christ, yet Christ cannot be truly exemplary since no one can undergo this approximation by one's own will.

At the center of the sermon, Donne links his analysis of conversion and the appropinquation of Christ with his discussion of change:

> *They changed,* says our Text; not their mindes; there is no evidence, no apparance, that they exercised any, that they had any; but they changed their passions. Nay, they have not so much honour, as that afforded them, in the Originall; for it is not *They changed,* but *They were changed,* passively; Men subject to the transportation of passion, doe nothing of themselves, but are meerely passive.[35]

Picking up on the middle passive voice of the Greek verb that "they changed" translates (*metabalomenoi*), Donne insists that conversion itself is an experience of passivity. Though Donne, in this instance, is insulting those who do not have the "honour" to change themselves and who are changed "passionately" to extreme positions by a "distemper" (such as thinking that Paul is a god), the precise claim about conversion nonetheless remains: one does not choose to convert; change is not an active choice in which one exercises one's will freely. Donne's theory of conversion is an experience of being "meerely passive."

Donne's account of conversion's passivity is essential for his discussion of martyrdom. After all, Donne's quotation from Dionysius bases our openness to being like Christ in *divina patitur*: to suffering divinely or like the divine. I have shown that Donne carefully considers the desire for and failure to achieve this instrumental passivity in "Batter my hart." Donne's understanding of martyrdom requires the clearing of a space for a pure passivity of reception in which the infinitude of the divine can annihilate the self and become present in the finite. But what does this clearing look like in Donne's writings on martyrdom?

This question has generally not been asked before because so much scholarship, from critics as diverse as Jonathan Goldberg, Annabel Patterson, Debora Shuger, and Jesse Lander, has assumed that Donne is too beholden to James I to question the sovereign's disdain for martyrdom and "fanaticall zeale" of all kinds, especially in the context of the Gunpowder Plot and its aftermath.[36] Donne's argument in *Pseudo-Martyr*, urging English Catholics to take the Oath of Allegiance while retaining their inner loyalty to the spiritual authority of Rome, has seemed like a conservative surrender to James I, a "remarkable act of submission to the system."[37] Yet one of Donne's main purposes in these tracts, and especially in *Biathanatos*, is to outline what he considered an authentic form of martyrdom rather than to dismiss martyrdom altogether. Donne's critique of martyrdom is limited: "I have a just and Christianly estimation, and reverence, of that devout and acceptable Sacrifice of our lifes, for the glory of our blessed Saviour."[38] In Donne's estimation, undergoing martyrdom because of a longing to obey the authority of the church or to follow an exemplary model is a false kind of sacrifice. This is not to say that Donne thinks that an unexemplary martyrdom free of willing is necessarily in conflict with or disconnected from questions of political efficacy or fidelity to community. It is a claim that only asserts the annihilation of the individual will as a prerequisite for true martyrdom, proposing that martyrdom itself cannot be a political action that a free individual willfully plans and executes. Nonetheless, the concept of unexemplary martyrdom does seem constructed to contain the political problem of collective martyrdom or fanatical rebellion.

In Donne's analysis, Catholic martyrdom is sullied by a Pope who "serve[s] his owne ambitions to your destruction,"[39] and it thus amounts only to a state-sponsored death, a fulfillment not of God's will but that of an institution. Institutionalized martyrdom, proposed as exemplary political intervention, serves merely to create a position of passivity to the state, not the true passivity by which God may annihilate the will and the self can be approximated to the divine. For Donne, those who swarm to institutionalized martyrdom, whether under Catholic or any other auspices, come to resemble the people who gather around the egalitarian Giant like flies in Spenser's *The Faerie Queene* Book V Canto 2: they are, at least according to Spenser's narrator, blindly led by a demagogue into believing that they are instruments of God, but in fact they are merely imitating models of generic action that are impure products of human will. Donne is unconcerned, though, with describing his productive martyrdom as Protestant, even if its outline becomes visible through a criticism of contemporary Catholic practice.

*Biathanatos* is where the unexemplary model of martyrdom is developed most precisely. The text was published only after Donne's death, and against his purported wishes; in its first printed edition from 1644, it was dedicated to Philip Herbert, whom Nigel Smith has described as "the decidedly mystical Earl of Pembroke, patron of various brands of radical Puritanism."[40] It was not a text that Donne, when closest to James I, would have wanted the world to see, and the fact that it was dedicated to a radical Puritan mystic in its first printing is only one sign of why it might have upset the Anglican establishment. But there is also a disturbing philosophical and political problem at the core of these considerations that Donne's writings never fully resolve: how can we describe the self-annihilation involved in martyrdom and religious zealotry without using the language of will, choice, and action?

*Biathanatos* seeks to awaken "charity" in interpreting the sacrifices of martyrdom. Donne argues that "self-homicide" can appear in the world in a form that is not sinful or heretical.[41] Selectively appropriating and departing from the arguments against suicide found in Augustine and Aquinas, Donne posits there is a natural inclination or drive to self-extinction, what he calls "a desire of dying which nature had bred."[42] By the end of his treatise, Donne goes so far as to claim, with reference to a genealogy of

arguments from Philippians 1:23, Augustine, Lombard, Serarius, and Aquinas, that the desire to be dissolved—"cupio dissolvi"—in Christ is the greatest perfection ("that than which none can be greater"):

> But when he [Augustine] comes to that than which none can be
> greater, he says then, the Apostle [Paul] came to *cupio dissolvi*. For, as
> one may love God with all his heart, and yet he may grow in that love,
> and love God more with all his heart, for the first was commanded in
> the Law, and yet counsel of perfection was given to him who said that
> he had fulfilled the first commandment, so, as St. Augustine found a
> degree above that charity which made a man *paratum ponere*, which is
> *cupere*, so there is a degree above that, which is to do it. This is that
> virtue by which martyrdom, which is not such of itself, becomes an
> act of highest perfection.[43]

Realizing "cupio dissolvi" is "that virtue by which martyrdom, which is not
such of itself, become an act of highest perfection." Here Donne is citing
Lombard on Augustine's concept of charity, which Lombard divides into
five categories: beginning, proficient, perfect, more perfect, and most perfect. Perfect charity is glossed as a readiness to die for another. "Cupio
dissolvi"—a love for self-dissolution—has an even higher degree of perfection than does willingness to die for a neighbor. It is the most perfect form
of charity. "To do it"—to dissolve the self—renders martyrdom an act of
highest perfection. Within the logic of *Biathanatos*, at least, there is a natural tendency to self-murder or self-sacrifice that is in constant conflict
with the institutions of state and church that require live agents, and this
natural inclination is perfected in the true martyrdom that releases the self
from the will, that makes that self, through annihilating its will, into an
organ of God.

The illustrative instance of self-homicide as true martyrdom in *Biathanatos* is Christ himself: with the divine immanent within him, Christ had the
proper inspiration to "giv[e] up His soul before He was constrained to do
it," and all who die in unconstrained self-sacrifice "therein imitate this act
of our Saviour."[44] "Giving up his soul"—giving up his will and releasing
himself into God's—initiates martyrdom and the imitation of Christ in
Donne's thinking, and any "constraining," whether by labors of the will or
by an institution such as the state or the church, ruins the real, passive imitation of Christ's self-sacrifice. Donne references *imitatio Christi* here but
disjoins imitation from a willful agent by insisting on loving self-dissolution
as the virtue that makes martyrdom most perfect. This is the reason, *pace*
Brad Gregory's work on early modern martyrdom, that martyrdom in

Donne's writing cannot exactly be *exemplary*: it requires a form of passivity that any model of martyrdom based on the idea of intentional imitation of an action cannot capture. Gregory argues, "The extremism of martyrdom should be understood not as a fanaticism of the fringe, but as exemplary action."[45] By contrast, if we wish to pursue this particular strand in Donne's thought, then we should instead think of true, charitable martyrdom as a fanaticism that, like Müntzer's receiving divine action, involves an unexemplary passivity so extreme that it requires a self-annihilation that one cannot seek out or work for. Donne is not always consistent on this point,[46] but in the most complex version of his theory, true martyrs imitate Christ, but without will; they undergo an annihilation of the very self that could choose to model its action on that of an exemplar.

Donne analyzes many biblical examples to illustrate the paradox of martyrs who are types of Christ but not examples to be followed. For instance, "the passive action of Eleazar," Donne notes with reference to the martyr of 1 Maccabees 6:46 who opened himself to execution rather than eat pork, is similar to Christ's sacrifice insofar as it is a self-exposure to destruction.[47] Eleazar's martyrdom reveals an annihilation of the will; this is the only way Eleazar could achieve "passive action."

Samson, the Jewish judge and martyr who pulls down the Temple of Dagon, provides the case of martyrdom on which Donne dwells longest after considering Jesus. Blinded and imprisoned, Samson kills himself and his Philistine captors in the Book of Judges. Turning to commentaries that range from Augustine to Calvin and Pererius, among others, Donne argues that it was the "special inspiration from God," the infusion of the spirit into Samson and the annihilation of Samson's will, that made Samson a true martyr. Donne concludes that Samson died "with the same zeal as Christ, unconstrained; for in this manner of dying, as much as in anything else, he was a type of Christ."[48] Donne insists on this true, unconstrained mode of martyrdom characterized by divine inspiration.

But to recall the question invited by Spenser in Chapter 1, how do we know whether someone is like Samson or Christ—a martyr or religious zealot moved by truly divine inspiration—or only a person claiming to be inspired for their own political or personal reasons, a demagogue or madman? As I discussed in my Introduction, and as we will see in Chapter 3, often in Renaissance political and philosophical thought, we witness an evasion of this question and a panicked attempt to classify all claims to inspiration as madness. But Donne foregrounds it at just the moment that he invokes Augustine's claim for Samson's divine inspiration, "which, because it appears not in the history, nor lies in proof, may with the same easiness be refused as it is presented."[49] And he repeats the concern a few lines later when worrying over the meaning of the nonsynchronous returns of Samson's strength and hair: "Doth this prove any impulsion, and incitement, and prevention of the Holy Ghost to that particular act, or rather only an habitual accompanying and awaking him to such actions by which God might be honored and glorified whensoever any occasion should be presented?"[50] Polemics against fanaticism would typically use this absence of definitive proof as grounds for dismissing the claim of divine inspiration and judge it as deception or delusion. By contrast, Donne is peculiarly drawn to the lacuna, not as a problem to be solved but as an open question on which to meditate.

Before analyzing Donne's precise response to the undecidable question of whether Samson was inspired, it is important to emphasize the extent of Donne's resistance to the tendency of critics of martyrdom to view the absence of proof of divine inspiration as itself proof of martyrs' madness. As Adam Kitzes has shown, Donne finds it a corruption of the primitive church to have turned even the proper kind of martyrdom into a sin or form of "madness."[51] By the time of the English Civil War, figures such as Hobbes will label martyrdom—and all other actions he groups under the category of fanaticism—as a kind of pathological madness. I will return to Hobbes's conflation of fanaticism and madness in Chapter 3. But for now it is worth noting that Hobbes's dismissal of fanaticism and martyrdom as madness becomes an increasingly popular strategy for the demystification of all claims to inspired action, and we find references to martyrdom as madness in thinkers as disparate as Meric Casaubon, Henry More, and Robert Burton.[52] The imputation of madness becomes a way of undercutting any justification for martyrdom—and, increasingly, any attempt to break with civil or natural law on the grounds of religious belief. But Donne, in advance of the proliferation of discussions of martyrdom as madness, preempts this interpretative strategy by historicizing the church's own shift away from considering martyrdom as sacred action:

> The blood of the martyrs . . . having as Nicephorus says, almost
> strangled the Devil, he tried by his two greatest instruments (when
> they are his), the magistrate and the learned, to avert them from this
> inclination. For, suggesting to the magistrate that their forwardness to
> die grew only from their faith in the resurrection, he procured their
> bodies to be burnt and their ashes scattered into rivers, to frustrate
> and defeat that expectation. And he raised up subtle heretics to infirm
> and darken the virtue and majesty of martyrdom. Of which, the most

pestilently cunning Basilides [a gnostic teacher who interpreted martyrdom as punishment for personal sin], foresuspecting that he should not easily remove that desire of dying which nature had bred and custom confirmed in them, tried to remove that which had root only in their religion, as being yet of tenderer growth and more removable than natural impressions. Therefore, he offered not to impugn their exposing themselves to death in all cases, but only said that it was madness to die for Christ, since He, by whose example they did it, was not crucified, but Simon, who bore the cross.[53]

Donne in this passage charts the historical convergence of the Christian church and state to reinterpret the widespread existence of martyrdom in the early church. By labeling martyrdom as "madness to die for Christ," the earlier interpreters of Christian martyrdom, such as Basilides (early in the second century AD), pushed martyrdom to the fringe of Christian piety. They made it into a mere pathological excess of feelings that led people away from actually bearing the cross of Christ's suffering in this life. In Donne's eyes, then, the description of martyrdom as madness in his own period is rooted in these prior debates over the earliest Christian martyrs and their likeness or unlikeness to Christ. Donne's research leads him to conclude that "our primitive church was so enamored of death, and so satisfied with it, that to vex and torture them more, the magistrate made laws to take from them the comfort of dying, and increased their persecution by ceasing it, for they gloried in their numbers."[54] So for Donne, the identification of martyrdom as madness has a history, one that is rooted in the biopolitical desires of both the church and the state to preserve the lives that they need in order to function. As Kitzes has argued, "church and state [have aligned] themselves in a campaign against suicide by reinterpreting it as a form of madness."[55] The very definition of madness that circulated in this debate over martyrdom is the product of a political contest rather than an objective diagnosis of its causes or diverse modes.

Though Donne is extremely critical of Catholic martyrdom in his own day, he refuses to equate martyrdom with madness and argues that the conflation itself fails to allow us to see what proper martyrdom might look like. Using Samson and Christ as his main examples, Donne insists that there is a kind of self-sacrifice or religious violence that is proper, and it is grounded in being fully inspired by God, by having God's will become one's own will in "passive action."

But by making this argument—by elaborating more fully on the conditions of self-emptying necessary for proper martyrdom or religious

violence—Donne leaves us with a couple of difficult but familiar questions. First, by what authority and method can such true inspiration be
known? And second, how can one become a proper martyr if one's self
stands in the way of the achievement of true inspiration? For these questions, the absence of evidence of divine inspiration in the case of Samson
becomes crucial once more. In the single mention of Samson in *Pseudo-
Martyr*, Donne writes:

> And though this secret and inward instinct and moving of the holy
> Ghost, which the Church presumes, to have guided not onely these
> martyres, in whose forwardnesse these authors have observed
> some incongruity with the rules of Divinity, but also *Sampson*, and
> those Virgines which drownded themselves for preservation of their
> chastity, which are also accounted by that Church as martyres;
> although (I say) this instinct lie not in proofe, nor can be made
> evident.[56]

Barring us from any proof of things that cannot be made evident, Donne
emphasizes as an intractable problem how one might interpret or know inspiration, how spectators to fanatical martyrdom can determine whether
they have witnessed true divine inspiration. "This secret and inward instinct and moving of the holy Ghost" is ultimately unknowable, even if
churches "presume" it. Donne does not suggest necessarily that they should
not be presuming it, only that it cannot "be made evident."[57] In Donne's
meditations on Samson, this is as difficult a problem for self-sacrificial martyrdom as it is for divinely inspired violence against the state, since Samson irrevocably enacts both at once.

In his famous treatise on secular authority, Luther claims that being
filled with the Holy Spirit requires grace, and Donne would agree with
this. But Luther continues to claim, in an oft-quoted citation: "If you
want to act like Samson, then first become like Samson."[58] And here Donne's consideration of martyrdom has led us to an essential point that must
be taken into account when considering violence to self or to state that is
claimed to be God's will: How does one *become* like Samson? And what
would it mean to become *like* Samson if his martyrdom can never be exemplary? (As Milton will reveal, this question is even relevant for Samson
himself: what does it mean for Samson, as his father claims in Milton's play,
to have "quit himself/Like Samson"?)[59] Is there an activity or labor one
could undertake to annihilate one's own will and make way for the passivity of divine inspiration? If so, does one actually become like Samson?
Or does divine inspiration just happen, an event for which there can be no

intellectual or physical preparation and around which similarities are projected in a retrospective narration that effaces the singularity of *this*
martyrdom? Donne does not answer these questions directly in his meditations on Samson, even if elsewhere, as I have shown, he will insist that
true martyrdom can never be the product of labor. But he wants to make
clear that martyrdom for him could never be exemplary in the sense of a
model to follow. One cannot labor or train to become like Christ or Samson. One can only be opened passively to that appropinquation in which
one becomes like God by losing oneself, by undergoing a conversion—a
transformation of self through its annihilation—that renders the initiation
of the act of martyrdom a form of passive openness. The martyr is a fanatical organ of God's ravishment.

In his final sermon, "Deaths Duell, or, A Consolation to the Soule,
against the dying Life, and living Death of the Body" (1631), a sermon that
some have called Donne's own self-elegy, Donne pauses to reflect again
on Samson's inspiration in this context:

> Stil *pray* wee for a *peaceable life* against *violent death*, and for *time* of
> *repentance* against *sudden death*, and for *sober* and *modest assurance*
> against *distempered* and *diffident death*, but never make *ill conclusions*
> upon persons overtaken with such deaths; *Domini Domini sunt exitus
> mortis*, to God the Lord belong the issues of death. And *he* received *Samp-
> son*, who went out of this world in *such* a *manner* (consider it *actively*,
> consider it *passively*, in his *owne death*, and in those whom he *slew* with
> himselfe) as was subject to interpretation hard enough. Yet the *holy
> Ghost* hath moved S. *Paul* to celebrate *Sampson* in his great *Catalogue*,
> and so doth all the *Church*.[60]

Donne lays bare the interpretative difficulties that Samson's death affords.
This is for Donne a "subject to interpretation hard enough": Was Samson's
sudden death, and the martyrdom that death brought, the way in which
Samson was "issue[d]" into passive sacrifice and united with God by becoming his instrument? Or was Samson being punished for a zeal that destroyed him and many others? The difficulty of this passage centers on the
phrase recorded cryptically in parentheses: "consider it *actively*, consider it
*passively*." I am not persuaded that the phrase is exactly or exhaustively
glossed by "in his *owne death*, and in those whom he *slew* with himself,"
which seems to cast Samson's activity as his killing others and his passivity as his own death. The implication of an inability to determine whether
Samson's violence is active—in the sense of undertaken by his own will—or
passive—in the sense of undertaken as a vessel of God—remains. Donne's

asyndeton exaggerates the parenthetical statement's ambiguity. We are left to wonder whether we must consider Samson's sudden violence as active or as passive, in temporal progression or dialectical paradox, or whether we must hold it in our minds both actively and passively at the same time, in an irresolvable parallax. We cannot know whether Samson's will was annihilated and he became a passive vessel of God's violence, or whether he labored to achieve his action of martyrdom and destruction.[61] Thrown back on the necessity of "interpret[ing]" the spectacle of Samson's martyrdom—"consider it *actively*, consider it *passively*"—we find that Donne has anticipated questions that generations after him, and Milton in *Samson Agonistes* especially, would find of the utmost importance. In enjoining us to consider Samson, Donne presents us with an aporia, and insists on the necessity of dwelling on that aporia, not reacting against it with panic or policing. In that interminable consideration, we should not forget that Samson cannot be exemplary; his martyrdom, if it is true, must be considered in its passive singularity. The only way out of this aporia is to be like Paul in Donne's description, to be released from the labor of interpretation by divine inspiration: "Yet the *holy Ghost* hath moved S. *Paul* to celebrate *Sampson*." As with martyrdom, however, one cannot work to be moved in this manner.

Donne's theorization of inimitable martyrdom has at least two consequences. First, it allows him to carve out a space for true martyrdom even as it renders the cause of fanatical acts (active will or passive inspiration) impossible to interpret definitively. Second, the antimimetic understanding of martyrdom enables Donne to contain the possible spread of self-annihilation and fanatical revolt, as we saw with Spenser's egalitarian Giant and his comrades, the fanatical "swarme of flyes," in Chapter 1. Donne's texts encourage a flexible mode of interpreting fanaticism, and reveal that poetry is intimately involved in that process of interpretation, even if it is productively inadequate as a technique for undergoing self-annihilation. Donne's poems are never ultimately the products of a vacant head, an inspired vessel. Donne's attempt to contain the proper martyrdom he has so carefully illuminated from mimetic diffusion is related to his discovery that poems, like any other kind of labor, ultimately delay the self-annihilation that makes possible fanaticism. The pragmatic effect of martyrdom's antirepresentational, unexemplary character is that it cannot be copied or spread like a contagion, and that no labor, not even the sacred labor of devotional poetry, can transform a self into an instrument of divine violence.

It is difficult to overstate how much Donne's positive elaboration of antimimetic martyrdom differs from the history of martyrology in early modern England. As Alice Dailey has convincingly demonstrated, in early modern martyrology, "imitation functions as the genre's principal strategy for martyr construction and authentication."[62] Martyrdom is meant to be neither unique nor illegible; it should be publicly verifiable and, just as importantly, exemplary, both an imitation of the ideal martyrdom, Christ's, and a model to be imitated by the faithful public that witnesses, whether in person or through textual mediation, the martyr's self-sacrifice. Donne's antimimetic stance on martyrdom sets itself, at least on this specific issue, against both the medieval tradition of *imitatio Christi* and Erasmian humanist discourses of exemplarity.[63] Timothy Hampton has shown that in most Renaissance humanist discussions of exemplarity, exemplars are understood to "'inflame' the reader, [to] 'incite' or 'animate' him to imitate them," and the same could be said, sometimes also with the brutally literal sense of inflaming, for the mimetic models of martyrdom that Donne sharply criticizes.[64] Donne takes Christ's self-annihilation and martyrdom as the most perfect example of martyrdom, but he also fears what happens when any martyr, even Christ, becomes an example to be imitated. He worries, in other words, about the possibility of exemplary martyrdom "inflam[ing]" witnesses to imitate figures like Samson—an even more politically vexed example than Christ is.

Donne's fear is based in both theological and political concerns. His writings suggest that mimesis, like verse technique, cannot be reconciled with a mystical theology of self-annihilation. This is why martyrdom is an exception to Donne's precept, in a sermon preached on the psalms, to "Doe nothing for which thou hast not an Example; for there is not a more dangerous distemper in either Beliefe or Practice, then singularity."[65] Donne needs martyrdom to be singular—which it why it is not properly a doing, since the doer needs to have been annihilated. To be more precise: Donne wants to disentangle the loss of will that takes place when one is "inflame[d]" to imitate a martyr from passive self-annihilation. Contrary to the example of the rhapsode in the *Ion*, contagious martyrdom would compromise but not utterly negate the will, Donne suggests. But that does not lessen his fear that martyrdom could actually spread to create a self-negating but indefinitely self-reproducing swarm, its mimetic transmission proliferating to an extent that it threatens the state's control over life and death. The theory of unexemplary, antimimetic martyrdom that Donne discovers in the *Holy Sonnets* and articulates explicitly in his prose writings is meant to solve this problem, to support a kind of martyrdom that is neither willed nor imitable, that can neither spread nor become an active political strategy. But the theory of unexemplary martyrdom brings to light as many problems as it solves, since Donne's honesty about the epistemological illegibility of the unexemplary martyr reveals that, unless inspired by the Holy Ghost, no one has the interpretive power to determine inspiration conclusively, and thus the distinction between a true and a pseudo-martyr is in crucial instances impossible to police. If it is true that only one inspired by God can determine whether Samson enacts his own or God's will—whether he is an agent or an instrument—then the same is true of a collective, of new kinds of community that emerge as collective organs of divine violence against self and state: fanatical swarms.

It is the threat of this kind of fanatical swarm that gives rise to Hobbes's monumental attempt to dismiss all martyrdom and religious violence as madness, to which I turn in Chapter 3. A supremely sophisticated example of the polemic that the poetics of fanaticism decline, Hobbes's sustained criticism of fanaticism as the utmost enemy of the state is rooted in a hypertrophied version of the same fear that Spenser and Donne work through: an alarm in the face of fanaticism's capacity to spread contagiously through a magnetic pulse or irresistible honeypot that shares with the multitude an illegible, self-annihilating divine immanence. But while Spenser and Donne addressed this alarm with a kind of epistemological humility—taking it as a profound challenge for their poetry—Hobbes develops a virulent and dismissive critique of fanaticism. Chapter 3 takes a momentary step back from what has been my primary emphasis on the poetics of fanaticism in order to look at one of the most far-reaching Renaissance polemics against it. As one of the most influential theorists of sovereignty, Hobbes sought to purge the state of the kinds of self-annihilation and inspiration that defined fanaticism and threatened to spread to create unruly, disobedient multitudes that broke with the sovereign contract. In unfolding the ramifications of Hobbes's polemic for his own equivocal attempt to make biblical texts an instrument of state power, my analysis offers a more concrete sense of the exclusionary violence that went into fashioning theories of the early modern state and also reveals how Hobbes's refusal to dwell in uncertainty about fanaticism is legible not only in the content of his polemic but also in its form—the mode of reading that it proposes as antidote to fanaticism, as well as the similes, metaphors, and rhetorical arrangements that constitute its local complexities.[66] My detour into Hobbes will throw into relief the significance of Spenser, Donne, and Milton's poetic experiments with fanaticism and the importance of their refusal to dismiss it as madness.

# CHAPTER 3

# Readerly Fanaticism:
# Hobbes's Outworks

Wherefore the deity must of necessity be removed and displaced,
to make room for the Leviathan to spread himself in.

—RALPH CUDWORTH, *The True Intellectual System of the Universe*

In "The Epistle Dedicatory" that prefaces *Leviathan, or The Matter, Forme, & Power of a Common-Wealth Ecclesiastical and Civill* (1651), Thomas Hobbes addresses possible reactions to his "discourse of Common-wealth." The single aspect of the work that Hobbes states may raise objections is his treatment of biblical text in *Leviathan*:

> That which perhaps may most offend, are certain Texts of Holy
> Scripture, alleged by me to other purpose than ordinarily use to be by
> others. But I have done it with due submission, and also (in order to
> my Subject) necessarily; for they are the outworks of the Enemy, from
> whence they impugne Civill Power.[1]

This concerns no minor part of Hobbes's treatise. The majority of Parts 3 and 4 of *Leviathan* (half the text) are devoted not only to the analysis of biblical texts but also to the construction of a biblical hermeneutic. These sections do much for his argument, allowing him to define ecclesiastical power and dismiss the possibility of divine or demonic possession. Hobbes is aware that his extensive and idiosyncratic analysis of biblical texts may cause offense—they did, and from many directions[2]—but he claims that everything he has done takes place "necessarily." This chapter examines what defines that necessity in Hobbes's work: the urgent threat that inspiration and biblical reading, as sparks for fanatical rebelliousness, present to Hobbes's model of the commonwealth. In the 1650s, Hobbes asked rhetorically, "What can be more pernicious to peace than the revelations that were by these *fanatics* pretended?"[3] Clearly framing fanatics as fraudulent, Hobbes's accusation that fanatics "pretended" their revelations—and, as we will see, any supposedly inspired actions—undercuts any possibility that what drives the fanatic is divine, or even that the origins of the fanatic's zeal might be ambiguous. But his apoplectic alliteration ("pernicious"/ "peace"/"pretended") registers rhetorically the intensity of their threat and of his response, nonetheless. Hobbes's polemic against fanaticism is worth sustained inquiry not only because of its complexity but also because of the effect its evasiveness has on Hobbes's own rhetorical forms.

Fanaticism presents for Hobbes's work a radical case of the dangers of passionate devotion and biblical interpretation. Hobbes attempts to neutralize the threat of fanatics not only by rejecting all kinds of millenarianism, as has been shown extensively, but also by condemning the interpretive practices that he saw as the source of their zeal, their deluded claims for divine inspiration, and the interpretive disputes that they raised with each other and with the sovereign. Hobbes undertakes a project of demystification, dismissing claims of self-annihilation and showing them for what they really are: the "vehement Passions" of the mad.[4] The methods that Hobbes develops for containing the spread of such vehemence and madness involve outlining a proper biblical hermeneutic, one that keeps readers wholly legible and produces affective responses that maintain readerly obedience to the sovereign. In his attempt to define and condemn anyone who would claim to be an instrument of the divine, Hobbes's account of biblical reading and inspiration also unfolds an argument about human interiority that has two difficult consequences: it allows for the possibility that the interior motives of fanatics may, despite the overarching purpose of his argument, be illegible, and it makes it difficult to disentangle the martyrdom of Jesus, which Hobbes claims is a necessary component of faith, from the actions of fanatical rebels, both of which elude the law of self-preservation on which Hobbes anchored much of his philosophy. This double analytic muddling, which Hobbes struggled with extraordinary rhetorical labor to contain, reveals the fraught nature of his polemic against fanaticism and the special epistemological and political challenge that fanaticism bore for any critic who still wished to maintain Jesus and Judeo-Christian biblical texts at the center of the cultural formation of citizens.

Hobbes's arguments are vexed on both of these fronts, and his dedicatory epistle begins to give a sense of how he arms himself to redeem the Bible from fanatical misuse. What does it mean that Hobbes describes texts of scripture as "the outworks of the Enemy, from whence they impugne Civill Power"? "Outworks" suggests that scripture is an outer defense, a site of fortification. (Hobbes's Latin *Leviathan* has "moenia"—city walls, bulwarks.)[5] Scripture is the fortification that enemies—including anyone who claims divine inspiration as the cause of disobedience—use to attack the state.[6] This is a peculiar formulation, not least because it gives the sense of fanatics as inhabiting a fortified city and the state as exposed besiegers, when one would expect the opposite—fanatics as the barbarians at the gates.[7] But Hobbes implies that fanatics have stolen what is proper to the state, "certain Texts of Holy Scripture," and built their own city out of them (or maybe their own temple—the meaning of *fanum*, the Latin root of "fanatic"), perhaps even claiming for themselves the state's moral integrity as an institution under attack. Hobbes wants to make the outworks the state's again and thus fully strengthen its borders. Yet the spatial metaphor is misleading, precisely because it seems to draw clear boundaries between the geography of the state and of the place from which the fanatics attack, when in fact the fanatics are already within the state. This initial confusion of place will have consequences for Hobbes's troubled attempt to pin fanatics in their place with the fixity to which Artegall's unchanging allegorical cosmos aspired, as described in Chapter 1. Hobbes's "impugne" registers etymologically this confusion of inside and outside: "the Enemy" fights from *within*, or fights *in* (*im-pugnare*) the space that should be properly ruled by civil power.[8] In this topography, Hobbes invites us to consider his political science as a physics that manages disputes between mobile forces, but also reveals the disorienting difficulty of fanatics' intimacy with what the sovereign claims as his own and essential for the state's security apparatus.

It is not controversial to argue that Hobbes dedicates his philosophical project to the creation and maintenance of civil order and obedience, and thus opposes all forms of religious violence and inspiration. But my approach to Hobbes's fight against the fanatics is different because I take his systematic polemic against fanaticism, which shapes a great deal of his writing, to be an attempt to foreclose the very questions about fanaticism's unknowable origins that this book's poets address in such sustained ways. Hobbes seems to think it is sufficient to reason backward from the evidence of a revolution (in the English Civil War) to demystify and indict the "pretended" divine motivations of fanatics. But this strategy allows horror about the effect of disobedience to rationalize avoiding the ambiguity of its cause. It is an especially noteworthy evasion of the epistemological obscurity at the heart of fanaticism, given that Hobbes himself claimed, perhaps more forcefully than any of the poets I study here, that the divine itself was unknowable, an assertion to which I will return. Hobbes argues, with absolute certainty, that self-annihilation and inspiration are both impossible, and suggests that the main source of fanaticism is the dangerous interpretive practices that have allowed biblical texts to become the "outworks of the Enemy." Hobbes's transformation of scripture into a text that unequivocally teaches obedience to the state is driven by this polemical denial and by his fear of fanaticism's contagious spread.

Hobbes constructs the fanatic as the negative image of his obedient citizen and reader. Scholars have tended to conflate Hobbes's fanatics with democrats or radicals in general or to focus on Hobbes's systematic and successful disarming of claims for divine inspiration rather than explore how fanatics become illegible to sovereignty in their collective disobedience.[9] Yet more powerfully perhaps than anyone before him, he thought of fanatics primarily as readers and interpreters, people who encountered scripture in such a way that it produced or expanded affects that led them to take individual or collective action (typically violent action) against the state. Recent scholarship has pointed out convincingly that Hobbes modeled different kinds of action around various readerly positions. *Leviathan* can be interpreted, as Victoria Kahn has powerfully demonstrated, as a "romance of political obligations" that chastens errant adventurers who have read too much romance and wish mimetically to enact the adventures of wandering heroes, valorizing instead the stereotypically docile and fearful "female subject of romance" as an exemplar for the early modern citizen.[10] Similarly, Hobbes develops in *Leviathan* a critique of fanatical modes of scriptural reading and interpretation that bars readers from the possibility of mistaking themselves as inspired, which should in turn make readers unable to transmit fanatical passion to others.

To pursue this line of thought, I first explore what Hobbes finds generally threatening about religion and the interpretation of scripture: how it is that a text can produce interpretive dispute and, by extension, fanaticism. Next, I examine Hobbes's biblical hermeneutic to offer a context for how he wished to police the reading of scripture. Finally, by way of a comparison of Hobbes's political and religious conceptions of representation and personation, I analyze the image of the fanatic, whom Hobbes defines as a subhuman madman and, in an elaborate simile, associates with a seditious collective roar of indiscrete, illegible parts, not unlike Spenser's swarm.[11] The fanatic and his passionately disobedient collectivities, along with the troubling example of Jesus's self-sacrifice, persist in subverting the ideal of sovereignty that Hobbes seeks to invent through redefining authority, authorship, and reading as they function within the commonwealth.

Even though Hobbes uses the term "fanatic" most frequently in texts published after the English-language *Leviathan*, I focus primarily on *Leviathan* in this chapter, rather than the later Restoration writings, because it tells us most about Hobbes's construction of the fanatic. *Leviathan* offers, as Leo Strauss has shown, Hobbes's most extensive and authoritative critique of revealed religion and the violence against the state that he thinks it can cause.[12] The fanatic in Hobbes's works is in a position of utmost antagonism to his vision of a politics of obedience in civil society, and therefore examining fanaticism within Hobbes's most robust critique of religion allows us to understand more fully the stakes of his polemic.

Historicity and textuality are the sources of Hobbes's concern about religion. As a diachronic event, religion unfolds over time—its founding events transmitted through text and history—and therefore cannot produce knowledge with certainty in the way that the sciences of logic, geometry, and civil philosophy can. Because religion is shaped by textual forms of mediation, it makes faith and belief difficult to protect from the disruptive process of interpretation. Interpretation can lead to dispute, and dispute to violent antagonism that the sovereign cannot control.

Hobbes contrasts religion's historicity most extensively with sovereignty's ahistoricity. J. G. A. Pocock has persuasively described how *Leviathan* depicts a competition between civil society and religion in precisely these terms:

> There exist then in *Leviathan* two structures of authority, one as
> a-historical as the other is historical, and they will come into direct
> and potentially competitive coexistence once the commonwealth
> constituted in books I and II becomes "a Christian Commonwealth"—
> words which, including the article, form the title of book III. The civil
> sovereign is set up by the a-historical processes of civil philosophy and
> natural reason, which among other things declare that God exists and
> commands obedience to the laws of nature which the sovereign also
> enjoins.[13]

The idiosyncrasy of this Hobbesian distinction is worth emphasizing. Hobbes disputes any argument that takes divine truth as transcendently ahistorical and civil authority as historically bound to the temporality of the earth. By contrast, he derives civil authority from the ahistorical laws of logic and geometry; it matters to Hobbes that these laws are not mediated by history because, once identified, they can be known without interpretation or disputation.[14] He proposes that the ontology of both God and human minds bars us from knowing the truths of religion in any other mode than their contingent and mediated manifestations.

Hobbes's analysis of religion begins in *Leviathan* with the claim that God is unknowable and that when we say the name "God" we do not signify a knowable signified but instead enact our praise of the incomprehensible divine: "there is no Idea, or conception of any thing we call *Infinite*. . . . And therefore the Name of *God* is used, not to make us conceive him; (for he is *Incomprehensible*; and his greatnesse, and power are unconceivable;) but that we may honour him."[15] After the original revelations of God's word, which turn out, in Hobbes's exegesis, to have been mediated to the prophets through angels, dreams, or visions, the only knowledge of God available comes through the mediation of scriptures. Thus, holy texts are multiply mediated: transcriptions of divine words that are communicated by some intermediary (angel, dream, or vision) to prophets, and which are then historically transmitted to readers in (potentially corrupted) textual form.[16] Hobbes suggests that he could never be persuaded by anyone who claims to have received God's word immediately: "If a man pretend to me, that God hath spoken to him supernaturally, and immediately, and I make doubt of it, I cannot easily perceive what argument he can produce, to oblige me to beleeve it."[17] According to Hobbes, a sovereign can oblige him not to speak publicly about his disbelief of anyone's claim to divine inspiration or revelation, but there are seemingly no arguments that can persuade him to change his mind. Even setting aside for the moment Hobbes's deep skepticism toward the possibility of divine inspiration or revelation, he makes clear that it is impossible for anyone to argue that biblical texts constitute an immediate transmission of God's word to its readers. Hobbes writes, "To say that God hath spoken to him [a person] in the Holy Scriptures, is not to say God hath spoken to him immediately, but by mediation of the Prophets, or of the Apostles, or of the Church, in such manner as he speaks to all other Christian men."[18] Hobbes thus contends both that God is inconceivable and that we can conceive with certitude that God no longer speaks to humans directly, let alone inspires or acts through them.

These claims, however, sit uneasily with each other. If God is incomprehensible, then how can anyone be certain that divine inspiration and revelation are impossible? The opposite deduction could be made: because God is incomprehensible, no one can be certain about the possibility of inspiration or revelation. But Hobbes knows that no one could prove this, definitely not to him, and so his position on inspiration's impossibility cannot be disproved.

Hobbes is nothing short of cunning here. What we are left with in his argument is multiple layers of mediation between the believer and God's word. Faith can never be *in* God as such, and God can never be present in any believer, at least no believer who is not Jesus. Faith is only ever faith in the words of the prophetic individual. A faith that asserts access to or inspiration from God would be a kind of fanatical pretending. As Kinch Hoekstra has shown, Hobbes views such claims to access divinity as either entirely deluded or intended to deceive and manipulate.[19]

"Beleefe" and "faith" will need to be radically redefined in order for Hobbes to demonstrate how no reader should ever be able to have an experience of inspiration sparked by an encounter with biblical text. Hobbes is careful with his terms:

> When a man's Discourse beginneth not at Definitions, it beginneth either at some other contemplation of his own, and then it is called Opinion; Or it beginneth at some saying of another, of whose ability to know the truth, and of whose honesty in not deceiving, he doubteth not; and then the Discourse is not so much concerning the Thing as the Person; And the resolution is called BELEEFE, and FAITH: *Faith, in* the man; *Beleefe,* both *of* the man, and *of* the truth of what he sayes. So that in Beleefe are two opinions; one of the saying of the man; the other of his vertue. . . . And consequently, when wee Believe that the Scriptures are the word of God, having no immediate revelation from God himselfe, our Beleefe, Faith, and Trust is in the Church; whose word we take, and acquiesce therein. And they that believe that which a Prophet relates unto them in the name of God, take the word of the Prophet, do honour to him, and in him trust, and believe, touching the truth of what he relateth, whether he be a true, or a false Prophet. And so it is also with all other History. . . . So that it is evident, that whatsoever we believe, upon no other reason, then what is drawn from authority of men onely, and their writings; whether they be sent from God or not, is Faith in men onely.[20]

So much for *sola scriptura.* Devotional readers do not find God's inspired word in the biblical text and will have no "immediate revelation from God himselfe." If they think they have faith in the Bible as God's word, it turns

out to be a "faith in men onely." Hobbes pushes faith in God's word to
the margins by making that word unreachable (even, in a strict sense, to the
biblical prophets).[21] Faith becomes a matter of relations between persons, of believing in the virtue of another person and the veracity of his
message.

Hobbes's ontology of scripture could not be further from the position
held by most Reformers, including Calvin, who insists on sacred presence
in scriptures. Calvin claims that the scriptures must be treated as having
"sprung from heaven" ("statuunt e coelo fluxisse"), as "the living words of
God" ("vivae ipsae Dei voces"), and that it was a "pernicious error" ("per-
niciosissimus error") and an insult to the Holy Spirit to claim that the
truth of scripture could "depend on the decision of men" ("hominum arbi-
trio niteretur"). For Calvin, faith is in part a matter of developing an affective relationship to scripture that can "banish all doubt" ("omnem
dubitationem eximant") and "prepare our hearts to reverence" God's word
("animos praeparent ad eius reverentiam").[22] By contrast, faith as Hobbes
defines it does not bear directly on the word of God since the latter is absent to the reader. He denies the possibility of imagining this inaccessibility as itself the grounds of a direct faith in God. If humans can only
ever have access to God through the mediation of human words, then
they could never receive immediate revelation, let alone become instruments of God's unmediated will.

Faith's entanglement with history is dangerous because it makes interpretation necessary and inevitable. Belief can give rise to "disputes" because
of its structure: humans read other human words, with a constant questioning of whether what the prophet "relateth" can be trusted. There is
only one way to deal with the contingency of belief's ineluctably historical
and textual nature: the sovereign must maintain the sole authority to determine the meaning of scripture. With only a single authorized meaning,
the fanatical enemy can never use biblical text as its outworks. Hobbes
proceeds to preclude the possibility of interpretative dispute through a
complex meditation on the first prophet, Moses, and the place that he holds
in the state:

> Whosoever in a Christian Common-wealth holdeth the place of
> Moses, is the sole Messenger of God, and Interpreter of his Com-
> mandments. And according hereunto, no man ought in the interpreta-
> tion of the Scripture to proceed further than the bounds which are
> set by their severall Soveraigns. For the Scriptures since God now
> speaketh in them, are the Mount Sinai; the bounds whereof are the

Laws of them that represent Gods Person on Earth. To look upon
them, and therein to behold the wondrous works of God, and learn
to fear him is allowed; but to interpret them; that is, to pry into what
God saith to him whom he appointeth to govern under him, and make
themselves Judges whether he govern as God commandeth him, or
not, is to transgresse the bounds God hath set us, and to gaze upon
God irreverently.[23]

As Moses is the "sole Messenger of God" and "Interpreter of his Com-
mandments," so the sovereign alone is the sole interpreter of scripture, the
texts of which Hobbes calls, using another perplexing spatial (and vertical) metaphor, "Mount Sinai" itself. Hobbes seems here to contradict his
earlier claim that the biblical texts are mediated and that belief in scripture is actually a belief in people—this is the effect, anyway, of claiming
that scriptures "are the Mount Sinai." But this is a sly displacement. Hobbes
maintains that Moses does have a special kind of relationship with God:
"Onely to Moses hee spake in a more extraordinary manner in Mount *Sinai*,
and in the *Tabernacle*."[24] But Hobbes is cagey about whether this "extraordinary manner" means that Moses immediately received God's word; he
only states that it is more extraordinary than the method the other
prophets received: dreams and visions. In his chapter "Of the Word of God,
and of Prophets," Hobbes's analysis of Moses makes two central points.
The first is that Exodus 33:11 (Hobbes supplies the following passage: "*The
Lord spake to Moses face to face, as a man speaketh to his friend*") should be
glossed to mean that God spoke to Moses "by mediation of an Angel, or
Angels, as appears expressly, *Acts* 7. ver. 35 and 53. and *Gal.* 3.19, and was
therefore a Vision, though a more cleer Vision than was given to other
Prophets."[25] In that sense, Moses simply received higher-quality mediation of God's word than other prophets. Hobbes has (not unambiguous)
textual evidence from Acts and Galatians to support the suggestion that it
may not be God but an angel who speaks to Moses. This seemingly applies to both the burning bush and the Mount Sinai episodes. But later in
the same chapter, Hobbes seems to change his mind. He specifies that it is
improper to state that Moses only received a dream or vision on Mount
Sinai. Instead, Hobbes rhetorically throws up his hands: "Therefore in
what manner God spake to those Soveraign Prophets of the Old Testament, whose office it was to enquire of him, is not intelligible."[26] Whatever
the extraordinary manner in which God spoke to Moses, we cannot know
anything about it, nor could the Jews depicted in Exodus. It is "not intelligible." This is a long way of suggesting that Hobbes introduces a great

deal of doubt into whether or not even Moses immediately received God's word; even if he did, the Jews then had no more direct access to the revelation he received on Mount Sinai than readers of the Bible in Hobbes's own day have to God's speech. The meaning that readers should receive from the Bible is not from God but rather from the sovereign; readers (to return to the passage that describes scripture as Mount Sinai) should passively "behold" this sovereign meaning and learn to "fear" not only God, but also, implicitly, the sovereign. To interpret is to "gaze upon God irreverently," which is of course a delusion in any case, given that God is "unconceivable."

But this is imprecise. Sovereign determination of reading is more comprehensive still, since it is the sovereign himself who constitutes what texts count as scripture and how they bear on civil law.

> By the Books of Holy SCRIPTURE, are understood those, which ought to be the *Canon*, that is to say, the Rules of Christian life. And because all Rules of life, which men are in conscience bound to observe, are Laws; the question of the Scripture, is the question of what is Law throughout all Christiandome, both Naturall, and Civill. . . . Seeing therefore I have already proved, that Soveraigns in their own Dominions are the sole Legislators; those Books only are Canonicall, that is, Law, in every nation, which are established for such by the Soveraign Authority. It is true, that God is the Soveraign of all Soveraigns; and therefore, when he speaks to any Subject, he ought to be obeyed, whatsoever any earthly Potentate command to the contrary. But the question is not of obedience to God, but of *when*, and *what* God hath said; which to Subjects that have no supernaturall revelation, cannot be known, but by that naturall reason, which guided them, for the obtaining of Peace and Justice, to obey the authority of their severall Common-wealths; that is to say, of their lawfull Soveraigns.[27]

Hobbes carefully argues that only the sovereign can authorize holy scripture as "Canon." So not only does the sovereign decide the single authorized interpretation of any given passage in scripture; he also determines what texts count as part of the scriptural canon to begin with, and how those passages are translated into laws. Less expected is Hobbes's proposal that someone to whom God spoke directly would have to follow God, "the Soveraign of all Soveraigns," before any "earthly Potentate." But Hobbes just as quickly undercuts that vexed possibility, since no subject is capable of having "supernaturall revelation." Since God's word "cannot be known" by subjects—his word is, again, as inconceivable as his being—the desire to obey God over any "earthly Potentate" actually leads directly back to obedience to the sovereign. In the absence of an impossible supernatural knowledge of God, all we have is our "naturall reason," which has "guided" any subject to obey the sovereign. To disobey the sovereign is to leave behind reason altogether—to become mad and, as we will see, potentially fanatical.

Scripture then becomes for Hobbes a supreme instance of the operation by which sovereignty produces rational subjects who will always have assented to and authored their own obedience. Reworking a classical topos, Hobbes claims that these subjects should have made "Artificiall Chains, called *Civill Lawes*, which they themselves, by mutuall covenants, have fastned at one end, to the lips of that Man, or Assembly, to whom they have given the Soveraigne Power; and at the other end to their own Ears."[28] These chains keep subjects bound in their fixed place. Anyone who does not obey the sovereign, and who claims divine revelation or inspiration as an excuse, parts ways with reason and has no place in the commonwealth or even within the bounds of humanity.

"The mysteries of our Religion," Hobbes notes in another bewildering metaphor, "as with wholsome pills for the sick, which swallowed whole, have the vertue to cure; but chewed, are for the most part cast up again without effect."[29] Religion cures only if it is consumed in its totality as the sovereign offers it, not broken down and interpreted. Swallowed whole, scripture has a medicinal, or one might say sedative, effect: it creates obedience. To chew the scripture up—or, presumably, to vomit it back up—makes for a sick and insane subject. In other words, the religious rebels Hobbes calls fanatics do not take their medicine. They interpret text and thereby chew their "pills"; they are not "cure[d]" of their belief in divine inspiration, and they do not think that obedience to God leads inevitably to obedience of the state. For Hobbes, fanatics cannot be organs of divine might because inspiration is impossible. Fanatics are simply sick with their own passions and reject their cure. They are always forming into a collective mob, refusing to fasten themselves into place with the "Artificiall Chains" of laws.

---

Seeing therefore Miracles now cease, we have no sign left, whereby to acknowledge the pretended Revelations, or Inspirations of any private man; nor obligation to give ear to any Doctrine, farther than it is conformable to the Holy Scriptures, which since the time of our Saviour, supply the place, and sufficiently recompense the want of all other Prophecy.[30]

"Pretended" again: revelation or inspiration could not be otherwise for Hobbes. With this conclusion to his chapter on the "Principles of Christian Politiques," Hobbes excludes prophecy, revelation, and divine inspiration from the present. Where there once were miracles, there is now only a void, and holy scriptures "supply the place" where they used to be. Though the doctrine of the cessation of miracles was widespread in the Renaissance since at least Calvin, Hobbes bends this ban to his own ends, making it a pretext for total obedience.[31] The canonization of scripture *as* the laws of the commonwealth forecloses the possibility of an inspired or interpretive power that might compete with that of the civil sovereign. Without such power, fanaticism has no place from which to act—no outworks.

"Supply the place" is an equivocal phrase, though, since it seems to promise compensation for a prophetic plenitude that has been lost, but actually suggests that the sovereign, as the sole designator and interpreter of scripture, is the one who offers "recompense." The etymology of Hobbes's "supply," from Latin *sub-plere* (*supplent* in Hobbes's Latin translation of *Leviathan*: "to fill from under"),[32] resonates evocatively with an essential scriptural concept: fullness. *Plērōma* in the Greek New Testament and *plentitudo* in the Vulgate refer to the "fullness" or "fulfillment" that the incarnation of Christ in corporeal form manifests in the world; these terms also refer, reciprocally, to the body of believers, the collectivity that is filled with the presence and power of Christ.[33] But this etymological resonance between Hobbes's "supply" and the Biblical *plērōma/plentitudo* is perverse. With holy scriptures "supplying the place" of prophecy, inspiration, and God's presence, Hobbes has rendered belief a relationship not of persons to God but between persons only. The fullness of divine presence could not be further mediated and distanced from the reader of scripture, and this is exactly how Hobbes wanted it; the only fullness available "now" is in obedience to the sovereign, and this is what scripture should supply.

The relationship between God and the sovereign is a more vexed one than it might seem in Hobbes's thought, and his writing about the history of Jewish kingship reveals that though the sovereign may himself demand obedience, civil sovereignty itself is created through a disobedient rejection of God. In this section, I focus on how Hobbes's history of Jewish kingship contrasts Moses and all other prophets before Saul, the first king of Israel, with civil sovereigns, despite the fact that he also draws an analogy between Moses and the civil sovereign. This differentiation leads Hobbes to a novel revision of eschatology, which allows him to undercut the millenarian longing for Christ's Second Coming and the justice that so many radicals in the English Civil War thought it would bring. In this elaboration of eschatology, Hobbes offers a negative image of fanatics as those that fundamentally misunderstand their relationship to God and the temporality of Christ's Second Coming. Being sick with their own interpretive passion, they experience cognitive breakdown in their devotional reading and millennial expectation. Hobbes's dense commentary on Jewish biblical history undercuts claims to divine inspiration as a justification for political efforts to bring about the end of a world ruled by civil sovereigns.[34]

Though Hobbes likes to represent Moses as the exemplary sovereign, he nonetheless understands the origin of a civil commonwealth as the consequence of a fundamental break with the Mosaic tradition in politics. Sovereignty may be derivable from the ahistorical laws of science, but kings come to dominate politics at a particular historical moment: the election of Saul.[35] In Hobbes's reading, the lineage of prophets that follows from Moses is deposed and replaced with civil sovereigns when the Jewish people come to Samuel and tell him that he is too old to lead them and that he should appoint a king instead. The key text for Hobbes here is 1 Samuel 8:5–8. The elders of Israel address themselves to Samuel, asking that he "now make us a king to judge us like all nations." Samuel feels slighted, and prays to God. Here is God's response:

> Hearken unto the voice of the people in all that they say unto thee: for they have not rejected thee, but they have rejected me, that I should not reign over them.[36]

The leaders of the Jews from Moses to Samuel were not technically kings; they were prophets of God.[37] God is upset about the Jewish elders' decision but tells Samuel to yield to their wishes, which amount to a desire to have a state separate from God. The civil kings that follow from Saul are confirmed as rulers of God's people, but they are sovereigns only because of this rejection of God. Rule by kings is like a second fall, taking the Jews further from God, and a new kind of commonwealth is the consequence:

> It is therefore manifest enough by this one place, that by the *Kingdome of God*, is properly meant a Common-wealth, instituted (by the consent of those which were to be subject thereto) for their Civill Government . . . which properly was a Kingdome, wherein God was King, and the High priest was to be (after the death of Moses) his sole Viceroy, or Lieutenant. But there are many other places that clearly prove the same. As first (I *Sam.* 8.7.) when the Elders of Israel (grieved with the corruption of the Sons of Samuel) demanded a King, Samuel

displeased therewith, prayed unto the Lord. . . . Out of which is
evident, that God himself was then their King; and Samuel did not
command the people, but only delivered to them that which God
from time to time appointed him.[38]

The Jewish people are from the beginning, for Hobbes, organized as a commonwealth, but first it was a commonwealth with God as king and leaders
from Moses to Samuel as God's lieutenants. With the election of Saul, the
first Jewish king marks a greater distance from God. This is a perverse
occasion for Hobbes because in this instance the demand for a king is cast
as a rebellion against God even though God also authorizes it. Paraphras-
ing Ezekiel 20:37, Hobbes glosses this paradoxical situation from the perspective of God: "I will reign over you, and make you to stand to that
Covenant which you made with me by Moses, and brake in your rebellion
against me in the days of Samuel, and in your election of another King."[39]

In these passages, Hobbes's civil sovereign emerges historically through
a transgression against God's will, and earthly sovereigns will remain in
power, Hobbes extrapolates, until the Second Coming of Christ. The king,
after Saul, must of course be obeyed as fully as the direct lieutenants of
God from Moses to Samuel were obeyed. But the situation is not easy for
Hobbes to parse, since it reveals that civil sovereigns are a product of the
very thing they exist to protect against: rebellion.[40] That this is a historically singular rebellion for rather than against kingship only minimally
muffles how it resonates with the rebellions that Hobbes worries so much
about in his own moment. Hobbes would hardly agree, but we could go as
far as to say that civil sovereigns are haunted by the rebellion that made
them possible. This is demonstrated by the fact that, a decade later, Hobbes
removed from the Latin version of *Leviathan* any suggestion that the election of Saul amounted to a deposition of God, an excision that, as Eric
Nelson has argued, may have been caused by role 1 Samuel 8 played in justifying antimonarchic rebellion in the 1650s. Some republican political
theorists took this passage of scripture to mean "that human kingship is
inherently a usurpation of the kingdom of God, and that monarchy is
therefore an instance of the sin of idolatry."[41]

The difficulty of sovereignty's historical origins does not end at the beginning. Sovereignty originates in rebellion against God, and it also includes rebellion against sovereignty as a possibility for action grounded in
religion. Hobbes repeats on several occasions his explication of these passages from 1 Samuel. Returning to his discussion of Jewish rebellion later
in *Leviathan*, he writes:

And afterwards when they demanded a King, after the manner of the nations; yet it was not with a design to depart from the worship of God their King; but despairing of the justice of the sons of Samuel, they would have a King to judg them in Civill actions; but not that they would allow their King to change the Religion which they thought was recommended to them by Moses. So that they alwaies kept in store a pretext, either of Justice, or Religion, to discharge themselves of their obedience, whensoever they had hope to prevaile.[42]

First, the Jewish people rebel against God by demanding a king—1 Samuel 8:7 makes this clear, and Hobbes's exegesis elaborates on it. In this instance, Hobbes tries, somewhat laboriously, to recuperate this rebellion as something other than a departure "from the worship of God their King." But what comes after is more perplexing. Hobbes suggests that even after the transition from God as king to civil sovereigns, the possibility of rebellion is "kept in store"; according to Hobbes, religion or justice—he seems almost to conflate the two terms here—can still be a "pretext . . . to discharge themselves of their obedience" to the sovereign.

One could argue that after Saul, the kings of the Hebrew Bible have not achieved sovereignty; Hobbesian sovereignty, in the most technical sense, can only exist insofar as there is no pretext for disobedience—but Hobbes makes clear that the demand for a king is the historical condition of possibility for earthly sovereignty to exist. Hobbes's mode of historicizing religion thus posits the possibility of rebellion grounded in religious reasons at the origin of civil sovereignty.

Hobbes discerns this originary disobedience, however, only to foreclose it as a possibility in the specific context of English Civil War millenarianism in which *Leviathan* most immediately intervenes. Hobbes's novel conception of eschatology—in particular, of the Second Coming of Christ—is integral to his fight against what he refers to as millenarian fanaticism, which during the English Civil War claimed religious inspiration as a cause of rebellion against sovereignty.[43] This is his striking claim: the return of Christ will not bring a new messianic age, defined in the minds of rebels by the emergence of a radically new order of justice, but will instead restore the kingdom that existed from Moses's rule through to Samuel, thereby redeeming the original political sin of disobedience. Hobbes's typological linking of Moses and Jesus illuminates this act of redemption. Hobbes calls Jesus's Second Coming "like (in Office) to Moses," a "similitude with Moses."[44] Hobbes thereby defines the Second Coming of Jesus as a restoration of the mode of divine, noncivil sovereign rule that existed before the rebellious election of Saul. When Hobbes asks, "To what end was his [Jesus's] first coming?," he answers: "It was to restore unto God, by a new Covenant, the Kingdom, which being his by the Old Covenant, had been cut off by the rebellion of the Israelites in the election of Saul."[45] The incarnation and resurrection of Christ here bears little on the redemption of mankind's original sinfulness or on the entrance of grace into the world, as it did for nearly every other major Reformer or Counter-Reformer of the period. Jesus's life and death offer merely a promise of restoration of the old covenant, the covenant that precedes the rule of men by earthly kings. The messianic promise is sovereignty, not salvation.

This restoration of the old covenant in Jesus's first coming is sealed only by the promise of his return. Any millenarian who sees the Second Coming of Jesus as the arrival of something that has never existed on earth is mistaken, since Jesus's kingdom can only be the restoration of the divine monarchy that will make civil sovereignty unnecessary: "So that it were superfluous to say in our prayer, *Thy Kingdome come*, unlesse it be meant of the Restauration of that Kingdome of God by Christ, which by revolt of the Israelites had been interrupted in the election of Saul."[46] Hobbes goes to great length to clarify what the kingdom of Jesus's Second Coming will look like. It will be exclusively on earth, in a prolongation of the material world as we know it, since Hobbes's monism requires that he discredit any belief in a spiritual kingdom that is not corporeal, just as he had earlier discredited the existence of incorporeal substances even when attributed to divinity or heaven.[47] Jesus's kingdom will take place in an indefinite extension of the time we know now, the time of material, earthly existence, rather than in a new messianic or eschatological time. Hobbes dismisses the idea of a messianic eternity, a "*nunc-stans*" in which "Eternity is the Standing still of the Present Time," as incoherent and absurd ("neither they [the scholastics] nor anyone else understand" what *nunc-stans* means).[48] And, finally, Hobbes defers indefinitely the Second Coming in order to underscore that no one could use rebellion against earthly sovereigns to speed its arrival: "the Kingdome of Christ is not to begin till the generall Resurrection."[49]

With this threefold redefinition of millenarian principals, Hobbes renders the possibility of disobedience on the grounds of religion a moot point, since only with the coming of the general resurrection, which no humans can precipitate, will the end of sovereignty be in sight. The pretext of disobedience that had been "kept in store" since the origin of sovereignty is rendered inoperative, for citizens cannot hope to "prevaile" without the rule of earthly sovereignty until the Second Coming creates a truly Christian kingdom. The first coming, therefore, promised a restoration of a prior kingdom only in an indefinitely deferred future; no action in the present could transform the world to make it a redeemed one, and God would not, in the time of this world, intervene to shape an individual or a community into instruments of his violent will to transform the world. Hobbes thus takes two central premises of radical millenarian thinking in seventeenth-century England—that actions in the world could encourage the overthrow of earthly sovereignty and accelerate the coming of Christ's kingdom, and that God could annihilate individuals and make them into the instruments of his violent will—and empties them of content.[50] In his *Behemoth*, Hobbes denounces as fanatics those who interpret the radical otherness of the *nunc-stans* (messianic time) and the spread of "Divine Inspiration"[51] as justification for disobeying political authority and rebelling against civil sovereignty: "A great number of Sects, as Brownists, Anabaptists, Independents, Fifth Monarchy men, Quakers, and diuers others, all commonly called by the name of Fanaticks."[52] Christ's Second Coming, for Hobbes, turns out to be an attempt to rethink Christ as sovereign without salvation, a formal restoration of the "place of Moses" that precludes indefinitely any disobedience.

The extreme lengths to which Hobbes is willing to go to appropriate Jesus more generally to the logic of sovereignty may be perhaps best viewed in his commentary on Luke 18:22: "Our Saviour added, *Sell all thou hast, give it to the Poor, and come and follow me*: which was as much as to say, Relye on me that am the King."[53] Hobbes's gloss could be mistaken for parody. Jesus's demand for the redistribution of material wealth, and his call for disciples to organize in a movement that directly questions political power, become confirmation of sovereignty: "Relye on me that am the King." It is not that Hobbes's labeling of Christ as a king is unique or without textual warrant, but Hobbes has departed perplexingly from Jesus's specific call for radical charity in Luke 18:22. Religious radicals in Hobbes's time often took this passage from Luke as a justification to disobey a law or practice that contradicted justice and charity; some, such as Gerard Winstanley and the Levellers, even thought it showed that the link between self and property was precisely what needed to be annihilated for Jesus's charity to fill them and act through them.[54] For these radicals whom Hobbes defamed as fanatics, eschatology could justify faith in a better way of living in this world, leading many to try to become the instruments of its divine transformation. That such desire for self-annihilation might begin from the reading of scripture was one of Hobbes's greatest fears. It contradicts the obedience that Hobbes believes scripture should instill.

And this is why Hobbes redefines eschatology: the Second Coming is not a fulfillment of charity, forgiveness, and generosity—a spiritual existence that exceeds and breaks from the justice of kings. Rather, for Hobbes, Jesus's return and his charity—in short, the democratic elements in Christ's kenotic love—are reduced to "rely[ing]" on a king.

That Hobbes envisions civil sovereignty as an interlude from Saul till the Second Coming presupposes the eventual deposition of earthly sovereignty in some undisclosed future. But humans can and should never participate in that deposition, either of their own will or as God's instruments.[55] Any attempt to bring about the messianic end, or to reform the world to make the coming of messianic time possible, is described as fanatical in Hobbes's polemical sense of the term, something that is pretended and that breaks with natural reason.

Sovereignty may depend on subjects that are in "perpetuall solicitude of the time to come," but for Hobbes, any attempt to "care of future time," to transform through the present political situation through ethical claims rooted in faith or scripture or even God's annihilating, transformative will, spreads fanaticism.[56] Our anxiety toward the time to come makes us, Hobbes argues, like Prometheus, with our heart and livers "gnawed on" every day and repaired proportionally at night.[57] Hobbes requires citizens to abide this suffering. Only obedience can minimize it.

As his revision of millenarian interpretations of the Second Coming makes clear, Hobbes sees fanatics as bad, irrational readers who are affectively moved to disobey or to imagine themselves as organs of divine might because of their ignorantly or willfully deluded interpretations of scripture. If they think they are organs of divine might, then "they take the tumour of their own hearts for the Spirit of God" in vainglory and madness.[58] Thus the construction of the category of the fanatic in Hobbes is tied to a rational discipline: readers are shaped to be rational citizens, and reason demands that they become citizens who obey. Anyone who breaks with this discipline is dismissed as a fanatical madman. It is this conflation of mad reader and fanatic to which I now turn.

Hobbes continues throughout *Leviathan* to view scripture as the outworks at which the sovereign and fanatics battle. The topography of the outworks—an ambiguous blur of interior and exterior—returns in Hobbes's construction of the difference between public and private spheres, a difference that allows him to elaborate how conscience can supposedly coexist with almost total obedience. Going against the grain of his argument, though, Hobbes's elaboration of the distinction between public and private produces a theory of interiority in which fanatical readers threaten to become illegible to sovereign power.

Hobbes's public and private realms, neatly divided, initially seem, as they will later be reworked in Locke's theory of an "infinite difference" or "absolute separation" between the claims of religion and the claims of the state,[59] to reduce religion's presence within the state to the private interiority of the subjects it produces. But this separation is unstable in Hobbes's thought. Carl Schmitt noted this, despairingly: he located in Hobbes's private/ public distinction a "barely visible crack in the theoretical justification of the sovereign state" that "contained the seed of death that destroyed the mighty leviathan from within and brought about the end of the mortal god."[60] The image of this barely visible crack offers an opportunity to view Hobbes's depictions of excessive internality as symptoms of his failure to exclude fanaticism from the state. Fanatics haunt the Hobbesian state from within; they hide in the fracture of the public/private distinction that Hobbes nonetheless feels the need to defend.

Hobbes's theory of privacy and publicity emerges in his attempt to prove the nonexistence of miracles, including, of course, the miracle of divine inspiration. Here he claims that we may not publicly confess belief in miracles in the present, since confession is a matter of public—which is to say, sovereign-approved—reason. Yet in this exclusion, Hobbes describes interiority as a site that sovereignty cannot influence:

> And the question is no more, whether what wee see done, be a Miracle; whether the Miracle we hear, or read of, were a reall work, and not the Act of a tongue, or pen; but in plain terms, whether the report be true, or a lye. In which question we are not every one, to make our own private Reason, or Conscience, but the Publique Reason, that is, the reason of Gods Supreme Lieutenant, Judge; and indeed we have made him Judge already, if wee have given him a Soveraign power, to doe all that is necessary for our peace and defence. A private man has alwaies the liberty, (because thought is free,) to beleeve, or not beleeve in his heart, those acts that have been given out for Miracles, according as he shall see, what benefit can accrew by mens belief, to those that pretend, or countenance them, and thereby conjecture, whether they be Miracles, or Lies. But when it comes to confession of that faith, the Private Reason must submit to the Publique; that is to say, to Gods Lieutenant.[61]

Impugning civil authority becomes a possibility within the heart of every believing citizen, so long as each also submits to public reason. One cannot cite a passage from scripture to justify the existence of miracles in public, but one can believe it in one's heart and mind "because thought is free." The shape of conscience presents a similar topographical ambiguity to that of the outworks: conscience is within the realm of civil authority, but it is also (uniquely in *Leviathan*—no other discussion of conscience in Hobbes has this aspect) outside of that realm insofar as it bears a "liberty" that the sovereign cannot determine or restrict.[62] While Hobbes maintains that disputes that take place at the outworks of scripture need to be policed by the sovereign, he still feels that questions of belief, when restricted to the heart of "a private man," bear a particular "liberty" that the sovereign cannot address, so long as those beliefs are not unfolded as "publique" confessions of faith. Michael Walzer has influentially read Hobbes's concept of private belief as a "secularized reduction of the Calvinist conscience" that poses little threat to civil order.[63] Yet it is possible as well to see in Hobbes's description of a private/public distinction a problem for sovereignty and the order it demands: What if interiority can become a potential site of fugitive evasion of sovereign authority? What if, despite being refused the capacity to confess in public, individuals privately store up pretexts of disobedience? And though Hobbes argues that it is ontologically impossible, what if their interior can be annihilated and inspired by God, and the sovereign could never know? This is the paradox of conscience for Hobbes: conscience, by not being confessed, should have no influence on the public, and yet conscience marks the limit of what sovereignty can know and control.

The Introduction to *Leviathan* orients the reader obliquely toward considering conscience as a problem for sovereign authority, one that cannot be wholly reduced to the privatization of belief. It is there that Hobbes first worries over interiority as a product of reading:

> There is another saying not of late understood, by which they might learn truly to read one another, if they would take the pains; and that is, *Nosce teipsum*, *Read thy self*: which was not meant, as it is now used, to countenance, either the barbarous state of men in power, towards their inferiors; or to encourage men of low degree, to a sawcie behaviour towards their betters; But to teach us, that for the similitude of the thoughts, and Passions of one man, to the thoughts, and Passions of another, whosoever looketh into himself, and considereth what he doth, when he does *think, opine, reason, hope, feare*, &c., and upon what grounds; he shall thereby read and know, what are the thoughts, and Passions of all other men, upon the like occasions. I say the similitude of *Passions*, which are the same in all men, *desire, feare, hope*, &c; not the similitude of the *objects* of the Passions, which are the things *desired*,

*feared, hoped,* &c: for these the constitution individuall, and particular
education do so vary, and they are so easie to be kept from our knowledge, that the characters of mans heart, blotted and confounded as
they are, with dissembling, lying, counterfeiting, and erroneous
doctrines, are legible onely to him that searcheth hearts.[64]

Hobbes famously translates the Greek inscription from the Delphic ora-
cle's temple in an unusual way; *gnōthi seauton* makes its way with fidelity
into Hobbes's Latin rendering, *nosce teipsum*, which Hobbes then translates in English not as "know thyself" but as "read thy self."[65] In the earlier *Elements of Law* (first circulated in manuscript form in 1640), Hobbes
paraphrases *nosce teipsum* as "reading over orderly one's own conceptions" (a better way to avoid error than reading books, he notes), but here in
*Leviathan* Hobbes simply translates it as "read thy self."[66] Knowing is
converted to reading. Hobbes depicts a model of drawing a "similitude
of the thoughts": by reading one's own passions, one can know the passions of every man "upon the like occasions."

Hobbes thus models reading as an activity of the commonwealth rather
than a private, reflective act. Readers of the Bible should find the sovereign inside, not divine inspiration. What each individual sees when he
reads himself is a likeness to other individuals—insofar as each individual
is properly inscribed with the cognitive and affective grid demarcated by
the sovereign. This is a kind of comparison, as Victoria Kahn has shown,
that is meant to neutralize the production and transmission of excessive
thoughts or affects, which might transmit between and collectively bind
individuals in disobedient multitudes.[67] Readers are thus barred from both
interpretation and imitative desire. Hobbes turns this privative reflective
act of reading oneself into a process for recognizing what is publicly
known through reason—which is to say, what the sovereign determines as
reason. Reading thyself here is codified: Hobbes's translation turns
reading not into a revelation of self-knowledge per se (the "reading over
orderly one's own conceptions" of the *Elements*), but rather into a recognition of the position that the sovereign has already constituted. The inhabiting of this position makes each reader legible to the sovereign. Despite
all the deceits that obscure the actual character of other humans' passions,
Hobbes proposes a model of reflexive reading here that can render the
passions of others legible, static, and alike.

Our singularity as unities, as legible individuals whose passions can be
read by a method based on similitude, depends on Hobbes's theory of
representation. Hobbes proposes in *Leviathan* that "it is the *Unity* of the

Representer, not the *Unity* of the Represented, that maketh the Person *One*. And it is the Representer that beareth the Person, and but one Person: And *Unity*, cannot otherwise be understood in Multitude."[68] Hobbes's concept of representation makes persons into the authors of both their own subjecthood and their own subjection, confounding agency by turning everyone into authors of their own actions but ultimately binding each individual's self-authoring capacity to a unity that never coincides with itself—the "Unity" of the sovereign representing the represented as asymmetrically disabled others who have no influence on how they are represented.[69] In other words, the internal unity and legibility of individuals are produced through their unity in the sovereign, whereby they internalize and assent to the sovereign's will as their own.

But what if individuals within the unity become illegible and cannot be appropriated to the logic of "similitude" by which sovereignty "beareth the Person"? In that case, the unifying internalization of sovereign will misfires; Hobbesian representation fails. Hobbes raises this possibility in his distinction between private belief and public confession. In hopes of dismissing the possibility, he declares that it is only a figure of "madnesse" who exhibits an excess of passions or who claims inspiration, but he does so in an elaborate simile that troubles the ability of the sovereign or anyone else to identify this madness:

> To have stronger, and more vehement Passions for any thing, than is ordinarily seen in others, is that which men call MADNESSE. . . . For they will clamour, fight against, and destroy those, by whom all their life-time before, they have been protected, and secured from injury. And if this be Madnesse in the multitude, it is the same in every particular man. For as in the middest of the sea, though a man perceive no sound of that part of the water next him; yet he is well assured, that part contributes as much, to the Roaring of the Sea, as any other part, of the same quantity: so also, though wee perceive no great unquietnesse, in one, or two men; yet we may be well assured, that their singular Passions, are parts of the Seditious roaring of a troubled Nation. And if there were nothing else that bewrayed their madnesse; yet that very arrogating such inspiration to themselves, is argument enough.[70]

Hobbes connects the madness of the individual to the madness of the multitude; both are refracted through his skepticism toward and pathologization of claims of divine inspiration. But the madness of the individual seems to become imperceptible because of its place within the madness of the multitude. It remains unclear how this individual fits into the multitude, whether through contagion, mimesis, consensual joining, or enthusiastic magnetism, or whether this individual even counts as an individual anymore, now that he is mad. What is clear is that this excess of passion makes an individual or a multitude illegible in the process of analogous reading that sovereignty's command to "read thy self" demands. As his simile unfolds, Hobbes contends that we "may be well assured" that such individuals are part of a "Seditious roaring" (louder even than Spenser's swarming flies), but Hobbes's "may be well" itself introduces a degree of doubt into the knowledge proposed, especially when it follows the already-tentative "he is well assured" in reference to the man at sea.[71] The simile is crucial to highlighting both the threat that Hobbes sees in madness and also the epistemological uncertainty that he condemns but cannot resolve. We *may* be well assured that this individual participates in the multitude like a single wave does in the roar of the sea, but we also may well *not* be assured: Hobbes notes that the individual madman, like the smallest movement of water at sea, is ultimately imperceptible ("though a man perceive no sound of that part of the water next him . . . though wee perceive no great unquietnesse, in one, or two men"), despite the fact that he demands we presuppose a kind of knowledge of these entities in their collective forms.

The image of seditious roaring is the antithesis of the antimimetic model of reading in which each individual knows himself insofar as he knows his individual place and internalizes the sovereign's will. By contrast, madmen, especially those who in their "vehement Passions" believe that they are inspired instruments of God, become like a wave in the sea, not perceptible in itself, and likewise illegible to a reader of hearts. They exist as parts of a transindividual roar that Hobbes labels seditious (from the Latin *sed-itio*, "going apart"—from the sovereign, presumably, and from the kind of reading that the sovereign institutes as a discipline of citizenship) for the same reasons that *The Faerie Queene* struggles with the hidden members in the swarm, but without the poem's genuine epistemological (and sometimes political) curiosity. This seditious roar is a figure of passionate and illegible interiority—madness—that is turned outward into collective disobedience, and it exceeds the model of conscience as private belief, a model that is meant to prohibit disruption or dispute. Even though the madman's singular "unquietnesse" cannot be perceived, he contributes to the collective roar. Overwhelmed by passion, the madman is overtaken by a violence that cannot be reduced to action or passion; his excess or idiosyncrasy of "vehement Passions" renders the actions he would take against the state something other than intentional and reasoned. As an instrument of passions that he cannot willfully control and declare, the madman or fanatic does not formally count as a person: the seditious roar of which he is a part, the multitude that he joins as he becomes illegible to the sovereign process of reading and representation, is beyond the voice of humanity.[72]

In his *Answer to Bishop Bramhall's Book called "The Catching of the Leviathan"* (1682), Hobbes addresses Bramhall's objection to his critique of inspiration by affirming that the fanatic's "pretense of *inspiration*," always "pernicious to peace," is a kind of madness: "What is a *fanatic* but a *madman?*"[73] Hobbes is writing there of fanatics in a specific context—"those men, which in the late civil war pretended the spirit"[74]—but he is nonetheless entrenching a more general paradigm. Instead of confronting the epistemological problem of fanatics' motivation and action, as the poets of fanaticism did, or labeling them heretics or beasts, as Martin Luther had a century earlier, Hobbes wants categorically to define fanatics as mad.[75] In arguing with Bramhall, Hobbes defines madness less as a specific condition and more as pure pretense: "The pretence or arrogating to one's-self Divine inspiration, is argument enough to show a man is *mad*."[76] But even that pretense is a symptom of "vehement Passions." To declare that one is—or to appear as though one is—inspired by God is in itself sufficient to prove that a person is mad. But we cannot know whether fanatics believe in their supposed inspiration or not, whether they take themselves to be divine instruments or demagogues, precisely because the heart of the fanatic as madman is illegible, enveloped within a seditious multitude.[77] Hobbes admits that the fanatics' motivations become unknowable, but at the same time, he attempts to scorn these motivations as deluded or deceptive. In short, he does not care if fanatics truly think they have become instruments of God or if they are knowing demagogues; these two options are, for Hobbes, different but equivalent kinds of madness. Both kinds of madmen need to be disarmed and punished by the sovereign, but illegible interiority still remains a problem. By redefining conscience as a space that the sovereign cannot access, Hobbes belies his insistence that it is transparently clear that fanatics are necessarily pretending their inspiration. Inspiration may be impossible in Hobbes's science or restricted only to Christ, but the sovereign cannot see the subject's interior to confirm that the impossible—divine inspiration—has not taken place. On account of their singular "vehement Passions," fanatics are those whose hearts remain illegible in the *fanum*, a temple that civil power cannot penetrate. Their illegibility presents itself as a political and epistemological problem that Hobbes cannot actually acknowledge but must label as a madness that must—but can never entirely—be destroyed.

Hobbes does not only leverage madness to exclude fanatics who attack the state directly. He also uses this charge to condemn martyrs who never threatened the sovereign with active disobedience. It is my final claim in this chapter that Hobbes cannot, by the time of *Leviathan*, avoid implicating Jesus in the inspired madness that he wishes to police, and this is perhaps the most serious sense in which fanaticism haunts his political theory.

Hobbes's position on martyrs evolves throughout his writing. Up to and including *De cive* (published first in Latin in 1642, and in English in 1651, the same year as *Leviathan*), Hobbes still thought martyrdom—as an act of dying for Christ—was in certain instances acceptable. In that text, Hobbes sees martyrdom as a form of nonresistant disobedience that is only acceptable when one is ruled by a non-Christian. To be a Christian ruler, the sovereign must believe in Jesus as Christ. If he does not, then one can passively disobey, but only in a particular manner:

> Must we resist [non-Christian] Princes when we cannot obey them [an principibus resistendum est vbi obediendum non est]? Truly no; for this is contrary to our civill Covenant. What must we doe then? Goe to Christ by Martyrdome [Eundum ad Christum per Martyrium]. Which if it seem to any man to be an hard saying, most certain it is that he beleeves not with his whole heart *THAT IESUS IS THE CHRIST* the *Sonne of the living God*, (for he would then desire to be dissolved, and to be with Christ [cuperet enim dissolui & esse cum Christo]) but he would by a feigned [simulatâ] Christian Faith elude [eludere] that obedience which he hath contracted to yeeld up unto the City.[78]

In phrasing that is uncannily similar to Donne's description of the most perfect desire in *Biathanatos*, *De cive* conceptualizes martyrdom as a desire to dissolve the self ("cuperet enim dissolui") and be with Christ. Hobbes makes clear that acting on this desire is not resistance to civil authority, but it is disobedience. To consider such a call to disobey "hard" would be merely to use a simulation of Christian faith to elude one's pact with the commonwealth. Interior belief becomes excessive—faith in Jesus makes obedience impossible—and translates into a public action, the self-dissolution of martyrdom, which Hobbes strains to define as nonresistant disobedience.

In *De cive*, then, martyrdom is an exception to the universal rule of self-preservation that is foundational in Hobbes's anthropology: it is disobedient but not seen as threatening to the state because it offers no active resistance to sovereignty. However, by the time Hobbes writes *Leviathan*, he has altered his definition of martyrdom. In *Leviathan*, a martyr is "a Witnesse of the Resurrection of Jesus the Messiah; which none can be but those that conversed with him on earth, and saw him after he was risen. . . . The word [martyr] signifieth nothing else, but the man that beareth Witnesse, whether he be put to death for his testimony, or not."[79] The transformation is decisive. In *Leviathan*, there are two kinds of martyrs: those who literally saw Jesus's death and resurrection, and those who witness— Hobbes's strategic use of mediation is active again—that their ancestors claim to have seen Jesus's death and resurrection ("Witnesses of other mens testimony; . . . second Martyrs, or Martyrs of Christs Witnesses").[80] Martyrdom is no longer actually defined by self-dissolution and death; it is witness and testimony alone. And even if a martyr does die, self-dissolution in and with Christ is no longer within the realm of the possible.

The evolution of Hobbes's account of martyrdom in *Leviathan*, and the solidification of his anthropology of self-preservation, make it increasingly difficult for him to separate Jesus entirely from the categories of fanaticism and madness as he defines them, and not only because Jesus claimed access to divine inspiration. Even as Hobbes transforms the definition of martyrdom in *Leviathan*, he makes it clear that the only time that dying for one's belief becomes acceptable is if the *unum necessarium* as he defines it— namely, the only faith necessary to salvation is a faith that Jesus is the Christ—is contradicted by the sovereign: "'Tis one Article onely, which to die for, meriteth so honorable a name; and that Article is this, that *Iesus is the Christ*; that is to say, He that hath redeemed us, and shall come again to give us salvation, and eternall life in his glorious Kingdome."[81] Yet Hobbes had earlier written, "A Covenant not to defend my selfe from force, by force, is always voyd": no man, according to Hobbes, can transfer or otherwise abnegate the right to defend himself physically "from Death, Wounds, and Imprisonment."[82] In other words, the only two times when citizens may actively disobey a sovereign are if that sovereign contradicts the claim that Jesus is the Christ or if the sovereign physically attempts to harm citizens, in which case they may not give up their right to resist.

These two propositions do not sit together comfortably. In the logic of *De cive*, Hobbes can take recourse to the fact that martyrdom is an acceptable exception to the law of self-preservation in select cases, but he does not do so in *Leviathan*. Instead, in this later text, Hobbes tries to redefine martyrdom as witness but cannot entirely elude the problem of death and self-dissolution. Hobbes's redefinition of martyrdom as witness transparently does not work in the case of Jesus. Jesus bears witness to and gives testimony about the fact that he is the Christ, of course, but his redemption of humanity essentially involves his refusal to defend himself from physical violence inflicted by the sovereign.[83] That is, Jesus's testimony is his death: his death, as precondition for resurrection, is the witness to the fact of his being Christ. Jesus sacrifices himself and allows the Roman state to imprison him and crucify his body so that humanity may be redeemed. Hobbes saw the potential conflict between these two claims—that we can resist the sovereign if he tries to harm us physically and that we may disobey if the sovereign contradicts that Jesus is the Christ—for the *unum necessarium* requires that Jesus relinquish the right to self-protection, an act Hobbes claims is void even in the case of martyrdom in *Leviathan*. There is an irreducible tension, then, between the single necessary article of faith (that is, that Jesus is the Christ insofar as he is both incarnation and sacrificial victim) and Hobbes's claim that we cannot give up our right to self-protection.

One counterargument would be that Hobbes grants that self-preservation is an inalienable right but that one could reasonably choose, given appropriate circumstances, not to exercise that right, and to sacrifice oneself. This counterargument would explain why it is, for example, that Hobbes seems to think it would be acceptable for a child to prefer to die rather than obey an order from the sovereign to kill his parent.[84] But that counterargument uses an exception to gloss over how fundamental self-preservation is to Hobbes's anthropology, and how unique Hobbes's example is of the son who prefers to die.[85] For Hobbes, self-preservation is not only an inalienable right that we may choose to exercise or not. It is the thing that, at root, drives us, and not to exercise that right—but instead to release oneself into sacrifice or annihilation—is more generally construed by Hobbes as a sign of madness. I do not point this out to say that Hobbes is being inconsistent but to claim that the kenotic self-emptying that defines Jesus's incarnation and death contradicts what Hobbes calls "A LAW OF NAURE, (*Lex Naturalis*) . . . a Precept or generall Rule, found out by Reason, by which a man is forbidden to do, that, which is destructive of his life, or taketh away the means of preserving the same; and to omit, that, by which he thinketh it may be best preserved."[86]

Hobbes's theory of self-preservation got him in no small amount of trouble in his own life. It was one of the doctrines that led to copies of Hobbes's books being burned at the University of Oxford in the wake of the Rye House Plot.[87] But not all Hobbes scholars agree that self-preservation is the driving force of the Hobbesian subject, so I should explain why

I find it to be so foundational for both his anthropology and his politics. Throughout the stages of his career, Hobbes is consistent in his insistence that self-preservation is a law of nature and that only through a failure of reason would one release oneself into self-sacrifice or self-destruction.[88] In *The Elements of Law*, Hobbes writes:

> And forasmuch as necessity of nature maketh men to will and desire *bonum sibi*, that which is good for themselves, and to avoid that which is hurtful; but most of all that terrible enemy of nature, death, from whom we expect both the loss of all power, and also the greatest bodily pains in the losing.[89]

Even more forcefully, in *De cive*:

> Among so many dangers therefore, as the naturall lusts of men do daily threaten each other withall, to have a care of ones selfe [cauere sibi] is not a matter so scornfully to be lookt upon; we cannot will to do otherwise [vt aliter velle facere non possimus]; for every man is desirous of what is good for him, and shuns what is evill, but chiefly the chiefest of naturall evills, which is Death; and this he doth, by a certain necessity of nature, no lesse then that whereby a Stone moves downward [idque necessitate quadam naturae, non minore, quam quâ fertur lapis deorsum]. . . . Therefore the first foundation of natural *Right* is this, That *every man as much as in him lies endeavor to protect his life and members* [quisque vitam & membra sua quantum potest tueatur].[90]

Self-preservation in Hobbes's world is a law of nature akin to gravity. Humans will protect themselves, and refuse to sacrifice or annihilate themselves, as surely as a stone will fall. They "cannot will to do otherwise." Everything that they are is inclined against annihilation. Leo Strauss has gone as far as to claim that Hobbes's entire science depends on precluding the possibility of self-annihilation.[91] The initial chapter of Hobbes's first major work, *The Elements of Law*, suggests this in its fictional experiment with the idea of the annihilation of the world:

> For the understanding of what I mean by the power cognitive, we must remember and acknowledge that there be in our minds continually certain images or conceptions of the things without us, *insomuch that if a man could be alive, and all the rest of the world annihilated*, he should nevertheless retain the image thereof, and of all those things which he had before seen and perceived in it; every man by his own experience knowing that the absence or destruction of things once imagined, doth not cause the absence or destruction of the imagination itself.[92]

In this definition of knowledge and cognition, Hobbes posits the possibility of the annihilation of the entire world, but insists implicitly on the self-preserving capacity of the individual who can know. The world annihilated, a self remains who retains the images of that world.[93] If in Hobbes's universe it is a law of nature that one preserve oneself, how then can Hobbes account for Jesus's sacrifice as anything other than a transgression of the laws of nature and reason? Hobbes would clearly admit that self-sacrifice happens in the world, but for Jesus, self-sacrifice is in some sense doubly constitutive. It constitutes Jesus's capacity for incarnation and redemption, the belief in which defines faith for Hobbes.

Jesus renounces the single right that Hobbes demands we not renounce even if the sovereign requires us to: the ability to protect ourselves from physical force that would harm us. Regardless of whether it is the passion inspiring self-sacrifice or the act of exposing oneself to self-annihilation itself that Hobbes sees as a transgression of the law of nature, it is clear that he finds something illegible to sovereign power in self-sacrifice. In fulfilling his role as Christ, Jesus disobeys precisely this claim; Jesus "fulfills the law" by opening himself to the ultimate physical harm.[94] This is the self-sacrifice of a fanatic.[95]

A second counterargument to my proposal that there is a contradiction between the single necessary article of faith (Jesus is the Christ) and Hobbes's insistence that self-protection is, like gravity, a law of nature would be that perhaps it is his uniqueness that enables Jesus alone to renounce what no one else could renounce: his own life. This is, for example, Grotius's solution to the problem, and it is related to Donne's attempt to develop a conception of inimitable martyrdom. Grotius claims that Jesus's martyrdom is absolutely unique and thus utterly inimitable because, as Debora Shuger summarizes it, "only as God did Christ have the right to lay down his life."[96] Yet Hobbes never makes such a claim. In his discussion of why Moses cannot be said to have been inspired by God, Hobbes does insist that Christ's divine inspiration is singular: "To say he spake [to Moses] by Inspiration, or Infusion of the Holy Spirit, as the Holy Spirit signifieth the Deity, is to make Moses equall with Christ, in whom onely the Godhead (as St. Paul speaketh *Col.* 2.9.) dwelleth bodily."[97] But that Jesus is the only being who has been inspired by the Holy Spirit does not necessarily mean that his inspiration authorizes his self-sacrifice. Many scholars have also suggested that Hobbes, despite his claim about Jesus's unique inspiration, disputed the divinity of Jesus.[98]

In both cases, Jesus cannot comfortably be claimed as the exception that proves the rule of self-preservation because his capacity for self-emptying sacrifice, for *kenosis*, is that which all Christians are meant to imitate, at least according to Philippians 2:5–8, a passage that links both Jesus's incarnation and death to a refusal to preserve himself:

> Let this mind be in you, which was also in Christ Jesus [Touto phroneite en hymin ho kai en Christō Iēsou]: Who, being in the form of God, thought it not robbery to be equal with God: But made himself of no reputation, and took upon him the form of a servant, and was made in the likeness of men: And being found in fashion as a man, he humbled himself [heauton ekenōsen: "emptied himself"], and became obedient unto death, even the death of the cross.[99]

Not preserving himself, as either God or man, is what makes Jesus's incarnation, death, and resurrection possible. His openness to annihilation—kenotically emptying himself of divinity and, through death, of humanity, too—is definitional. In other words, Jesus is defined as much by what he loses as by what he is: self-annihilation is paradoxically what characterizes him. And, as I suggested in the Introduction, it is the obedience to the formative principle of self-sacrifice that this passage sets out as exemplary, meant for readerly imitation (just what Hobbes wishes to resist in his own theory of sovereign reading): "Let this mind be in you, which was also in Christ Jesus" ("Touto phroneite en hymin ho kai en Christō Iēsou"). That is, the self-annihilation that defines Jesus as Christ is precisely the thing that his followers, at least according to Paul, are meant to imitate. This stands in stark contrast to Hobbes's investment in obedience and self-preservation and his characterization of Christ as the ultimate sovereign. And though Hobbes's counterargument might, in fact, be that only Jesus could be obedient unto death—that is, only Jesus's singular *kenosis* could rightly contradict the principle of self-preservation—Paul nonetheless makes clear that this *kenosis* is an example to be followed, even if, as my chapter on Donne sought to illuminate, the undergoing of self-annihilation was sometimes understood necessarily as an utterly passive experience. Self-annihilation and disobedience thus remain irreducible possibilities for followers of Jesus even as Hobbes designs a state and citizenry that would make them impossible. The exemplarity of Jesus's self-annihilation and disobedience threatens to multiply into uncontrollable and illegible resistances.

Our debt to Hobbes's paradigm of fanaticism is twofold. We inherit many of Hobbes's characterizations of fanatics and his project to define fanatics as the enemies of civil power, as madmen who claim the impossible—namely, inspiration—and who are beyond the bounds of the human.

Reducing fanatics to madmen and excluding them from humanity altogether has made us unable to think about the irresolvable issues of authority, inspiration, and excessive passion that they raise. Like martyrs who store up possibilities of disobedience grounded in holy scripture, the figures of the madman and fanatic move along lines of flight in *Leviathan* by which inner conviction and excess of passion cannot be reduced to sovereign forms of representation. Hobbes never stops worrying that fanatics (the madmen and martyrs whose specific characteristics he constructs) may well act as forces outside the appropriation of sovereignty that, from within the state, threaten to impugn civil authority as a seditious roar that renders each of its members imperceptible.

In a passage in *De cive*, Hobbes quotes Martial to claim that prayers themselves make gods: "Qui fingit sacros auro, vel marmore vultus,/Non facit ille deos: qui rogat, ille facit."[100] The prayers of fanatics, Hobbes fears, threaten to unmake that mortal God, sovereign power, whose existence is the condition of possibility of true commonwealths.[101] We may still not yet be able to imagine what lies on the other side of that unmaking. In Milton's *Samson Agonistes*, the subject of Chapter 4, we can see the depth of the epistemological and aesthetic conundrums that the fanatical unmaking of this mortal God introduces to modernity. Rather than conflate fanaticism with madness, Milton addresses fanaticism's epistemological obscurity directly in his depiction of Samson's vexed relationship to divine inspiration. As a poet of fanaticism, Milton experiments with the techniques of tragic drama in verse to cultivate a very different reading practice from Hobbes's, for *Samson Agonistes* demands of its readers an interpretive orientation that dwells with and responds to the unknowable origins of fanaticism.

CHAPTER 4

# Tragic Fanaticism:
# Milton's Motions

Poets are the hierophants of an unapprehended inspiration.

—PERCY BYSSHE SHELLEY, "A Defence of Poetry"

In my study of Donne in Chapter 2, I showed that Samson's suicidal zeal made him a frequent vessel for anxieties about fanaticism in the Reformation. In his only mention of Samson in *Leviathan*, Hobbes works carefully to separate Samson from fanaticism as definitively as possible. To his relief, he finds that Samson's violence does not actually threaten civil peace, since it is meant to protect God's people as a commonwealth. Samson's violence should only be construed as zealous action and willful courage used to reconstitute a state's sovereignty:[1] "In the Book of *Judges*, an extraordinary Zeal, and Courage in the defence of Gods people, is called the *Spirit* of God; as when it excited Othoniel, Gideon, Jephtha, and Samson to deliver them from servitude, *Judg.* 3.10. 6.34. 11.29. 13.25. 14.6, 19."[2] Emerging in his taxonomy of the term "spirit" in the Bible, Hobbes's discussion of Samson asserts that the judge is only moved by his own "affections" (zeal and courage) in his attempt to defend a Jewish commonwealth.[3] No divine inspiration is involved.[4] The fact that Samson famously does not preserve his life during his final act in "defence of Gods people" is noticeably omitted.

Hobbes's diremption of Samson's zeal and the Holy Spirit displays his characteristic desire to conceal the interpretive ambiguity that makes an example like Samson a dynamic site for meditation in the poetry of fanaticism. What haunted Spenser and Donne so deeply—the idea of a self annihilated and turned into an instrument of God—is dismissed as an impossibility in *Leviathan* for not only political but also ontological reasons. Hobbes rationalizes his stance against the ambiguity of Samson's violence with reference to his version of monist materialism, the position that everything is composed of a unitary matter. According to Hobbes's monism, divine inspiration is impossible because anyone who claims such inspiration believes—or so Hobbes proposes—that God's spirit is incorporeal. In his deductive argument that spirit, since it cannot be incorporeal, must then be only a metaphor for human affect, Hobbes of course ignores the possibility that fanatics in the wake of Thomas Müntzer might have theorized God's immanence and inspiration not as incorporeal but as material action, moving in and through the annihilated self. But whereas *Leviathan* employs a monist demystification of spirit polemically to flatten the complexities inherent to fanaticism, Milton, by contrast, envisions monism as calling for a sustained poetic investigation into the dilemma of Samson's fanaticism.[5]

As Chapter 3 demonstrated, Hobbes sees fanatics as dangerous in part because their vehement passions render them illegible to sovereign power. This illegibility, for Luther as well as for Hobbes, is the justification for severely policing or killing fanatics; it marks their expulsion from the category of the human. Milton, however, inherits Donne's "passive action" as a serious problem for thought and for poetry.[6] *Samson Agonistes* (1671) transforms the framework of inquiry, though. Witness, rather than legibility, becomes the crucial locus of exploration. Contrary to what most scholarship on the play would lead us to believe, the most crucial question of *Samson Agonistes* is not whether fanatics' motivations can be known but how, in the absence of such knowledge, witnesses to their violence, including readers, should respond. At the very end of his poetic and political career, at the moment when Hobbes's attempts to expel the transgressive energies of fanatics from civil power seem to have momentarily succeeded during the Restoration, Milton explores as tragedy the irresolvable problem of the origins of fanaticism, crystalized in the irresolvable dispute about whether Samson is a willing actor of brutal vengeance or a passive vessel of divine violence. *Samson Agonistes* demands that we tarry with the difficulty of understanding the motions and motivations of Samson's brutal final act, his destruction of himself and many of the

Philistines who hoped to use him as an incarcerated laborer.[7] In this play, Samson's fanatical revolt against servitude and state power complicates the relationship between action and passivity, particularly in its return to the dramatic and physiological problem of passion (a term I define in some detail below, but which refers here, as it did in the Introduction, to an external force affecting one's will). Milton thus recasts a series of problems about willful violence and instrumental inspiration that Hobbes meant to foreclose. Milton does so by ostensibly sidestepping the problem of fanaticism's mimetic spread that preoccupies the other authors I have studied. Part of what makes Samson such an important case, of course, is his separateness as a Nazarite. But the play also has a tendency to erode any conception of Samson's singularity, and thus in its conclusion returns to the problem of Samson's exemplarity explicitly.

Hobbes locates the only site of religious disobedience within the interior space of conscience, and attempts to regulate severely the kind of affects that religion should cultivate in the readers of its scriptures. *Samson Agonistes* reimagines the possibilities and horrors of fanaticism after Hobbes's battle against religious insurrection and inspiration.[8] My analysis attempts to explain how Milton's encounter with fanaticism's instrumental model of passive action and divine immanence produces such a complex poetic and dramatic meditation on Samson's violence. My reading of the play begins with an examination of how Milton's translation and gloss of a passage from Aristotle's *Poetics* in the Preface to *Samson Agonistes*, "Of that sort of Dramatic Poem which is call'd Tragedy," blocks the reader in advance from knowing whether to categorize Samson's violence as action or passion. I show how Milton revises the generic and technical norms of tragic verse as a necessary way of responding to the question of whether Samson is an organ or agent. Representations of purgation and sacrifice in the play offer illuminating textual cruxes for exploring how the concept of divine calling further complicates the relationship between action and passion first staged in the play's Preface. Finally, I interpret the closing scene of the play and revise claims about the inaccessibility of Samson's violence and its motivations, demonstrating how this inaccessibility is explored through formal means. This chapter will then return to the question that Milton himself raises and leaves purposefully ambiguous—whether Samson's violence was, to quote the *Defensio Prima* (1651), "instigated by God or by his own virtue" ("sive Dei, sive propriae virtutis instinctu").[9] Instead of attempting to answer this question, I use it to frame the series of seeming dichotomies—action or passion, actor or organ, individual will or divine disposal, strength or weakness—that the play puts into motion to invite us to think with, rather than to resolve, the fundamental ambiguity that Milton located in Samson.

What I have named "passion" might sound like a philosophical category that was readily available to Renaissance readers: involuntary action. The distinction between passion and involuntary action is instructive, though. Involuntary action gains a canonical definition in Book III of Aristotle's *Nicomachean Ethics*, which was readily available to Renaissance readers in Samuel Heilan's 1581 Latin edition.[10] In his analysis of Aristotle's distinction between willed and unwilled action and its Renaissance reception, Bradin Cormack describes how the philosopher links virtue exclusively with voluntary action: "Aristotle differentiates the voluntary act, which he later defines as one whose 'origin lies in the agent [in ipso agente], who knows the particular circumstances in which he is acting [singulas actionis circumstantias]' (III.i.20), from the involuntary act done under compulsion, which has 'its origin from without [foris]' (III.i.2)."[11] Passion in *Samson Agonistes* is radically different from an involuntary action that originates in compulsion by others or by circumstance. The possibility that Samson's passive action is divinely dispensed—that it is not Samson who acts, but God immanently through Samson—radicalizes the sense in which involuntary action originates "from without" and also collapses the distinction between internal and external origination of an action, since God would have to be understood as both internal and external to Samson's annihilated self.

Much recent scholarship on *Samson Agonistes* assumes that the necessary response to the play's provocation is to take a decisive position on whether Samson's violent action is a product of his will or of his transformation into God's vessel. Criticism on the play has often sought to adjudicate claims about Samson's final relationship to God, setting out, for example, "to settle beyond reasonable doubt the question as to whether Milton meant to show Samson's final act as praiseworthy," the legal language of trial—"beyond reasonable doubt"—revealing the desire to convict or exonerate Milton and his Samson.[12] The illegibility of fanatical passion and action, which I have in this book traced through Spenser, Donne, and Hobbes, has led to endless debate among critics who wish to claim Samson as, alternatively, a divinely inspired vessel of God's action or a vengeful self-willed terrorist. Critics' polemics about *Samson Agonistes* thus often resemble Reformation attempts to police the border drawn between proper religious heroes and madmen.

Critical studies of the play should call into question the usefulness to literary analysis of the norms of the courtroom, which are often counterproductive. My account starts from the claim that we cannot, from the material the play offers us, know whether Samson was inspired, whether he is an active agent or passive organ. Our desire to indict or to absolve a work as complex as *Samson Agonistes*—and a figure as opaque as Samson—obscures the fundamental epistemological and aesthetic problem the play poses. This problem is not simply an interesting interpretive crux, nor is the play's commitment to opacity merely an example of how Milton so often frustrates the very hermeneutic desires he draws us into. Fanatical inspiration's unknowability is a problem with more specific and significant religious and political stakes. And this unknowability is not focused solely on Samson's last moment of suicidal violence. It is diffused through Samson's own reflections on himself and his God, and the burden in my analysis of the play will be to show how the play incrementally unfolds a series of undecidable ambiguities in advance of—but also because of—that culminating mystery of self-annihilation and slaughter.

In one of the most penetrating recent additions to the debate over whether Milton's Samson is a terrorist or suicide bomber (discussed briefly in my Introduction), Feisal Mohamed argues that *Samson Agonistes* succumbs in its conclusion to Milton's "favored cultural narrative: God's special favor for heroes of faith and execution of justice upon His idolatrous enemies, be they the flower of Palestine or of Restoration England."[13] Against critics who have argued for Samson's violence being rooted in willful vengeance rather than divine inspiration, Mohamed claims that Milton unambiguously valorizes Samson as an instrument of God's violence. According to Mohamed, Samson loses his subjective individuation and becomes a "vessel of God's wrath."[14] Similarly, Victoria Kahn claims that at the end of the play, it is "God who acts here, bearing witness to Samson, rather than vice versa," and Helen Lynch writes, "Acknowledging, embracing and channeling God's sole and supreme causality, Samson . . . becomes most 'Like' himself, inhabits and departs himself most completely, at the moment he allows himself to be fully the instrument of divine will."[15] In their emphasis on Samson as a "vessel of God's wrath" or an "instrument of divine will," these critics perceptively analyze one interpretive option that the play offers, but it is far from unambiguous. Most polemically, Mohamed declares that Milton's play participates in a culture that immortalizes acts of religious violence because it celebrates Samson's terrorism. Yet by attempting to read *Samson Agonistes* as a "conduct manual for failed revolutionaries,"[16] we lose sight of Milton's technical experiments with tragic verse, which emerge for precisely the purpose of thinking about how and

why we cannot know the source of Samson's violence. The play is structured around the impossibility of knowing anything certain about what
Samson calls the "rousing motions" that incite him to his final act of destruction, and my account of the play's poetic and dramatic experiment
requires a refusal to evade that impossibility.

Milton's insistence on the ambiguous causality of sacred violence emerges,
as this book has shown, at the end of a long line of Renaissance poets who
attempted to grapple with fanaticism's irreducible opacity.[17] The play's ambiguity cannot be overcome through a process of interpretive adjudica-
tion. But though this chapter insists on the irreducibility of its specific
ambiguity, I am not so much looking to offer a new context—the context
of fanaticism—for the old claims about the ambiguity of *Samson Agonistes*. I
want to propose instead that Milton's attempt to deal with the problem of
action and passion inherent to fanaticism *causes* the ambiguity, or takes the
ambiguity as a formal problem internal to its poetics.[18] In *Of Reformation*,
Milton writes that "every true Christian may be called to be a martyr," but it
is the ambiguity of what *being called* to be a martyr looks like that makes the
problem of fanatical passion and action so complex in *Samson Agonistes*.[19]

Stanley Fish makes a related claim: that because we cannot know whether
Samson is inspired, we therefore have no basis from which to judge Samson's
actions and must see them as virtuous.[20] Unlike Fish, I do not think that
the inability to judge requires an assumption of virtue. The play's formal
unknowing of fanaticism renders its illegibility a political, religious, and
aesthetic problem of utmost importance, one that we are barred from seeing by claims about Samson virtuous action. The impossibility of definitively assigning Samson an identity as an organ or agent is a structural
feature of Milton's experiment with tragedy.

I have argued throughout this book that fanaticism figures the possibility of passion at its extreme limit. Fanatics are those who, through a process of self-annihilation, may become passive instruments of God's will.
The reckoning with fanaticism is why the poem is so intractably ambiguous. The unknowability of fanatical inspiration generates Milton's insistence on aesthetic and epistemological uncertainty, and demands that he
reform the techniques of tragic poetry.

Refusing to decide whether Samson is a passive organ or willful agent, Milton is faced with a difficult task, one that requires a transformation of
tragic form. Not surprisingly, "action" and "passion" are central terms in
Milton's description of his poetic and dramatic innovations in the play's

Preface. Though many have surveyed how Milton signals his synthesis of ancient Greek, Italian, and Christian tragic forms,[21] I focus on an unsettling and understudied detail: the suggestive inconsistencies in his translation and description of the Aristotelian theory of tragedy he inherits. Milton's abbreviated citation of Aristotle's definition of tragedy, his partial translation of Aristotle's Greek into Latin, and his gloss of both Greek and Latin in the English Preface to *Samson Agonistes* have proved enduring problems for readers trying to make sense of Milton's theorization of tragedy, but the role of Milton's linguistic shift from "action" to "passion" is more fundamental than has been noted.[22] Here are the trilingual versions of Aristotle's definition of tragedy:

> Tragōdia mimēsis praxeōs spoudaios, &c.[23]

> Tragoedia est imitatio actionis seriae, &c. Per misericordiam & metum perficiens talium affectuum lustrationem.[24]

> Tragedy, as it was anciently composed, hath been ever held the gravest, moralest, and most profitable of all other poems: therefore said by Aristotle to be of power by raising pity and fear, or terror, to purge the mind of those and such-like passions, that is to temper and reduce them to just measure with a kind of delight, stirred up by reading or seeing those passions well imitated.[25]

The most significant of Milton's changes here is easy to overlook because it occurs not in his translation from Greek to Latin on the title page but in his English paraphrase in the Preface. At issue is Aristotle's famous definition of tragedy as an imitation of action, *praxeōs*.[26] In his translation of Aristotle into Latin, Milton renders *praxeōs* as *actionis*—this is clear enough. Action remains the focus. But Milton's English, more gloss than translation, transforms what might otherwise seem like a negligible difference between *praxeōs* and *actionis* by using a peculiar phrase: "passions well imitated." With the shift into English, Milton implies that he is submitting Aristotle's concept of praxis to a conversion into its seeming opposite, "passions," a term that is, of course, essential to *Samson Agonistes*, which ends with "all passion spent" (1758). Here is the first alteration that Milton makes to tragedy; it seems *catharsis* will be caused by witnessing a mimesis of passions rather than a mimesis of action. But Greek and Latin remain on the title page, which leaves the nature of the relationship between passion and action obscure. That obscurity will trouble not only the play's achievement of catharsis but also its representation of what determines Samson's violence.

As Elizabeth Harvey has shown in her study of *Samson Agonistes*, "passion" was a resonantly ambiguous term in the Renaissance. From the Latin *patior*, "to suffer," a translation of the Greek *pathos*, "passion" could signify "a condition of intense affective receptivity" (the exemplary model of which is the passion of Christ); the *patho-logical*, which evokes the medical study of the emotions or, more literally, the writing or speaking of the emotions; and grammatical passivity, "the syntactical position of being acted upon."[27] Milton's "passions well imitated" bears this considerable interpretive equivocation. The Preface to *Samson Agonistes* necessarily poses—and pointedly leaves unresolved—the extent to which we as readers and Samson himself are witnessing a mimesis of an experience of praxis or passion—of willed activity or passive receptivity. The grammatical meaning of "passion" remains in play as well: is Samson subject or object, active agent or receptacle, when it comes to what he will call the "sentence" (1369) of his fate at the end of the play, his entanglement in the "dire necessity" (1666) that means death for both him and the Philistines who have imprisoned him? The question of the extent to which Samson's "great act" (1389) at the end of the dramatic poem signals his willful agency or his transformation into a passive vessel of God is one of the major and unresolvable cruxes of the play, and organizes its poetics. Here I diverge from Kahn's estimation that Milton's *Samson Agonistes* is "about the power of mimesis or representation to turn passion into action,"[28] since no such transformational "turn" can be said to occur with certainty: the play places a demand on us to envision passion and action as essentially and inextricably related. This is perhaps why *praxeōs* and *actionis* remain on the title page to frame our experience of the play; they are not simply overcome and supplanted by "passions." Their mutual presence requires that we consider passion and action dialectically rather than imagine them as opposites.[29]

The slippery relationship between *praxeōs*, *actionis*, and passion is more complex still because the original term for the effect of witnessing this action or passion, *catharsis*, has been elided in the quotation of Aristotle's Greek and replaced with "&c." *Catharsis* is, of course, crucial to Aristotle's definition of tragedy, in which it is described as the telos (*teleias*) of witnessing the mimesis of praxis.[30] In Aristotle's Greek, *catharsis* can mean purging, purification, cleaning, and evacuating; in Biblical Greek, the term gains the additional meanings with which Milton must have been familiar: purification from sin, consecration, or the pronouncement of cleanliness, as in Hebrews 9:22: "And almost all things are by the law purged [katharizetai] with blood; and without shedding of blood is no remission."[31] The concept of *catharsis* does appear in the Preface's Latin translation, where

Milton renders Aristotle's text as "per misericordiam et metum perficiens talium affectuum lustrationem" (by pity and fear perfecting the lustration of such affects). As a translation for *catharsis*, *lustratio* proves to be especially complex in this field of ambiguous translation; it, too, bears on the Preface's meditation on action and passion.[32] Late sixteenth- and seventeenth-century Latin translations of Aristotle's passage supplied Milton with a number of terms for *catharsis*. *Purgatio, expiatio*, and *mundo* would have been sensible choices given Milton's English use of "purge" in his English gloss. Debora Shuger has shown that a number of Renaissance Greek lexicons that were available in England, Guillaume Budé's *Commentarii linguae Graecae* (1529) and Henricus Stephanus's *Thesaurus Graecae linguae* (1572) in particular, define *catharsis* in terms of both *lustratio* (which Budé glosses via Livy as *lustrationis sacro peracto*, "purification by sacrifice") and *purgatio* (which Budé glosses as "a cleansing or religious purification"). *Lustratio*, these lexicons make clear, had the sense both of sacrificial expiation and personal or national salvation.[33] Current lexicographers tell us that *lustratio* belongs to the traditions of Roman sacrifice that typically involved a ritual "action of going round or traversing."[34]

Elsewhere in Milton's oeuvre, *lustratio*, as Jason Rosenblatt has demonstrated, generally evoked "pagan and Hebraic lives of abstinence and purification,"[35] but in the Preface to *Samson Agonistes*, Milton's usage is more multivalent.[36] The term evokes multiple meanings as a translation for *catharsis*: ritual purgation, sacrifice, and lustrative cleansing most immediately, but these, too, are yoked to the term's resonance with an ending, a *perficiens, telos*, or fulfillment, the effect of which is achieved with the literal sacrifice of Samson. *Lustratio* returns us to the complex relation of action to passion that we glimpsed in Milton's substitution of passion for *praxis* and *actio*. *Samson Agonistes* foregrounds *lustratio* both as a series of purifying acts that Samson undertakes and as a kind of passive sacrifice that Samson may undergo as a divine vessel.

Milton's ostensibly clarifying gloss of tragic *catharsis* ("by raising pity and fear, or terror, to purge the mind of those and such-like passions, that is to temper and reduce them to just measure with a kind of delight, stirred up by reading or seeing the passions well imitated")[37] only introduces more equivocation. Do *catharsis* and *lustratio* "purge the mind" of pity, fear, terror, and "such-like passions"? Or do they "temper and reduce" (to make more proportionate and draw back, *re-ducere*) these passions "with . . . delight" to a "just measure," the justness and quantity of which remain strikingly unspecified? And given the final words of the play—"all passion spent"—what does it mean that passion is purged, deprived of strength, or fully actualized only in the play's violent catastrophe? Do *catharsis* and *lustratio* in Milton's hands transmit a tempered, aestheticized version of the experience of self-annihilation that Samson may undergo? Neither the Preface nor the play offers answers to these questions. But the discourse of purification that Samson employs throughout the play will be important for explicating fanaticism's relationship to *catharsis* in Milton's experiment with tragic form, for the judge himself oscillates between conceiving of his calling as an active work of purification and a passive undergoing of divine sacrifice. The play is structured so that readers are called on to witness not only Samson's violence but also their own inability to adjudicate between his passion and his action, his status as holy vessel and as vengeful and suicidal murderer.

The story of Samson that Milton inherits has the hero's bodily strength at its center, a strength related to his purifying asceticism and betrayed ultimately in his revelation of its source to Dalila. Milton takes pains to orient the reader to Samson's body as an agent of action, both his heroic actions in the past and his milling labors in the present. And yet the play spends a great deal of time, as Samson's self-reflections develop in between encounters with his visitors, rendering the location and source of Samson's strength increasingly difficult to determine. In this way, the play alternates between suggesting that Samson produces his own strength by the work he performs on and through his body—his asceticism as a kind of muscular training—and that his body may in fact be a vessel for God. Samson's reflections on his separateness, and how that separateness bears on his relationship to Jewish law, alternately cast him as exemplary actor and singular instrument, and the play uses this self-undoing separateness to undermine Samson's inclination to self-deification.

Samson is something of a paradox for the play. As chosen exception, he is separate and singular, evincing an antinomian extravagance that is in excess of Jewish law. In this sense, Samson seems not unlike Donne's inimitable martyrs—at least insofar as his actions are inimitable. Samson's separateness concentrates and extends the chosen status of the Nazarite tribe as a whole: "Nazarite" comes from the Hebrew root *nazir*, meaning one "separated" or "consecrated"; it is also closely related to the Hebrew verb *nazar*, "to abstain," and the noun *nader*, "vow."[38] Numbers 6:1–21 specifies that the separateness is defined by ascetic refusal: restrictions on what to eat and drink, a ban on having a razor taken to one's head, and a prohibition on approaching a corpse. Yet even as Samson is held up as singular, he is—or rather he was, before the start of the play finds him imprisoned—an exemplary model of potent strength for others to imitate. This exemplarity militates against his singularity. The tension between Samson's singularity and his exemplarity will come to a head at the end of the poem when Samson seems to become at once illegible, an analogue to God's "unsearchable dispose" (1746), and a visible monument of "matchless valour," an example to be collectively followed (1740). But the Chorus registers this ambiguity already on first approaching Samson. Seeing him imprisoned and weakened through his grinding labors at the Philistine mill, fallen from his great potency to "this, this . . . carelessly diffused" (115, 118), the Chorus addresses Samson: "O mirror of our fickle state, / Since man on earth unparalleled!" (164–65). Both a mirror in which we can see ourselves ("our fickle state") and "unparalleled," Samson's fraught exemplarity frames the Chorus's narration of his condition.

In his initial soliloquy, Samson announces his separateness and yet suggests that it has failed to be a "promise" of his life's unique "design," and this equivocation presses forward his confusion about whether his strength is his own or God's:

> O wherefore was my birth from Heaven foretold
> Twice by an angel, who at last in sight
> Of both my parents all in flames ascended
> From off the altar, where an offering burned,
> As in a fiery column charioting
> His godlike presence, and from some great act
> Or benefit revealed to Abraham's race?
> Why was my breeding ordered and prescribed
> As of a person separate to God,
> Designed for great exploits; if I must die
> Betrayed, captived, and both my eyes put out,
> Made of my enemies the scorn and gaze;
> To grind in brazen fetters under task
> With this heaven-gifted strength? O glorious strength
> Put to the labour of a beast, debased
> Lower then bondslave! Promise was that I
> Should Israel from Philistian yoke deliver;
> Ask for this great deliverer now, and find him
> Eyeless in Gaza at the mill with slaves,
> Himself in bonds under Philistian yoke;
> Yet stay, let me not rashly call in doubt

Divine prediction; what if all foretold
Had been fulfilled but through mine own default,
Whom have I to complain of but myself?

(23–46)

In this passage's first sentence, the redoubled announcement or "foretell-
ing/Twice" of Samson's birth, a gift from God to Manoa's barren wife, is
what initially seems to define Samson's separateness. Samson's life, his
"breeding," has been "ordered and prescribed"—both arranged and pre-
written in advance of his birth. He was cast even before being brought to
life "as of a person separate to God/Designed for great exploits," unique
even among the Nazarites. But this "as" introduces an undercurrent of
doubt. The conjunction suggestively makes us unsure of whether Samson
is such a separate being, "designed" as a vessel to be filled with God's
strength, or only like ("as") one. The metapoetic significance of this "as"
is stressed by the fact that it initiates the second comparison compressed
in the beginning of this speech, which offers us a sense of the poem's own
"[design]," its line-by-line poetic exploration of the dizzying difficulty of
determining whether Samson is like an agent or like a divine instrument.
The sacrificial covenant that is relatively unambiguous in Judges—Manoa
and his wife make a ritual offering to God before they receive the gift of
Samson's birth—is obscured here by the repetition of "as" at the beginning of lines 27 and 31. Moreover, "where an offering burned" gives no
indication of the agent behind this offering, and the burning comes to be
almost indistinguishable from the angel's flaming ascension, underscored
by that first use of "as," "where an offering burned,/As in a fiery column
charioting/His Godlike presence."

Despite the ambiguity in this initial plaint, Samson locates in the past
that "Promise was that I/Should Israel from Philistian yoke deliver," even
if he implies failure on the part of God. Samson never settles into any
given assertion, though, and he interrupts and revises this reading of
"promise" and failure, too: "Yet stay, let me not rashly call in doubt/
Divine prediction; what if all foretold/Had been fulfilled but through mine
own default,/Whom have I to complain of but myself?" What had seemed
a "promise" potentially broken now appears to Samson in his revision—
"yet stay"—as his own "default," his own failure or imperfection. Had it
not been for this "default," what was "foretold" and "predict[ed]" would
have been "fulfilled." It is as though Samson was meant to be a vessel for
God's word ("Divine pre[-]diction"), the passive instrument that could have
"fulfill'd"—or been filled with—God's will, except "through mine own

default," a default that Samson realizes may be rooted in his persistent attachment to himself, his refusal to annihilate himself: "Whom have I to complain of but myself?"

Samson will continue throughout the soliloquy—indeed, throughout the play—to alternate between blaming God and himself for his imprisonment. Immediately following this shift from a narrative of broken "promise" to one of personal "default," Samson questions the meaningfulness of the strength he has been given by God ("But what is strength without a double share/of wisdom?" [53–54]) only then to refute and correct himself again ("But peace, I must not quarrel with the will/Of highest dispensation, which herein/Haply had ends above my reach to know" [60–63]). Samson's perpetual equivocation is itself an enactment of the complex relationship between passion and action that the Preface initiates. Is Samson's "living death" (100) his own "default"—a consequence of his action, his investment in self rather than God—or is it a passionate station of suffering along the course of God's unreachable "ends"?

Samson's speech about the relationship between promise and default—metonymies for passion and action—bears on the play's inquiry into the source of his power to undertake such impressive acts of violence. Samson returns repeatedly to the question of how it is that he lost his power and where in his body it was "lodged," and thus whether the strength itself is his or God's:

> Who this high gift of strength committed to me,
> In what part lodged, how easily bereft me,
> Under the seal of silence could not keep,
> But weakly to a woman must reveal it,
> O'ercome with importunity and tears.

(47–51)

At this moment, even before Samson revises himself yet again to refer to his strength as a gift so "slight" that it was merely "hung" in his hair (59), it becomes unclear what Samson's gift is and what "seal[s]" it in his body: his silence (a stoic refusal to disclose the secret) or simply the presence of his hair? The play refuses to allow Samson or us as readers to be certain of the source and seal of the strength that keeps him separate. Likewise, the play never allows us to know whether Samson is being punished for having failed to maintain the ascetic rituals that could have kept him separate.

Samson's separateness does at times, however, seem to be predicated upon his actions, his adherence to these ascetic rituals. The image of a body or mouth sealed and protected from weakness recurs throughout the poem as a mark of the failure of Samson to care sufficiently for the ascetic practices that at least seem to allow his body the strength to act according to God's promise. Synecdoches for that body's weakness are various: the breaking of the seal of silence, the cutting of his hair, and Dalila's penetrating "feminine assaults, / Tongue-batteries" (403–4). The possible vulnerability of particular body parts is vexed largely because of Samson's perpetual fear of feminization, a screen for his own ambivalence about passion and passivity.[39] Early in the tragedy, while contrasting his current state with the Chorus's recollection of him as God's "mighty champion, strong above compare" (556), Samson describes Dalila's deception as penetration of his otherwise "defen[ded]" body and mind: "What boots it at one gate to make defence, / And at another to let in the foe / Effeminately vanquished?" (560–63). Desire for Dalila is imagined here as a failure of border patrol—it leads to a penetration that opens up the seemingly impenetrable Samson. This exposure "let[s] in" a force that vanquishes, a vanquishing that is done "effeminately"; it is accomplished by a woman, of course, but it also seems to have an effeminizing influence on Samson, whose firmness is breached. The grammatical doubleness of "effeminately" as an adverb that modifies both Dalila's action of vanquishing and Samson's own state mirrors Samson's reinterpretations of the cause of his own weakness, which he first understands as Dalila's fault but then reworks as his own: "Of what now I suffer / She was not the prime cause, but I myself" (233–34). And yet the Chorus's description of Samson breaking "his vow of strictest purity" by wedding Dalila's "uncleanliness" (319–21) alerts us to the fact that it is not only Samson's "effeminate" weakness that renders void his ability to act; it is also his marital transgression, his failure to obey a law that guarantees his ability to act with such unique strength.

Whether Samson's marriages—first to a Philistine woman from Timna, then to Dalila—constitute acts for which he is to blame or whether he is moved by God to marry remains a dilemma for the play's interpreters, even if the need to resolve it has seemed less than that provoked by Samson's tearing down of the temple. The inability to confirm whether his marriages are divinely inspired looks ahead to the inability to read the "motions" that Samson claims inspire him to his final act of violence.[40] In his first justification for marrying someone outside of the Nazarite tribe, Samson argues:

>         They knew not
> That what I motioned was of God; I knew
> From intimate impulse, and therefore urged
> The marriage on; that by occasion hence
> I might begin Israel's deliverance,
> The work to which I was divinely called.
>
>                                                              (221–26)

The syntax of line 222 makes it hard to determine whether Samson is active or passive here: "I motioned" grammatically designates Samson as agent, but the cryptic "was of God" makes it seem as though he is passive, an instrument of God's motions. The passive sense is underscored by the echo of Judges in the King James Version. "And the Spirit of the Lord began to move him at times"[41] suggests that the cause of Samson's movements is God. Is it Samson's breaking of the vow of "strictest purity" that makes it impossible for him to fulfill the work that is his unique calling, or does "intimate impulse" override his submission to the law in order to offer him "occasion" to deliver Israel? Do God's motions, through "intimate impulse," make Samson into a vessel, or does his will ("urged") coexist with God's will? It becomes that much more unclear when Samson refers to his choice to marry Dalila with terms—"I thought it lawful from my former act, / And the same end" (231–32)—that leave unanswered whether the first transgression of Nazarite law was lawful because Samson understood himself as being moved by God or whether this "former act" was itself a work that violated law despite Samson's exceptional, separate status.

Despite the ambiguity, it becomes clear at this point in the play that Samson understands weakness as interfering with his ability to be separate and to act, and that weakness must be overcome by a return of potency and a purgation of effeminate passion. Yet the middle of the play demystifies the idea that Samson's strength lies in one particular body part, which begins to unsettle with increasing urgency the extent to which the strength Samson has shown was ever his to possess. Samson's shift away from seeing his strength embodied in his hair crystallizes the question of whether Samson's attempted salvation of Israel depends upon his strength and will. Whereas earlier in the play Samson repeatedly insists on the fact that his strength resides in his hair, he changes his tune when Harapha, the blistering Philistine hero, accuses him of having "feign[ed]" the fact that his strength "was given thee in thy hair, / Where strength can least abide" (1135–36):

My trust is in the living God who gave me
At my Nativity this strength, diffused
No less through all my sinews, joints and bones,
Than thine, while I preserved these locks unshorn,
The pledge of my unviolated vow.

(1140–44)

Samson refutes the idea that his strength is located in his hair, claiming that his strength has been "diffused" through the entirety of his body. His hair is merely the "pledge" of his "unviolated vow."[42] It remains uncertain whether the vow itself is violated when its "pledge" is, since "my unviolated vow" could indicate either that Samson's vow was unviolated while he "preserved these locks unshorn" or that the vow remains still unviolated, even though the mark of its pledge has been cut. Either way, in shifting focus from the shearing of his locks to the disclosure of a secret, Samson puts emphasis back on his body, its ability to perform works on account of his will. The question of how to read this "diffus[ion]" as a measure of the extension of Samson's bodily potency is a difficult one, and not least because the Chorus first spies Samson, in his blindness and bondage, as one who "lies at random, carelessly diffused" (118). Such local uncertainties, symptoms of fanaticism's unknowability, texture the entirety of the poem.

That the image of "this strength, diffus'd" appears earlier in the poem helps us ascertain how diffusion relates to the play's account of activity and passivity. Samson begins the play by lamenting his own blindness and envisioning it as a second form of imprisonment. But just before referring to "myself my sepulcher, a moving grave" (102)—in which his self-entombment suggests the emptiness of self-enclosure rather than the self-annihilation required to be God's organ—Samson recuperates his blindness with a narrative that casts the diffusion of his sight, like the diffusion of his strength, as an even greater awareness and potency:

Since light so necessary is to life,
And almost life itself, if it be true
That light is in the soul,
She all in every part; why was the sight
To such a tender ball as the eye confined?
So obvious and so easy to be quenched,
And not as feeling through all parts diffused,
That she might look at will through every pore?

(90–97)

Echoing passages from Luke 11:34,[43] Augustine's *De Trinitate*,[44] and Milton's own Proem to Book III of *Paradise Lost*, this passage moves from a syllogism about light, the soul, and life to evoking a body that, less "tender" in its differentiation of organs, could feel and see through every pore. Like strength, vision could function through a diffused yet totalized "will." The image of an eye in every pore for Samson, made blind by consequence of what may or may not have been the violation of his vow, at first seems like a fantasy of overcoming the weakness of a single body part's vulnerability. John Rogers has described this as a monist fantasy that strength and sight could be multiplied and spread throughout every pore.[45] If strength were diffused through the body equally and Samson could see, feel, and will in every single pore without differentiation, then the body itself would become something like light in its total union with the soul ("She all in every part" refers us back to the conflation of light and the soul) and could not be so easily damaged. And yet, it is essential to note that the play brackets this fantasy of diffusion *as fantasy*—something that gives Samson hope while imprisoned but that hypertrophies the will and abets an image of self-idolatry. In the course of the play, Samson departs from idolization of his strength and instead dwells in his blindness, accepting weakness and passion as signs of his possible transformation into an instrument of the divine. Samson starts to imagine the source of his strength as, paradoxically, his capacity to be a passive vessel.

Samson's embrace of weakness arises in the play again where we might least expect it: in a moment of meditation on his own supposed feminization at the hands of Dalila.

> Famous now and blazed,
> Fearless of danger, like a petty god
> I walked about admired of all and dreaded
> On hostile ground, none daring my affront.
> Then swoll'n with pride into the snare I fell
> Of fair fallacious looks, venereal trains,
> Softned with pleasure and voluptuous life.
>
> (528–34)

Though weakness here seems to index the privation of masculinity that renders Samson's action impotent in lines such as these, wherein the phallic "swoll'n . . . pride" of Samson's body is "softened" by Dalila's domestic ensnarement, it is also true that Samson's reference to himself as "like a petty god" evinces the self-idolatry that Samson criticizes elsewhere in the poem. Hence self-fetishized puissance is precisely what Samson seems to discard later in the play; it leads him too often to define himself as "a petty god," rather than as God's passive instrument. Samson's criticism of his own conception of himself as "a petty god" also offers a way to reinterpret Rogers's analysis of Samson's monistic fantasy, in which sight becomes "diffused" in every pore of the body, as a kind of idolatry in which the body itself is made to become ensouled light, nearly the essence of life itself.[46] Samson's turning against his own deification puts pressure on Joanna Picciotto's analysis of the judge's "diffusion," which posits it as the mechanism by which Samson's transformation from "petty god" to "public person" occurs.[47] Picciotto elegantly traces how Samson comes to be released from his individual, private self in order to become a public person, a symbol of the multitude. But in context, it is hard not to worry that Samson's wish for diffusion of sight and strength conforms to his reiterated fantasy of deified will—a fantasy, that is, of being a self with divine strength, not a desire to unmake the self so that God can immanently be present in him. As the play proceeds, it suggests that this fantasy may be overcome by a diffusion of weakness in which the will is annihilated and Samson seeks to become an instrument of God rather than a public person—even though the play will never allow us to confirm that such annihilation has taken place. Though Milton embraced monism as a philosophy that informed both his theology and his poetry, and *Samson Agonistes* may be considered one of the great experiments in what a monist tragedy might look like,[48] in the instance of the eye's "diffus[ion]" the play registers a worry about the misappropriation of monism for an ontology of individual strength and sight. It is the negation of the fantasy of an eye in every pore, maximizing sight's "will," that leads to Samson's self-emptying embrace of passion and weakness.

For Samson, the imagining of a sight diffused "as feeling through all parts" (96), which makes sight seem like feeling but also suggests a sight that itself feels, gestures toward the achievement of an overabundance of "will": "that she might look at will through every pore" (97). Yet departing from the narrative that names his body as the potent instrument of his own will, Samson late in the play increasingly understands the passive position of his potential instrumentality. Unlike earlier in the play, where his separateness signified his personal strength, his late revision of calling recasts his action as passion, his work as an unmaking by divine disposal. Yet the language of the poem at once tempts us to and prevents us from interpreting Samson's action as produced by God's inspiration, and this tension is most acute in Samson's meditation on "dispensation" and "dispos[al]" before he agrees to attend the festival of Dagon.[49]

Samson's reactions to the officer leading up to his act of violence demonstrate his legal predicament. When the officer first comes to Samson to demand that he perform at the "solemn feast" dedicated to Dagon and entertain the Philistines, Samson responds: "Thou know'st I am an Hebrew, therefore tell them, / Our law forbids at their religious rites / My presence; for that cause I cannot come" (1319–21). In this exchange, Samson's relation to the law necessitates his action: the syntax of "I am an Hebrew, therefore" signifies that the law has already prescribed what Samson can and cannot do. His actions proceed from this law: he acts, or refuses to act, in order to conform his will to it. Samson almost immediately revises this "cannot come," however, in his iterations of "I will not come" (1333, 1342). Inability becomes willful refusal with a slight modal substitution. Just before the second encounter with the officer, Samson has an exchange with the Chorus in which the question of whether he can or will go along to the festival of Dagon becomes a meditation on the nature of law and divine permission, activity and "constrain[t]":

> *Chor.* Where the heart joins not, outward acts defile not.
> *Sam.* Where outward force constrains, the sentence holds
> But who constrains me to the temple of Dagon,
> Not dragging? the Philistian Lords command.
> Commands are no constraints. If I obey them,
> I do it freely; venturing to displease
> God for the fear of man, and man prefer,
> Set God behind: which in his jealousy
> Shall never, unrepented, find forgiveness.
> Yet that he may dispense with me or thee
> Present in temples at idolatrous rites
> For some important cause, thou need'st not doubt.
> *Chor.* How thou wilt here come off surmounts my reach.
> *Sam.* Be of good courage, I begin to feel
> Some rousing motions in me which dispose
> To something extraordinary my thoughts.
> I with this messenger will go along,
> Nothing to do, be sure, that may dishonour
> Our Law, or stain my vow of Nazarite.
> If there be aught of presage in the mind,
> This day will be remarkable in my life
> By some great act, or of my days the last.
>
>                                                              (1368–89)

The Chorus here initially offers a reading of the situation that disjoins "heart" from "outward act." If heart (that is, inner conscience and emotion) is not joined to the act in its outward performance, then the law is not transgressed and the self is not defiled. An "act" defiles only if the heart commits to it. The Chorus thereby suggests that the question of permissibility does not primarily bear on action's relationship to law but on inner conscience. Samson's response contextualizes and revises the problem in iambs so smooth that it is easy to elide how vital this different interpretation of his situation is to become: "Where outward force constrains, the sentence holds." Only where external constraints on the body are present does this "sentence" have "hold" over the body. Samson then qualifies this glossing of "outward . . . constrain[t]"—which seems radically different from the earlier constraint of "I am an Hebrew, therefore"—by differentiating subtly between "commands" and "constraints," such that he links obedience to freedom ("If I obey them,/I do it freely"). Samson makes freedom the condition of his obedience to the Philistines just before he makes his obedience to God a condition of an even greater freedom, and in this questioning of the bases on which freedom and subjection are evaluated Samson envisions passion—becoming God's sacrificial vessel for violence—as more important than self-preservation.

This is a question that this study of fanaticism cannot help but repeat: What does it mean to do something "freely," if freedom in this instance is constituted by annihilating the self and becoming an instrument of God's dispensation and disposal? Samson's narrative of his own transformation in this passage turns on these precise terms, "dispense" and "dispose": "Yet that he may dispense with me or thee/ . . . Some rousing motions in me which dispose." From Latin *dispenso*, the Vulgate translation of the Greek *oikonomeō*,[50] "dispense" here, as in the play's earlier use of it (314: "For with his own laws he can best dispense"), means at once to order and to negate, to pardon by means of grace and to do away "with me" through annihilation. "Yet that he may dispense with me or thee" suggests, on the one hand, the determination of Samson's will and, on the other, the abolition of Samson's capacity to will his action. This duality is signaled, too, by the unresolved "or" of Samson's last line directly delivered to us in the play: "By some great act, or of my days the last" (1389). God's dispensing with Samson may lead to "some great act" (though what it is ostensibly remains hidden to Samson) *or* to his last days, the latter implying both death and a sense of apocalyptic end time, the interruption of divine will and temporality within the play. "Dispense," directly in the middle of line 1377, is linked with "dispose" at the end of line 1382, both sonically and semantically: God can dispense with Samson so that—the shift in line position and the stress on both "-pense" and "-pose" (from Latin roots meaning to suspend and then to place) suggests this causality—he may dispose him to an action that breaks with the ordinary norms imposed by law: "I begin to feel/Some rousing motions in me which dispose/To something extraordinary my thoughts." His dispensation directs him to his disposal; he is unmade as he is motioned to become a vessel of God's will. God has disposed of Samson so that he may fulfill his fatal mission, making it impossible to know whether God has created a disposition within Samson or gotten rid of his will entirely and replaced it with God's own.

The Chorus's unsatisfying maxim at the play's conclusion does nothing to resolve this ambiguity, since it implicitly links Samson's disposition to God's "unsearchable dispose": "All is best, though we oft doubt,/What the unsearchable dispose/Of highest wisdom brings about" (1745–47). The play gives us no solid ground on which to account for the shift from Samson's solitary desperation to his dispensation and disposal. Like the characters in the play, readers are unsure whether God has emptied Samson and made him into a vessel of divine violence, or whether Samson has persuaded himself that he is now ready to return to his path as willful, violent liberator of Israel.

Much depends on what we—and Samson himself—make of these "rousing motions." In his Preface, Milton avoids mentioning these "motions" at all; there, he comments only that Samson was "at length persuaded inwardly that this [which seems to refer only to the demand to perform at the Philistine feast] was from God."[51] But the term "motions" is present repeatedly in Samson's understanding of his relationship to divine agency in the play itself. Mediated to us by Samson without any other confirmation, these motions mark the inception of his ambiguous "something extraordinary." The Chorus labels this transformation a return of the heroic, willful Samson ("the man returns" [1390]), but Samson describes these motions as a novel initiation into something that will be seen as remarkable within—and thus in some sense not continuous with—the narrative of his heroic life. This is now the second time that Samson has described his breaking of a Nazarite law as receiving motions of God (see line 222) and here, as before, the emphasis is on a "dispos[al]" to something extraordinary, to a divinely inspired calling.

Seemingly a transparent term, "motion" has complex resonances in seventeenth-century English. From the Latin *motus*, "motion" most simply signifies physical movement or emotion. For some in the seventeenth century, physical movement is a model for emotion and the senses, as in

Hobbes's famous definition of sense as "Motion in the organs and interior parts of mans body, caused by the action of the things we See, Heare, &c." and passions as "the Interiour Beginnings of Voluntary Motions."[52] Renaissance Latin dictionaries reveal more expansive definitions for *motus*: "A motion or moving; a stir, trouble, commotion or disturbance; any passion of the mind; gesture or carriage, a measure in dancing; a cause or occasion; a mutiny; the remove of an Army."[53] In classical rhetoric, Quintilian suggests that *motus* can mean not only motion or emotion or commotion but even "trope,"[54] and in scholastic philosophy, *motus* and *dispositio* were terms often used to explore whether salvation was initiated by work or by grace, by the internal will or by God's external charity.[55] We might even hear in "rousing motions" an echo of Müntzer's claim about the movement of God coming into his heart and emptying him so that so that he may receive God's action. Milton's phrase, "rousing motions," remains multivalent in part because what the "something extraordinary" to which they "dispose" him is, exactly, remains obscure, an effect possibly of emotion, commotion, trope, inordinate passion, or divine inspiration.

"Extraordinary" poses another interpretive crux. In *De Doctrina Christiana*, Milton explicates the term *extraordinaria* as signifying God's miraculous interventions in the world, those that break with the natural order of cause and effect.[56] The fact that Samson is motioned to this "something extraordinary" only further underscores the question of whether Samson is in fact actor or passive vessel of God's miraculous intervention. In an analysis of Milton's gloss of "extraordinary," Rogers suggests:

> In *Christian Doctrine*, Milton had clung to a residual orthodox belief in God's miraculous powers of intervention, naming God's capacity for voluntary intervention in his "extraordinary providence" (*"providentia Dei extraordinaria"*), which is that power "whereby God produces some effect out of the usual order of nature." Here, however [in Samson's motioning toward "something extraordinary"], as if to shake off forever the vestiges of voluntarism that had shackled the argument of *Christian Doctrine*, Milton shifts this loaded adjective, "extraordinary," from God to God's creature.[57]

Rogers's gloss of "extraordinary" is extremely useful, but his conclusion that "extraordinary" has shifted to apply now to God's creature rather than to God himself precludes the possibility of Samson's self-annihilation, which precisely undoes the distinction between God and God's creature. If Samson's will has been annihilated by these "motions" and replaced with God's, then what is to come is still God's extraordinary intervention, with Samson as his instrument. Milton presents what may be Samson's inspiration as "rousing motions," but the various connotations of "motion" do not allow us to determine whether the motions are extrinsic—a gift from God that is required to "begin . . . some great act" or that will annihilate and replace Samson's will altogether—or whether they are intrinsic, such that he feels them "in me" by having undergone dialogic exercises to purify his will, which have now prepared him to say "I will" to the officer.

Samson's own description of his "rousing motions" makes it impossible for us to judge the source of Samson's inspiration, and the question of whether his final "presage" is stirred on by a passional experience of divine dispensation or a willful self-generated decision is made even more complicated by the passage's numerous other ambiguities. Samson "feel[s]" the motions, and yet they directly "dispose . . . my thoughts," which renders the motions' influence on the senses or thoughts equivocal. Likewise, Samson insists that he would do "nothing, . . . be sure, that may dishonour/ Our Law, or stain my vow of Nazarite" at the moment when it seems as though that law has been suspended so that he could obey the "commands" of the Philistine's against his "prescri[ption]" as a Hebrew. And, finally, the term "dispose" itself could mean either to be placed passively by God or to activate a "disposition," a *habitus* of action, that Samson has now finally achieved through his ascesis of self-interrogation.

The equivocation between "dispose" as passion or action is central to what the play forces us to consider when we encounter fanaticism such as Samson's. Despite the ambiguity, Samson's meditations late in the play suggest that he abnegates his heroic strength and embraces his weakness— the weakness of not himself being able to know the event to which these motions dispose him. Samson goes along with the officer despite having no knowledge of what yet will happen to him: "I with this messenger will go along," Samson says, in an image that mirrors the blindness of Samson at the first lines of the play, in which he cannot know where he is going ("A little onward lend thy guiding hand/To these dark steps" [1–2]). It is this blindness that signifies Samson's openness to following what he interprets with faith, but cannot grasp with knowledge, as God's "motions," a weakness that a surviving eyewitness to Samson's final performance describes to us in striking terms:

> He patient but undaunted where they led him,
> Came to the place, and what was set before him
> Which without help of eye might be assayed,

To heave, pull, draw, or break, he still performed
All with incredible, stupendous force,
None daring to appear antagonist.

(1623–29)

Blind Samson must commit himself to movement without knowing where he is; he is "patient but undaunted" in his weakness, embracing it as the deprivation through which he tentatively "might . . . assay" his still-unknown progress to sacrificial destruction. He must give himself over to weakness, dwell in his own deprivation rather than overcoming it. As Milton wrote of Jesus in his *Defensio Prima*, the embrace of weakness becomes the foundation of a different kind of freedom, in which passion and action are brought together without being synthesized: "Who does not know that he [Christ] put himself into the condition not only of a subject, but even of a servant, that we might be free? Nor is this to be understood of inward liberty only, to the exclusion of civil liberty."[58] Even at this moment when Samson's performance is characterized by the massive totality— the "all"—of his "stupendous force," Samson seems to be defined as fundamentally "patient." We only reach the verb "came" after the line break, which suggests that having been disposed to this place is itself an experience of patience, passivity, and suffering. Samson is not only waiting calmly for the arrival of an unknown future but also undergoing the suffering that is inflicted on him. Understanding Samson's blindness as a figure for his passivity prepares us to read the final event of Samson's life, which entwines passion and action, sacrifice and purgation.

He unsuspicious led him; which when Samson
Felt in his arms, with head a while inclined,
And eyes fast fixt he stood, as one who prayed,
Or some great matter in his mind revolved.

(1635–38)

This passage defines for us the problem of interpreting fanaticism in a way that does not simply dismiss it as delusion. Samson is "led" here to his final, passionate stance of violent action; he gives himself over to that which he cannot know in advance. Whereas in Judges 16:28 Samson's prayer to God is unambiguous, here we are again confronted by another "as" that darkens our view of the scene: Samson stands "as one who prayed/Or some great matter in his mind revolved." From this scene, mediated to us many times over (the messenger tells Manoa and the Chorus, "For so much such as nearer stood we heard" [1631]), we cannot know—we cannot see—whether Samson is praying to God or not; he looks like ("as") one who prays, but might also just be considering "some great matter," or, if not considering, then at least having it "revolve" in his mind. Unlike many other Renaissance martyr dramas, from George Buchanan's *Baptistes sive Calumnia* (1577) to John Dryden's *Tyrannic Love: A Royal Martyr* (1669),[59] in which the martyr desires and wills his own death, Milton's play does not give us evidence that Samson's violence is a willed expression to become a martyr. Indeed, the Chorus observes that the only way to understand what has happened is to see that Samson has released himself from his will and been delivered into the workings of God's necessity: "Among thy slain self-killed / Not willingly, but tangled in the fold, / Of dire necessity" (1664–66). Samson's fanaticism here can certainly not be reduced to direct, immediate access to God that outstrips the limits of human reason; we are much closer to witnessing the realization of the will of God precisely in its unrealizability and unknowability. It appears to enter the world, if it does in this moment, through Samson as vessel. Samson appears to become an instrument of divine violence, unable to know or will what he does, but the "as" also bars us from knowing that he has become God's organ here with certainty.

Is Samson becoming in this moment what Augustine saw him as, a "vessel [vas]" that is "emptied [exinaniri]" and "filled [impleri]" by God, unmade and reconstituted through God's immanent action?[60] Or is Samson becoming yet again the angry hero whom Calvin envisioned, driven less by God's self-annihilating "righteous zeal [probi zeli]" than by a willful and "vicious longing for vengeance [vitiosa cupiditas vindictae]"?[61] Even if one were to believe that Samson were inspired, who then commits the final act of violence: God through and as an inspired Samson or Samson himself? The bifurcated structure of these questions confuses rather than clarifies what the play insists upon: that we cannot differentiate Samson's passion from his action, or determine whether he is an organ or agent.

In Hobbes's *Leviathan*, the only space in which religion can be allowed to come into conflict with civil power is the internal space of conscience; conscience can only offer a privatized form of religious protest in *Leviathan*. The unknowability of divine disposal and action in *Samson Agonistes* cannot be reduced to a concept of private conscience; it blurs the topography of inclusion and exclusion on which Hobbes depends to ban the fanatic. Though Samson states that his final action is undertaken "of my own accord" (1643), the messenger's description of the violence itself is divided between representing the act as God's apocalyptic violence ("As with the force of winds and water pent, / When mountains tremble"

[1647–48]) and as Samson's gestural achievement: "He tugged, he shook" (1650).[62] Indeed, "accord" itself maintains in Samson's mouth a double meaning: of my own will *and* of my attunement to God's immanence as his self-emptying instrument.[63] The scene has a kind of necessity and inevitability to it ("Samson with these immixt, inevitably/Pulled down the same destruction on himself" [1658–59]), but this moment of climax of the play represents a *catharsis* that embodies the meanings of *lustratio* as both sacrifice and purgation, as passion and action, as the suspension of law (Samson is now "immixt" with the unclean, uncircumcised) and its fulfillment as Jewish apocalyptic prophet.[64] That Samson is "with these immixt" at once underscores his singularity and literally mixes his body with others, "inevitably." Such "immix[ing]" seems to suggest his nonseparateness, entangled as he is with other bodies, but it also insinuates the possibility of divine violence (if that is what causes Samson's act) to assemble multiple bodies together in a new mixture—though here of course it is a dead one, very different than the fugitive life of Spenser's swarm. The presence or nonpresence alike of God in Samson leads to the obliteration of his body and its inevitable mixture with others.

Samson's singular fanatical mission works to restore the vocation of a collective; as an (indeterminate) organ of divine might, his violence and death become at once an action of purgation and a passional obedience. That this violent act has seemed to some critics to be ultimately "meaningless," to use Richard Halpern's term, because it does not liberate the Jews offers us no certain evidence that Samson is not a vessel for God's violence; the future we know does not eliminate the irreducible unknowability of the instant in which Samson may (or may not) become an instrument of God.[65] Our inability to see Samson's internal disposition—to determine whether or not he is inspired by God, whether his violence is action or passion, cathartic purgation or sacrificial annihilation—mirrors Samson's blindness ("O mirror of our fickle state"): it is our weakness, which is also the weakness of those who witness the violence within the play, to be unable to see Samson's motives or motions. In rendering Samson's refusal of what I explored in Chapter 3 as Hobbes's inalienable right of self-protection,[66] Milton makes Samson illegible, uncountable.

The end of the play confronts us with what it means to witness his violence—or, more precisely, to witness his violence as it circulates in a story. That story does not allow us to turn away from the illegibility of Samson's "rousing motions." And our witness is staged within the play, as the Chorus and Manoa gather to process the unnamed messenger's story of what Samson has done.[67] Their reflection on the messenger's story situates Samson within the kind of monumentalizing "gaze[s]" from which he tended to distance himself earlier in the play ("Made of my Enemies the scorn and gaze" [34]; "to visitants a gaze, / Or pitied object, these redundant locks / Robustious to no purpose clustering down, / Vain monument of strength" [567–70]).[68] The Chorus, allusive and elusive, describes Samson as something like a singular instrument of God, dying and being reborn like the phoenix: "then vigorous most / When most unactive deemed" (1704–5). Manoa's speech insists on God's "favouring and assisting [Samson] to the end" (1720) but places a heavier emphasis on heroism, and on the exemplary nature of Samson's deed:

> Nothing is here for tears, nothing to wail
> Or knock the breast, no weakness, no contempt,
> Dispraise, or blame, nothing but well and fair,
> And what may quiet us in a death so noble.
> Let us go find the body where it lies
> Soaked in his enemies' blood, and from the stream
> With lavers pure, and cleansing herbs wash off
> The clotted gore. I with what speed the while
> (Gaza is not in plight to say us nay)
> Will send for all my kindred, all my friends
> To fetch him hence and solemnly attend
> With silent obsequy and funeral train
> Home to his father's house: there will I build him
> A monument, and plant it round with shade
> Of laurel ever green, and branching palm,
> With all his trophies hung, and acts enrolled
> In copious legend, or sweet lyric song.
> Thither shall all the valiant youth resort,
> And from his memory inflame their breasts
> To matchless valour, and adventures high.

$$(1721–40)$$

Here is a literal lustration, proleptically anyway. Washing the gore from Samson's body demonstrates Manoa's desire to dissociate Samson as an exemplary heroic self from his shattered body. "Clotted gore" must be cleaned away so that Samson can be translated into a text on which Manoa can "enroll" (1736) his own meaning, transforming Samson's "acts" into that which Samson detested: a "monument," an idol of heroic grandeur to be imitated by "valiant youth." Manoa hopes to turn Samson into an institutionalized fanatic, assisted by God but still defined by his "matchless valour."

In casting Samson as monumental hero, Manoa imposes an explanatory narrative on an event that he has not himself witnessed. The narrative goes like this: God gave Samson his strength back so that he could again become a hero for future generations to imitate, and for that reason we have no reason to mourn. As though working out a compromise between Redcrosse's austere claim to be an organ and the Palmer's emphasis on achievement, Manoa's story pointedly sidesteps the question of whether Samson underwent his violent martyrdom as heroic actor or passive instrument of God's will by suggesting that God's assistance made Samson heroic again. Manoa and the Chorus quickly set to work on a regulating framework for our—and their own—mediated witness of Samson's mysterious violence. But Manoa also raises here a potential future that so many Renaissance thinkers feared, one in which fanaticism can be transmitted or imitated. Samson can be set up as a monument, and his memory will "inflame" the breasts of "valiant youth" to undertake "adventures high." It is as though after the death of his son, Manoa is generically transported and finds himself in a chivalric romance, hoping it could be an antidote to tragedy, except that Milton himself suggests, in the Preface, that this transmission of passion is itself an effect of his experiment with tragic form, an experiment in which *catharsis* and *lustratio* distribute self-emptying passion. But Manoa's strange account of Samson's having "quit himself/Like Samson" (1709–10) implies that Samson might, in that final act, somehow have been imitating himself (and emptying himself through imitation), which is to say either that he took his earlier self as a willful model to replicate or that in losing himself (perhaps through self-annihilation), he became again what Samson was: a vessel of God. Samson's speeches before his death and the play's multiplication of ambiguities make it difficult not to experience Manoa's discourse of monumentalization as an unpersuasive compensation for unknowability. Manoa's disjunctive speech cannot wash away the consequential effects of the play's lingering with the irresolvable dialectic of passion or action, but it does turn them outward by returning to what the emphasis on Samson's singularity and separateness seemed to occlude: the possibility of an *Ion*-like transmission of divine rapture that will "inflame" a collectivity, though this time institutionalized and canonized, and therefore less anarchic than a Spenserian swarm.

In short, the play provides interpretative frameworks for Samson's violence—and the potential acts of violence that it may spark in those inflamed hearts—but we are asked to look at them quizzically. Insofar as the surviving characters' interpretive dilemma mirrors our predicament, we are warned off them. Neither the Chorus's confidence in Samson's annihilation and rebirth nor Manoa's monumentalization of Samson as a hero favored and assisted by God can be grounded in anything like evidence. The play thus reveals how our responses to Samson's violence and death are, as Judith Butler has argued about suicide bombing, fashioned first in affects that are "tacitly regulated by certain kinds of interpretative frameworks,"[69] and acknowledging these frameworks allows us to see that one's body, passion, and action are never entirely one's own, but can be circulated in the world in ways that cannot be anticipated. We register Samson's violence as bound up in his trials of *lustratio*, oscillating between active purification and passionate sacrifice, between willful violence and a passive entanglement (see 1665). Without having access to his motivations or "motions," we recognize that Samson becomes for us a site in which history and the desire for radical vision emerge at the point where active will and organal disposal—action and passion—become at once mutually determining and mutually obscuring. *Lustratio* figures fanaticism in *Samson Agonistes* as ritual *catharsis* that sacrifices not only Samson but also our ability to know if he performs his action or God enacts it through him.

The state of "amaze" with which Samson's violence strikes us, even when encountered third- or fourth-hand—"as with amaze shall strike all who behold" (1645)—marks our position as spectators who cannot know the source of the "rousing motions" that make this violence possible. This unknowing is part of a tragic condition that only a few poets can bear to think as a problem immanent to both their world and their verse.[70] It also implicates us in those motions, suggesting that we, too, amazed by the violence, mirror Samson's passion (if it was passivity after all), emptied of knowing if not entirely of self. This is the tragedy of Samson's fanaticism. We bear witness to this revolt, and its potentially contagious dissemination of sacrificial energy horrifies. This horror is redoubled by our inability to determine whether it is divine violence or heroic attack, passive martyrdom or active "strike." Milton's Samson is thus not easily connected with the chauvinist figure of Samson as "tough Jew" and purveyor of "mythic violence" that Talal Asad ably analyzes.[71] To name him as national hero, as Israel has so often tried to do, is to perpetuate (in inverted political circumstances) the narrative that Manoa creates at the play's ending, evading fanaticism's complex, irresolvable economy of passion and action.

If fanaticism for Spenser introduces an absolute and unintelligible force that disrupts the allegorical system of *The Faerie Queene*, and for Donne incites a formal problem of will and interpretability uncovered in lyric experiment and translated into prose meditation (recall how Donne hails us regarding Samson: "Consider it actively, consider it passively"), then for Milton fanaticism becomes a problem of tragic recognition, a question of how witnesses respond in the face of unknowable violence in which they are implicated. Spenser's swarms and Donne's mimetic contagion have mostly fallen out of the story of Milton's Samson, except in Manoa's wish for a monument that would spark imitation, but what takes its place is a concern with how the witness of fanaticism itself creates the condition for new kinds of collectivities—potentially ones more open to unknowing as a condition of communal struggle and liberation. The witness of fanaticism requires that we dwell with a violence only intelligible in light of its abject residues of catastrophic upheaval, a dramatic experience of bodies and their damage not as a monumental fact to be known but as an occasion for contingent identification and dis-identification. Not knowing whether Samson's "rousing motions" initiate an annihilation through which he becomes an inspired vessel of divine and "dire necessity," we come to the end of *Samson Agonistes* with the knowledge—if that name does not obscure its obscurity—that we cannot see our way out of the aporia of action and passion, that the problem of fanaticism requires us to encounter that aporia as a defining and irreducible feature of our political and epistemic situation, one that verse can think in minutely subtle ways. Those who wish instead to police fanaticism as the utmost enemy of the state do so at their—and our—peril.

I have benefited from the advice, support, and engagement of many people while writing this book—more than I can remember and name. I would especially like to thank my mentors. Jeff Dolven, Daniel Heller-Roazen, D. Vance Smith, and Nigel Smith have been extraordinary teachers and interlocutors. This book would not have been possible without them. They remain models of intelligence, generosity, engagement, and writerly style.

I owe a large debt to the other friends, colleagues, and teachers who have read and commented on pieces of this book at various stages and who have left their own unique marks on me and significantly improved my writing and thinking: Leonard Barkan, Alex Dubilet, Will Evans, Victoria Kahn, Russ Leo, Giulio Pertile, Ramsey McGlazer, Warren Montag, Matthew Spellberg, Amelia Worsley, and Emily Vasiliauskas.

Others have discussed with me ideas related to this book, asked incisive questions when I have presented shorter drafts of chapters, or helped me reflect on the stakes of this kind of work; their impact has been extremely important. I am thankful to David Alff, Kristel Faye Baldoz, Zahid Chaudhary, Bradin Cormack, Nadja Eisenberg-Guyot, Andrea Gadberry, Rae Gaubinger, Bill Gleason, Zoe Gibbons, Leon Grek, John Guillory, Matthew Harrison, Brook Henkel, Jessie Hock, Nat Lippert, Sangina Patnaik, James Martel, Meredith Martin, Andrew Miller, Joe Moshenska, Subha Mukherji, Philip Pettit, Orlando Reade, Eileen Reeves, Sarah Rivett, Lindsay Reckson, Francisco Robles, John Rogers, James Rutherford, Gayle Salamon, Bea Sanford Russell, Elias Sacks, Starry Schor, Debora Shuger, Kelly Swartz, Elise Wang, Julianne Werlin, Rowan Williams, Melanie Webb, Andrew Norman Wilson, Jessica Wright, Liesl Yamaguchi, and Dora Zhang. Thank you to audiences at the University of Cambridge and its Centre for Research in the Arts, Social Sciences and Humanities, the University of Colorado–Boulder, New York University, Princeton University (especially forums at the Renaissance Workshop, the University Center for Human Values, and the Center for the Study of Religion), the

Renaissance Society of America, and the American Comparative Literature Association. My earlier teachers may not have engaged this work
directly, but their influences are here, too; thanks especially to Kim Ben-
ston, Stephen Finley, Laura McGrane, Ulrich Schönherr, and Christina
Zwarg for their formative care and commitment. Kim was my first guide
through the poems of Donne and Milton, and his instruction continues
to influence how I read.

As I recast and completed this book at Occidental College, my ideas for
it evolved in conversation with, and thanks to the support of, Mijin Cha,
Dan Fineman, James Ford III, Jane Hong, Kathy Izumi, Sarah Kozinn,
Ainsley LeSure, Krystale Littlejohn, Warren Montag, Kelema Moses,
Leila Neti, Kristi Upson-Saia, and Jean Wyatt. I am grateful as well
to Wendy Sternberg, dean of the college, and to the Louis and Hermione
Brown Humanities Support Fund for financial support that aided this proj-
ect at a late stage.

I have discussed some of the texts and ideas addressed in this book with
my students at Occidental, at Princeton, and at the Garden State and Al-
bert C. Wagner Correctional Facilities in New Jersey; their insights and
energy have made me productively reconsider what I thought I knew from
fresh perspectives. In my teaching and writing, I try to stay true to what
my student David Martinez once suggested literature and philosophy can
do: "pierce the armor we build around ourselves with words and habits,"
allowing us openly to encounter other people, new concepts, or the world
in ways we have not already anticipated. I hope this book contributes something to that project.

It has been a pleasure to work with everyone at Fordham University
Press who helped to bring this text into the world; there, I owe special
thanks to Tom Lay, who has been a supportive and thoughtful editor
from start to finish. Thank you to Eric Newman for keeping the book on
track through production. The book's no-longer-anonymous readers for
the press, Julia Reinhard Lupton and Dennis Austin Britton, offered
shrewd commentary and exacting counsel that have strengthened my argument. Many thanks as well to E. A. Williams, who provided painstaking
copyediting, and to Amy Sherman and Sarah C. Smith, who were vigilant
proofreaders.

I am grateful to my family for always supporting me, and especially to
Leslie, Marilyn, and Ellen Wolfson, whose teacherly examples have influenced me greatly.

Special thanks to Katie Kadue, who read and commented on every page
of this book and improved it substantially. Her thousand decencies, daily,

have fermented and tempered my thinking in ways that have made it more than it ever could have been otherwise.

I am grateful to Duke University Press and Palgrave Macmillan for permission to use herein earlier and shorter versions of Chapters 1 and 2, which appeared in print as "Donne's Annihilation," *Journal of Medieval and Early Modern Studies* 44, no. 2 (Spring 2014): 407–27; and "Allegories of Fanaticism," in *Literature, Belief and Knowledge in Early Modern England: Knowing Faith*, ed. Subha Mukherji and Tim Stuart-Buttle (New York: Palgrave Macmillan, 2018), 153–72. Thanks as well to New Issues Poetry & Prose for their permission to use lines from Jericho Brown's "Burning Bush" as an epigraph in the Introduction; the poem is published in *Please* (Kalamazoo, Mich.: New Issues Poetry & Prose, 2008), 42.

INTRODUCTION. RECEIVING DIVINE ACTION:
FANATICISM AND FORM IN THE REFORMATION

1. Unless otherwise noted, citations of *The Faerie Queene* are given parenthetically by book, canto, and stanza taken from *The Faerie Queene*, edited by A. C. Hamilton, with Hiroshi Yamashita, Toshiyuki Suzuki, and Shohachi Fukuda, 2nd ed. (London: Longman, 2007).

2. For a useful reconstruction of polemics against "fundamentalism" in America since the word's inception in 1920, see David Harrington Watt, *Antifundamentalism in Modern America* (Ithaca, N.Y.: Cornell University Press, 2017). For a refusal to accept "terrorism" as "a single causally coherent phenomenon," see Charles Tilly, "Terror, Terrorism, Terrorists," *Sociological Theory* 22, no. 1 (May 2014): 5–13. On rendering lives ungrievable, see Judith Butler, *Frames of War: When is Life Grievable?* (London: Verson, 2009), 38: "An ungrievable life is one that cannot be mourned because it has never lived, that is, it has never counted as a life at all."

3. For a particularly cavalier example of this tendency, see Jan Miernowski, "Can a Human Bomb Be Human? Humanist and Antihumanist Perspectives on War and Terrorism," in *Early Modern Humanism and Postmodern Antihumanism in Dialogue* (London: Palgrave, 2016), 139–71, which defines religious fanatics as "uneducated and underprivileged or brainwashed and psychologically manipulated individuals incapable of making rational decisions" (139).

4. Ralph Cudworth, *True Intellectual System of the Universe*, vol. 1 (1845; repr., Bristol: Thoemmes, 1995), 513. Cudworth here is adapting an analysis of Plutarch's to his own day, and though he is conflating a great number of ideas (his nineteenth-century annotator, Johann Lorenz von Mosheim, suggests Cudworth is branding Spinozism, the negative theology associated with Jacob Böhme, and the English Paracelsian Robert Fludd with the label of fanaticism), and not speaking particularly of the possibility of religious violence that is this book's focus, his definition is nonetheless suggestive: "The other, who altogether neglecting the natural and necessary causes of

things, resolved all into the divine cause, as it were swallowing up all into God, as guilty of a kind of fanaticism. . . . Some fanatics of latter times have made God to be all, in a gross sense, so as to take away all real distinction betwixt God and the creature."

5. Stanley Fish, *Self-Consuming Artifacts: The Experience of Seventeenth-Century Literature* (Berkeley: University of California Press, 1972), 156–223.

6. For example, John Calvin, *Institutio Christianae Religionis* (Paris, 1559), 1.13.7.

7. John Owen, *[Pneumatologia]: A Discourse Concerning the Holy Spirit* (London, 1674), 115. For an excellent analysis of the potentially antinomian implications of Owen's argument about inspiration, see Sharon Achinstein, *Literature and Dissent in Milton's England* (Cambridge: Cambridge University Press, 2003), 162–64.

8. One possible exception, analyzed in Chapter 1, is Spenser's Britomart, who is neither unambiguously feminine nor fanatical.

9. For examples focused on seventeenth-century England, see Phyllis Mack, *Visionary Women: Ecstatic Prophecy in Seventeenth-Century England* (Berkeley: University of California Press, 1992); and Carme Font, *Women's Prophetic Writing in Seventeenth-Century Britain* (New York: Routledge, 2017). For a more historically expansive study, see Diane Watt, *Secretaries of God: Women Prophets in Late Medieval and Early Modern England* (Suffolk, Eng.: D. S. Brewer, 1997).

10. A study of such male fantasies of passivity in this context would be fascinating, and could be usefully informed by Amy Hollywood's argument in *Sensible Ecstasy: Mysticism, Sexual Difference and the Demands of History* (Chicago: University of Chicago Press, 2001) that versions of mysticism associated with medieval European women have often been influential for later writers drawn to meditations on self-annihilation, ecstasy, and gender. See also Hollywood's claim, in the context of the Middle Ages, that "the complete loss of will or of the self in the divine, which legitimates almost all women's and some men's textual production and religious authority, is often explicitly gendered. Not only is the soul often (although not always) read as feminine in relationship to a male divinity, but also women's putative passivity and malleability render them particularly apt sites of divine agency on earth. Medieval women make use of the very gender subordination that constrains them as the condition for and source of agency, an agency ultimately ascribed not to religious women themselves, but to God" (*Acute Melancholia and Other Essays: Mysticism, History, and the Study of Religion* [New York: Columbia University Press, 2016], 117). The essay in *Acute Melancholia* from which this previous quotation is drawn, "Gender, Agency, and the Divine in Religious Historiography" (117–28), analyzes acutely the

historiographical difficulty of attributing agency to medieval women who claim that they have submitted their wills entirely to God.

11. Jordana Rosenberg, *Critical Enthusiasm: Capital Accumulation and the Transformation of Religious Passion* (Oxford: Oxford University Press, 2011), 6. Rosenberg conflates, in passing, enthusiasm and fanaticism at, for example, 21, 43, and 70, likely in response to the premodern trend of using them to define each other. It is in the late Enlightenment and Romantic moment that thinkers became especially invested in distinguishing enthusiasm from fanaticism—to save the former from the threat of the latter. See for example Samuel Taylor Coleridge, *Notes on English Divines*, ed. Derwent Coleridge (London: Edward Moxon, 1853). Coleridge makes a sharp correction (likely influenced by his reading of Immanuel Kant's essay "Von einem neuerdings erhobenen vornehmen Ton in der Philosophie," which he admired) to Richard Baxter's *Reliquiae Baxterianae*: "Baxter makes the usual mistake of writing Fanatic when he clearly means Enthusiast. The Field-Methodists are fanatics, *i.e. circà fana densâ turbâ concalefacti*; those who catch heat by crowding together round the same Fane. Fanaticism is the fever of superstition. Enthusiasm, on the contrary, implies an undue (or when used in a good sense, an unusual) vividness of ideas, as opposed to perceptions, or of the obscure inward feelings" (39–40).

12. See René Descartes, *The Philosophical Writings of Descartes*, vol. 1, trans. John Cottingham, Robert Stoothoff, and Dugald Murdoch (Cambridge: Cambridge University Press, 1985), 396. In his comments there on self-satisfaction in *Les Passions de l'âme*, Descartes speaks critically of those who "imagine themselves such close friends of God that they could not do anything to displease him," including "the greatest crimes that man could commit, such as the betrayal of cities, the killing of sovereigns, and the extermination of whole nations for the sole reason that the citizens do not accept their opinions." For a compelling analysis of Descartes's account of zeal's origin as rooted in hatred of the self and others, see Warren Montag, "Commanding the Body: The Language of Subjection in *Ethics* III, P2S," in *Resistance and Power in Ethics*, vol. 1 of *Spinoza's Authority*, ed. A. Kiarina Kordela and Dimitris Vardoulakis (New York: Bloomsbury, 2017), 155–56. Though I have stated that Descartes, in his criticism of self-satisfied piety, is much less motivated by a need to justify state violence than Luther or Hobbes are in their polemics against fanatics, his diagnosis is not devoid of the desire to protect sovereignty, and his list of the "greatest crimes" implicitly links the genocidal impulse in zealous self-satisfaction with the betrayal of cities and murder of sovereigns, as though they were acts intrinsically of a kind.

13. See for example James Simpson, *Burning to Read: English Fundamentalism and Its Reformation Opponents* (Cambridge: Belknap, 2010).

14. Achinstein's *Literature and Dissent* is one such exception; see for example her resistance to assuming that Milton's claim to have written inspired poetry was meant to disguise subversive political intent: "Perhaps obscurity did not hide an interior or veiled meaning, but, as in a Calvinist account such as John Owen's, could stand for the obscurity of inspiration itself, a very otherworldliness that was irrational and a potential threat to civil society or state" (171). Robert Appelbaum's recent study of Renaissance "terrorism," *Terrorism before the Letter*, quotes on its second page a poem describing the assassination of George Villiers, Duke of Buckingham ("the last major incident of terrorist violence in England in the time period being studied in [*Terrorism before the Letter*], 1559 to 1642") that suggests that "God's hand was in it"—that is, that God's hand drove or participated in the action of the killing. But the ambiguity of agency and knowledge that Appelbaum provides a glimpse of at the beginning of his study is not the object of his analysis, and it quickly passes from view. See Appelbaum, *Terrorism before the Letter: Mythography and Political Violence in England, Scotland, and France 1559–1642* (Oxford: Oxford University Press, 2016), 2. In religious historiography, other relevant exceptions to the skepticism toward claims to divine possession exist as well, of course, including Nigel Smith, *Perfection Proclaimed: Language and Literature in English Radical Religion* (Oxford: Oxford University Press, 1989); Brad Gregory, *Salvation at Stake: Christian Martyrdom in Early Modern Europe* (Cambridge: Harvard University Press, 2001); the studies by Dipesh Chakrabarty and Ranajit Guha cited in the next two notes, respectively; Mary Keller, *The Hammer and the Flute: Women, Power, and Spirit Possession* (Baltimore: Johns Hopkins University Press, 2005); and Amy Hollywood, "Gender, Agency, and the Divine in Religious Historiography," in *Acute Melancholia*, 117–28.

15. Dipesh Chakrabarty, "Minority Histories, Subaltern Pasts," in *Provincializing Europe: Postcolonial Thought and Historical Difference* (Princeton: Princeton University Press, 2000), 97–113.

16. See Ranajit Guha, *Elementary Aspects of Peasant Insurgency in Colonial India* (Delhi: Oxford University Press, 1983); Guha and Gayatri Chakravorty Spivak, eds., *Selected Subaltern Studies* (New York: Oxford University Press, 1988); and Timothy Mitchell, "Nobody Listens to a Poor Man," in *Rule of Experts: Egypt, Techno-Politics, Modernity* (Berkeley: University of California Press, 2002), 153–78. In Guha and Spivak, *Selected Subaltern Studies*, see especially Guha, "The Prose of Counterinsurgency," 45–84.

17. "Der Legitimitätsgründe einer Herrschaft." See Max Weber, "Politik als Beruf," in *Gesammelte politische Schriften* (Munich: Drei Masken, 1921), 398.

18. See Walter Benjamin, "Zur Kritik der Gewalt," in *Gesammelte Schriften*, vol. 2.1, ed. Rolf Tiedemann and Hermann Schweppenhäuser (Frankfurt am Main: Suhrkamp, 1999), 179–203. There, Benjamin discusses the distinction between *göttliche Gewalt* (divine violence that interrupts the worldly order and destroys the structures of law that institutionalize violence) and *mythische Gewalt* (mythical violence that institutes and pre-serves law).

19. *The English Works of Thomas Hobbes of Malmesbury*, ed. Sir William Molesworth (London, 1839–45), 4:328.

20. This is Weber's famous phrase: "Das Monopol legitimer physischer Gewaltsamkeit." See Weber, "Politik als Beruf," 397. Weber there clarifies that any associations or individuals who use violence must be authorized by the state, and in that sense the state is the sole source of law for violence ("alleinige Quelle des 'Rechts' auf Gewaltsamkeit").

21. On the fanatic as "stock character," see William Cavanaugh, "The Invention of Fanaticism," *Modern Theology* 27, no. 2 (2011): 226–37. See also Cavanaugh, *The Myth of Religious Violence: Secular Ideology and the Roots of Modern Conflict* (Oxford: Oxford University Press, 2009), for a useful analysis of the incoherent logic that underwrites scholarly attempts to uncover a generalizable tendency toward violence in "religion" as a universal category. Dominique Colas has developed the most historically elaborate case for "fanaticism" as the antithesis to civil society and the state, begin-ning with the Reformation, in *Le Glaive et le Fléau: Généalogie du fanatisme et de la société civile* (Paris: B. Grasset, 1992). For studies of how the early modern state produced stereotypes of extremist others in order to justify its own violence and necessity, see Lori Anne Ferrell, *Government by Polemic: James I, the King's Preachers, and the Rhetorics of Conformity* (Stanford: Stanford University Press, 1998); and Ethan H. Shagan, *The Rule of Modera-tion: Violence, Religion, and the Politics of Restraint in Early Modern England* (Cambridge: Cambridge University Press, 2011).

22. By "limit-experience" I mean to echo the sense that Foucault gave the phrase in his comments on Nietzsche, Blanchot, and Bataille's concept of experience; there, limit-experience has "the task of 'tearing' the subject from itself in such a way that it is no longer the subject as such, or that it is com-pletely 'other' than itself so that it may arrive at its annihilation, its dissociation. It is this de-subjectifying undertaking, the idea of a 'limit-experience' that tears the subject from itself, which is the fundamental lesson that I've learned from these authors." Michel Foucault, "How an 'Experience-Book' Is Born,"

in *Remarks on Marx: Conversations with Duccio Trombadori*, trans. R. James Goldstein and James Cascaito (New York: Semiotext[e], 1991), 31–32.

23. John Locke, *An Essay Concerning Human Understanding* (Oxford: Clarendon Press, 1975), bk. 4, chap. 19, par. 14.

24. All quotations of Donne's *Holy Sonnets* are from the Westmoreland sequence as reproduced in *The Variorum Edition of the Poetry of John Donne*, ed. Gary A. Stringer, vol. 7, pt. 1, *The Holy Sonnets*, ed. Gary A. Stringer and Paul A. Parrish, 11–20.

25. I have already insinuated that there are important differences between fanaticism and enthusiasm, and I return shortly to the relationship between the two in an attempt to define more precisely what I mean by each in this study, but since they were rarely used with consistency in early modern Europe, I will bracket the difference for a moment, since it is the negation of the possibility of unmaking, of self-annihilation, that is most pertinent in Locke's text.

26. Locke, *Essay Concerning Human Understanding*, bk. 4, chap. 19, par. 3.

27. Locke, *Essay Concerning Human Understanding*, bk. 4, chap. 19, par. 11.

28. Achinstein, *Literature and Dissent*, 160–61.

29. Locke, *Essay Concerning Human Understanding*, bk. 4, chap. 19, par. 11.

30. Locke, *Essay Concerning Human Understanding*, bk. 4, chap. 19, par. 8.

31. Locke, *Essay Concerning Human Understanding*, bk. 2, chap. 1, par. 19.

32. Locke, *Essay Concerning Human Understanding*, bk. 2, chap. 27, par. 13: "The same consciousness being preserved . . . the personal Identity is preserved." For more on consciousness as self-ownership, see Étienne Balibar, *Identity and Difference: John Locke and the Invention of Consciousness*, trans. Warren Montag (New York: Verso, 2013). See also Montag, "A Parallelism of Consciousness and Property: Balibar's Reading of Locke," in *Balibar and the Citizen Subject*, ed. Warren Montag and Hanan Elsayed (Edinburgh: Edinburgh University Press), 157–81.

33. Locke, *Essay Concerning Human Understanding*, bk. 4, chap. 19, par. 4.

34. On Donne's *Holy Sonnets* as devotional acts, see Louis Martz, *The Poetry of Meditation: A Study in English Religious Literature of the Seventeenth Century* (New Haven, Conn.: Yale University Press, 1976); and David Marno, *Death Be Not Proud: The Art of Holy Attention* (Chicago: University of Chicago Press, 2016).

35. Giorgio Agamben, *The End of the Poem: Studies in Poetics*, trans. Daniel Heller-Roazen (Stanford: Stanford University Press, 1999), 114.

36. Donne, *Holy Sonnets*, 5, lines 9–10.

37. Judah Stampfer also refers to the zealous figure projected past the end of the poem as an "extreme fanatic" in *John Donne and the Metaphysical Gesture* (New York: Funk and Wagnalls, 1970), 270.

38. Locke, *Essay Concerning Human Understanding*, bk. 4, chap. 19, par. 10.

39. "We ought to seek our conviction in a higher place than human reasons, judgments, or conjectures, that is, in the secret testimony of the Spirit [ab arcano testimonio Spiritus]." John Calvin, *Institutes of the Christian Religion*, ed. John T. McNeill, trans. Ford Lewis Battles (Louisville: Westminster Press, 1960); and Calvin, *Institutio Christianae Religionis* (Paris, 1559), 1.7.4. See also Calvin, *Institutes of the Christian Religion*, 3.1.1, 3.1.3, 3.2.15. Compare Milton, *The Works of John Milton*, ed. Frank Allen Patterson (New York: Columbia University Press, 1931–38), 11:282–83, which suggests that such secret testimony forces belief even if it is only reason that proves or yields understanding: "And divine testimony affirms or denies that a thing is so and brings about that I believe; it does not prove, it does not teach, it does not cause me know or understand why things are so, unless it also brings forward reasons (et divinum quidem testimonium affirmat vel negat rem ita esse, facitque ut credam; non probat, non docet, non facit ut sciam aut intelligam cur ita sit, nisi rationes quoque adhibeat)." Feisal Mohamed suggests intriguingly that these passages from the *Institutes* and *Artis Logicae* help to explain Milton's occasional "plain style," used to compose the speeches of "inspired plainness" by the Father and Abdiel in *Paradise Lost*, "direct expression[s] of heavenly light." Mohamed, *Milton and the Post-Secular Present: Ethics, Politics, Terrorism* (Stanford: Stanford University Press, 2011), 29–31. I explain in more detail later how I part ways with Mohamed's application of the concept of "plain style" to the representation of Samson's unverifiable inspiration in *Samson Agonistes*. For more about Calvin's meditations on *autopistia* (scripture's immanent production of faith in the reader, beyond reason or argument), see Henk van den Belt, *The Authority of Scripture in Reformed Theology: Truth and Trust* (Leiden, Neth.: Brill, 2008).

40. Locke, *Essay Concerning Human Understanding*, bk. 4, chap. 19, par. 13.

41. Sarah Rivett, *The Science of the Soul in Colonial New England* (Chapel Hill: University of North Carolina Press, 2011). See Introduction and Chapter 1 in that book for a helpful analysis of the ways that seventeenth-century Protestants and natural philosophers "applied the experimental method to witness, observe, and record the manifestations of grace on the souls of others." Rivett, *Science of the Soul*, 6. On the idea of the visibility of sainthood, see Geoffrey F. Nuttall, *Visible Saints: The Congregational Way, 1640–1660* (Oxford: Blackwell, 1957); and Edmund S. Morgan, *Visible Saints: The History of a Puritan Idea* (Ithaca, N.Y.: Cornell University Press, 1965).

42. I write "so-called wars of religion" to acknowledge the suggestive argument by Cavanaugh that the narrativization of the violence in

sixteenth- and seventeenth-century Europe as "wars of religion" has created
a foundational myth, one used to justify the marginalization of public
religion and the secure transfer of legitimate violence to the secular state. See
Cavanaugh, *Myth of Religious Violence*, 123–80. See also Benjamin J. Kaplan,
*Divided by Faith: Religious Conflict and the Practice of Toleration in Early Modern
Europe* (Cambridge: Harvard University Press, 2010), which argues that
Reformation historiography tends to obscure the fact that the end of the
"wars of religion" did not actually produce great religious toleration.

43. For Stephen Greenblatt's overview of this long-held narrative about
the "increased self-consciousness about the self-fashioning of human identity"
in the Renaissance, see the Introduction to Greenblatt, *Renaissance Self-
Fashioning: From More to Shakespeare* (Chicago: University of Chicago Press,
1980). For more recent accounts, see Elizabeth Hanson, *Discovering the
Subject in Renaissance England* (Cambridge: Cambridge University Press,
1998); and Udo Thiel, *The Early Modern Subject: Self-Consciousness and
Personal Identity from Descartes to Hume* (Oxford: Oxford University Press,
2011). For the turn against privileging early modern subjectivity, see pieces as
various as David Aers, "A Whisper in the Ear of Early Modernists; or,
Reflections on Literary Critics Writing the 'History of the Subject,'" in
*Culture and History, 1350–1600: Essays on English Communities, Identities, and
Writing*, ed. David Aers (Detroit: Wayne State University Press, 1992),
177–202; the essays in Margreta de Grazia, Maureen Quilligan, and Peter
Stallybrass, *Subject and Object in Renaissance Culture* (Cambridge: Cambridge
University Press, 1999); Timothy Reiss, *Mirages of the Selfe: Patterns of
Personhood in Ancient and Early Modern Europe* (Stanford: Stanford University
Press, 2002); Brian Cummings and Freya Sierhuis, *Passions and Subjectivity in
Early Modern Culture* (London: Ashgate, 2013), especially Part 1; and Monique
Allewaert, *Ariel's Ecology: Plantations, Personhood, and Colonialism in the
American Tropics* (Minneapolis: University of Minnesota Press, 2013), 1–27.

44. Martin Luther, *D. Martin Luthers Werke: Kritische Gesamtausgabe*,
ed. J. K. F. Knaake, et al. (Weimar: H. Böhlau, 1883–2009), 18:551–787.

45. On the importance and temporal complexity of the Aristotelian
distinction between voluntary, involuntary, and mixed action to Renaissance
ideas of will, see Bradin Cormack, "On Will: Time and Voluntary Action in
*Coriolanus* and the Sonnets," *Shakespeare* 5, no. 3 (2009): 253–70.

46. See Cynthia Marshall, *The Shattering of the Self: Violence, Subjectivity,
and Early Modern Texts* (Baltimore: Johns Hopkins University Press, 2002).
Marshall claims that in the Renaissance "an aesthetic of shattering or
self-negation took hold: it constituted a counter-force to the nascent ethos of
individualism" (17). My aim is to offer a more contextually specific account
of the religious discourse of self-annihilation than one finds in Marshall's

book, tracing a constellation of concrete epistemological and poetic questions that emerge around the figure of the fanatic in the period. Marshall's definition of self-shattering draws on Leo Bersani, one of queer theory's most sustained proponents of self-shattering as an aesthetic and erotic practice. For Bersani's most succinct formulations, see Bersani, "Is the Rectum a Grave?," *October* 43 (Winter 1987): 197–222; and Tim Dean, Hal Foster, Kaja Silverman, and Leo Bersani, "A Conversation with Leo Bersani," *October* 82 (Autumn 1997): 3–16. More recently, Rebecca Lemon has incisively applied Bersani's understanding of self-shattering to what she theorizes as the "radical giving of the self" and the "paradox of willing away one's will" that is involved in early modern addiction. Lemon, *Addiction and Devotion in Early Modern England* (Philadelphia: University of Pennsylvania Press, 2018), 57, 138.

47. For a recent, capacious narrative about early modern attempts to control, appropriate, evade, and indulge the passions, see Christopher Tilmouth, *Passion's Triumph over Reason: A History of the Moral Imagination from Spenser to Rochester* (Oxford: Oxford University Press, 2007).

48. Erich Auerbach, "Excursus: *Gloria Passionis*," in *Literary Language and Its Public in Late Latin Antiquity and in the Middle Ages*, trans. Ralph Manheim, 67–82 (Princeton: Princeton University Press). See also Auerbach, "*Passio* als Leidenschaft," in *Gesammelte Aufsätze zur romanischen Philologie* (Bern, Ger.: Francke Verlag, 1967), 161–75.

49. "Per enthusiastas intelligimus homines fanaticos, qui afflatum et inspirationem Dei vel fingunt, vel præsumunt, et vel Diabolicis, vel melancholicis, vel voluntariis illusionibus divinam revelationem tribuendo se aliosque circumducunt." Friedrich Spanheim, *Disputationum Anti-Anabaptisticarum Decima-sexta . . . De Enthusiasmo* (Leiden, Neth., 1646), thesis 4. Cited in Michael Heyd's thorough discussion of Spanheim's polemics, "*Be Sober and Reasonable*": *The Critique of Enthusiasm in the Seventeenth and Early Eighteenth Centuries* (Leiden, Neth.: Brill, 1995), 19–20; I quote Heyd's English translation of Spanheim. See also Spanheim, *Englands VVarning by Germanies Woe* (London, 1646), 26.

50. Plato, *Ion*, in *Plato: The Complete Works*, ed. John M. Cooper (Indianapolis: Hackett, 1997), 533d–e, 534b, 536b.

51. The classical discourse of enthusiasm is of course not entirely encompassed by the question of poetic inspiration and rhapsody. There are numerous other examples of divine possession in ancient poetry, and a particularly intriguing one can be found in Book VII of Virgil's *Aeneid*, when the Fury Allecto, sent by Juno, shakes her favorite snake out of her hair and throws it at the Rutulian Queen Amata to possess her, an act of inspiration that is, like Ionic enthusiasm, described both as a kind of encircling

and as a force that spreads: "ille inter vestis et levia pectora lapsus/volvitur attactu nullo, fallitque furentem/viperam inspirans animam; fit tortile collo/ aurum ingens coluber, fit longae taenia vittae/innectitque comas et membris lubricus errat" (Gliding between her raiment and smooth breasts, it winds its way unfelt, and, unseen by the frenzied woman, breathes into her its viperous breath. The huge snake becomes the collar of twisted gold about her neck, becomes the festoon of the long fillet, entwines itself into her hair, and slides smoothly over her limbs). Virgil, *Aeneid*, bks. 7–12, *Appendix Vergiliana*, ed. G. P. Goold, trans. H. R. Fairclough, Loeb Classical Library (Cambridge: Harvard University Press, 2001), 7.349–53. When Amata begins to scream about her daughter's commitment to Bacchus, her divine fury catches on contagiously: "fama volat, furiisque accensas pectore matres/ idem omnis simul ardor agit nova quaerere tecta" (Fame flies abroad, and the matrons, their breasts kindled with fury, are driven on, all by the same frenzy, to seek new dwellings) (7.392–93). Before she runs into the woods and spreads her frenzy to others, Amata is whirled by her possession through the city like a spinning top (*turbo*), impelled by a force that is at once internal—"penitusque in viscera lapsum/serpentis furiale malum totamque pererrat (The serpent's maddening venom has glided deep into her veins and courses through her whole frame) (7.374–75)—and external: "dant animos plagae" (The blows [of the children spinning the top] give it life) (7.383).

52. Spanheim, *Englands VVarning*, 24.

53. An extremely useful history of the critique of enthusiasm can be found in Michael Heyd, *"Be Sober and Reasonable."* See Heyd's Introduction on the medicalization of this critique, and Chapter 3 on Casaubon and More. J. G. A. Pocock argues, by contrast, that the generalization of enthusiasm as a term of abuse across Europe in the sixteenth and seven- teenth centuries, meant to dehumanize the "fury of millennial sects" from the Peasants' Revolt in Germany onward, never really lost its original meaning of "the in-pouring or in-breathing of the divine." See J. G. A. Pocock, "Enthusiasm: The Antiself of Enlightenment," *Huntington Library Quarterly* 60, nos. 1/2 (1997): 9–10.

54. See for example Cicero's description of "superstitious philosophers" as fanatics in *De Divinatione* 2.118 (Cicero, *On Old Age, On Friendship, On Divination*, trans. W. A. Falconer, Loeb Classical Library No. 154 [Cam- bridge: Harvard University Press, 1923]): "sed nescio quo modo isti philosophi superstitiosi et paene fanatici quidvis malle videntur quam se non ineptos" (But, for some inexplicable cause, those superstitious and fanatical philosophers of yours would rather appear absurd than anything else in the world). Quoted in Dominique Colas, *Civil Society and Fanati-*

*cism: Conjoined Histories*, trans. Amy Jacobs (Stanford: Stanford University Press), 372n6.

55. Colas, *Civil Society and Fanaticism*; Alberto Toscano, *Fanaticism: On the Uses of an Idea* (New York: Verso, 2010).

56. In his vital study *Thomas Münzer als Theologe der Revolution*, Ernst Bloch reproduces the caption on a portrait made of Müntzer: "Archifanaticus patronus et capitaneus seditiosorum rusticorum." See Bloch, *Thomas Münzer als Theologe der Revolution* (Frankfurt am Main: Suhrkamp, 1960), 127.

57. Colas, *Civil Society and Fanaticism*, 12. Colas suggests that English texts sometimes use "fanatic" and other times use "phanatic." Occasionally texts use both spellings—for example, in George A. Fox, *A Distinction between the Phanatick Spirit, and the Spirit of God* (London, 1660). Calvin will sometimes, in French versions of his texts, translate the Latin *fanaticus* as *phantastique*. Colas says the "phanatic" or "phanatik" (or, in French, *phantastique*) spelling is based on the mistaken but suggestive assumption that the term "fanatic" derived not from Latin *fanum* but from the Greek *phantasma* (from the root *phos*, meaning "light"), implying an association between fanaticism and vision (or mistaken visions: phantasms or hallucinations).

58. Colas, *Civil Society and Fanaticism*; and Toscano, *Fanaticism*, respectively. Toscano draws heavily on Bloch's *Münzer als Theologe*.

59. Friedrich Engels, *Der deutsche Bauernkrieg* (Berlin: Neuer Weg, 1945). Karl Marx comments that the radical possibilities of the German Peasants' Revolt were ruined because of theology: "Damals scheiterte der Bauernkrieg, die radikalste Tatsache der deutschen Geschichte, an der Theologie" (The Peasant War, the most radical event in German history, failed because of theology). Marx, "Zur Kritik der Hegelschen Rechtsphilosophie," in *Marx-Engels-Werke*, vol. 1, by Karl Marx and Friedrich Engels (Berlin: Dietz Verlag, 1976), 386.

60. See Colas's polemical anti-Marxist Preface to the English edition of Colas, *Civil Society and Fanaticism*, xx.

61. Toscano, *Fanaticism*, 67.

62. Alain Badiou, *Saint Paul: La foundation de l'universalisme* (Paris: Presses Universitaires de France, 1997).

63. The literature on the Luther-Müntzer dispute is voluminous and many particularly helpful analyses are available. Niklaus Largier, "Mysticism, Modernity, and the Invention of Aesthetic Experience," *Representations* 105 (2009): 37–60, discusses "inspired, mystical reading practices" and Luther's investment in secular power as a way of limiting biblical hermeneutic possibilities. Cynthia Grant Schoenberger, "Luther and the Justifiability of Resistance to Legitimate Authority," *Journal of the History of Ideas* 40, no. 1 (1979): 3–20, addresses the malleability of Luther's position on individual

resistance to authority. Bloch, *Thomas Münzer als Theologe*, 143–71, demonstrates the ways in which Luther's Christology, natural-law theory, and selective reading of Paul's Letter to the Romans informed Luther's stance against collective resistance. Steven Ozment focuses on the politics of mysticism in Luther's and Müntzer's respective works; see Ozment, *The Age of Reform, 1250–1550: An Intellectual and Religious History of Late Medieval and Reformation Europe* (New Haven, Conn.: Yale University Press, 1980), 80–134; *Mysticism and Dissent: Religious Ideology and Social Protest in the Sixteenth Century* (New Haven, Conn.: Yale University Press, 1973); and "Eckhart and Luther: German Mysticism and Protestantism," *Thomist* 42, no. 2 (1978): 259–80. Karl Gerhard Steck, *Luther und die Schwärmer* (Zurich: Evangelischer Verlag, 1955) examines the political implications of Müntzer's critique of Luther's dualism. James Stayer, *The German Peasants' War and Anabaptist Community of Goods* (Quebec: McGill-Queen's University Press, 1994) provides an analysis of the threat of communization. And Jacob Taubes, *Occidental Eschatology*, trans. David Ratmoko (Stanford: Stanford University Press, 2009), 111–20, studies Luther's conviction that the authorities should murder the peasants in good conscience, and the influence of the Anabaptist revolts on English chiliasm during the Civil War.

64. The essential texts by Luther on fanaticism are collected primarily in volumes 15 and 18 of *D. Martin Luthers Werke*, and translated in volumes 40 and 46 of *Luther's Works*, ed. Jaroslav Pelikan and Helmut T. Lehmann (Saint Louis: Concordia, 1955–), including: "Ein Brief an die Fürsten zu Sachsen von dem aufrührischen Geist" ("Letter to the Princes of Saxony Concerning the Rebellious Spirit," [1524]), "Ein Brief an die Christen zu Straßburg wider den Schwärmergeist" ("Letter to the Christians at Strasbourg in Opposition to the Fanatic Spirit" [1524]), "Wider die himmlischen Propheten," Parts 1 and 2 ("Against the Heavenly Prophets" [1525]), and, most venomous of all, "Wider die Räuberischen und Mörderischen Rotten der Bauern" ("Against the Robbing and Murdering Hordes of Peasants" [1525]).

65. In *German Peasants' War*, Stayer outlines the debates about whether "'omnia sunt communia' was Müntzer's own principle or a projection of princely fears tortured out of him by an interrogator" (107–11).

66. On how Tauler, according to a pastor who worked with Müntzer, "seduced" Müntzer and the peasants, see Eric Gritsch, *Thomas Müntzer: A Tragedy of Errors* (Minneapolis: Fortress, 1989), 13. Ozment's *Mysticism and Dissent* compellingly makes the case for Müntzer as the one who yoked together mystical self-annihilation (in the tradition of Eckhart and Tauler) and collective rebellion in the Reformation. On crucial differences between

Tauler and Eckhart regarding the doctrine of self-emptying, see Alex
Dubilet, *The Self-Emptying Subject: Kenosis and Immanence, Medieval to
Modern* (New York: Fordham University Press, 2018), 33. Dubilet theorizes
Eckhartian mystical immanence as, among other things, "the breakdown
of the difference between man and God. . . . Eckhart's kenotic movements
problematize the very locus of subjective interiority that could be posited as
opposed to an external God" (33). In this, Eckhart more than Tauler should
perhaps be seen as Müntzer's intellectual forbear. This is not to say that
Müntzer's language shares the theoretical density or sophistication of
Eckhart's. But to my mind, Müntzer—at least in the passage I explicate
below—did not "hold fast to the distinction between the creature and the
creator" in the way that Dubilet argues that Tauler and then Luther tended
to in their theories of mystical self-annihilation (33). This is another crucial
way in which Müntzer disagreed with Luther, and though this disagreement
has not been studied in detail, its political and theological consequence are
decisive; it is precisely why Müntzer is able to see himself as a vessel for
God's violent action. Unlike certain strains of thinking in Tauler and
Luther, that is, Müntzer's self-emptying does not prepare the soul for ascent
to the divine, but annihilates the self so that God's action can become
immanent within, and thus undifferentiated from, the self.

67. Müntzer, *Schriften und Briefe: Kritische Gesamtausgabe*, ed. Günther
Franz (Gütersloh, Ger.: Gütersloh Verlaghaus Gerd Mohn, 1968), 251 (my
translation).

68. Ozment, *Age of Reform*, 89.

69. Müntzer, *Schriften und Briefe*, 499 (my translation).

70. Toscano, *Fanaticism*, 67.

71. On this kind of pronomial slippage in the history of mystical discourses, see Michael Sells, *Mystical Languages of Unsaying* (Chicago: Chicago
University Press, 1994).

72. Michael Coogan, Marc Z. Brettler, Carol Newsom, and Pheme
Perkins, *New Oxford Annotated Bible*, 4th ed., new rev. standard version
(Oxford: Oxford University Press, 2001), Philippians 2:5–8.

73. 1 Corinthians 14:2 (NSRV). Acts 2:3–4 describes unambiguously
the divine inspiration that is involved in glossolalia on the day of Pentecost:
"Divided tongues [diamerizomenai glōssai], as of fire, appeared among
them, and a tongue rested on each of them. All of them were filled with the
Holy Spirit [eplēsthēsan pantes Pneumatos Hagiou] and began to speak in
other languages, as the Spirit gave them ability [edidou apophthengesthai
autois]." On the significance of glossolalia in ancient, medieval, and modern
thought, see Daniel Heller-Roazen, "Speaking in Tongues," *Paragraph* 25,
no. 2 (2002): 92–115.

74. Some scholars question whether the category of mysticism is actually useful for understanding the theology of figures such as Eckhart and his followers (among whom I am including, perhaps controversially, Müntzer). One of the most polemical of such calls to do away with the category of "mysticism" is in Kurt Flasch, "Meister Eckhart und die 'Deutsche Mystik'— Zur Kritik eines historiographischen Schemas," in *Die Philosophie im 14 und 15 Jahrhundert*, ed. Olaf Pluta (Amsterdam: B. R. Grüner, 1988), 439–63. A subtler response is found in Alain de Libera, "L'Un ou la trinité? Sur un aspect trop connu de la théologie eckhartienne," *Revue des sciences religieuses* 70, no. 1 (1996): 31–47. I retain "mysticism" as a way of (perhaps reductively) referring to the tradition of self-annihilation and divinization that Müntzer saw himself taking to its more explicitly political conclusion. See Dubilet, *Self-Emptying Subject*, 62–63, on the significance of this debate.

75. Ian Munro, *The Figure of the Crowd in Early Modern London: The City and Its Double* (New York: Palgrave Macmillan, 2005), 39.

76. Talal Asad, *On Suicide Bombing* (New York: Columbia University Press, 2007), 91. Mohamed, whose work I discuss more in this Introduction and in Chapter 4, has made use of Asad's work to discuss what he refers to as terrorism in early modern England. Despite my resistance to the conflation of all suicide bombing with a longing for uncoerced freedom, the value of Asad's contribution remains for me significant. On martyrdom as "exemplary action," see Gregory, *Salvation at Stake*, 8.

77. "Were [Wäre] er gut, er würde sich zuvor prüffen und demütiglich urteilen lassen." *Luther's Works*, 40:52; *D. Martin Luthers Werke*, 15:213.

78. *The Works of Lancelot Andrewes, Sometime Bishop of Winchester*, ed. J. P. Wilson and James Bliss (Oxford: J. H. Parker, 1841), 3:374, 3:392–93.

79. Debora Shuger, *Habits of Thought in the English Renaissance: Religion, Politics and the Dominant Culture* (Toronto: University of Toronto Press, 1997), 101–2.

80. For an illuminating discussion of the seventeenth-century enterprise of "Anglicizing the central mystical anthropology of Medieval German spiritualism as it had been interpreted by the sixteenth-century German spiritualist and Anabaptist Movement," see Smith, *Perfection Proclaimed*, 107–43 (quotation on 136). On Anabaptism's presence in Nashe and Spenser, see David Loewenstein, *Treacherous Faith: The Specter of Heresy in Early Modern English Literature and Culture* (Oxford: Oxford University Press, 2013), chap. 4.

81. For a survey of different understandings of poetic inspiration in the Renaissance, see Gordon Teskey, "The Ethics of Inspiration," in *Reading Renaissance Ethics*, ed. Marshall Grossman (New York: Routledge, 2007), 193–205. Teskey introduces but does not explore in detail the implications of

the epistemological and poetic questions inspiration raises: "What ethical responsibility can there be in a poet who is letting another force into the world, a power over which the poet has no control, and indeed over which society, the giver of the system of ethics, has no control? Will this spiritual power be demonic or divine, or will the very starkness of that choice, which was achieved by the fathers of the church in suppressing the roman country religions, be lost?" (294). For a recent analysis of William Blake's poetics of self-annihilation, see Steven Goldsmith, *Blake's Agitation: Criticism and the Emotions* (Baltimore: Johns Hopkins University Press, 2013).

82. See for example Julia Reinhard Lupton and Graham Hammill, eds., *Political Theology and Early Modernity* (Chicago: University of Chicago Press, 2012); and Victoria Kahn, *The Future of Illusion: Political Theology and Early Modernity* (Chicago: University of Chicago Press, 2014). On the development of the modern state form as a "detheologization of public life," see especially Section 3 of Carl Schmitt, *The* Nomos *of the Earth in the International Law of the* Jus Publicum Europaeum, trans. G. L. Ulman (New York: Telos, 2003).

83. Julia Reinhard Lupton, *Citizen-Saints: Shakespeare and Political Theology* (Chicago: University of Chicago Press, 2005), 21.

84. Lupton, *Citizen-Saints*, 1 (my emphasis). In my turn away from such an emphasis on agential self-election in the context of fanaticism, I have been influenced by Saba Mahmood, *The Politics of Piety: The Islamic Revival and the Feminist Subject* (Princeton: Princeton University Press, 2004).

85. Alice Dailey, *The English Martyr from Reformation to Revolution* (Notre Dame, Ind.: Notre Dame University Press, 2012), 8. I should note that, despite my relative narrowing of the category of form, Dailey's study is illuminating and thought-provoking; I have learned much from her rigorous analysis of martyrdom as a genre.

86. By contrast, for acute attempts to recuperate a materialist or historicist formalism in Renaissance English literary studies, see for example Heather Dubrow, "Guess Who's Coming to Dinner? Reinterpreting Formalism and the Country House Poem," *MLQ* 61, no. 1 (2000): 59–77; and Dubrow, *The Challenges of Orpheus: Lyric Poetry and Early Modern England* (Baltimore: Johns Hopkins University Press, 2008). See also Richard Strier, "How Formalism Became a Dirty Word, and Why We Can't Do without It," in *Renaissance Literature and Its Formal Engagements*, ed. Mark David Rasmussen (New York: Palgrave, 2002), 207–15; Henry Turner, "Lessons from Literature for the Historian of Science (and Vice Versa): Reflections on 'Form,'" *Isis* 101 (2010): 578–89; and Ben Burton and Elizabeth Scott-Baumann's Introduction to *The Work of Form: Poetics and Materiality in Early Modern Culture* (Oxford: Oxford University Press, 2014), 1–22. For an overview of new

formalism as a movement, see Marjorie Levinson, "What is New Formalism?," *PMLA* 122, no. 2 (Mar. 2007): 558–69. To designate those critical studies that articulate a historical reading of form, Levinson makes use of the concept of "activist formalism," as articulated in Susan Wolfson, "Reading for Form," *MLQ* 61 (2000): 1–17. For an account of form's relationship to passion and time, see Anne-Lise François, "'The feel of not to feel it,' or the Pleasures of Enduring Form," in *A Companion to Romantic Poetry*, ed. Charles Mahoney (Oxford: Wiley-Blackwell, 2011), 445–66. François suggestively describes form "not as that which endures, inured to the effects of time, but as that which requires 'enduring'—the object of a transitive, ongoing action as well as a verb in its own right, rather than the finished shape supposed capable of outlasting the history from which it has emerged" (446).

87. Jonathan Kramnick and Anahid Nersessian, "Form and Explanation," *Critical Inquiry* 43 (Spring 2017), 664.

88. Theodor Adorno, *Ästhetische Theorie* (Frankfurt am Main: Suhrkamp, 1970), 320; Adorno, *Aesthetic Theory*, trans. Robert Hullot-Kentor (Minneapolis: University of Minnesota Press, 1997), 216. I have silently altered Hullot-Kentor's translation. For a provocative defense of interdisciplinary studies of poetry rooted in Adorno's sense of the "collective undercurrent" of poetry, see Brent Hayes Edwards, "Specters of Interdisciplinarity," *PMLA* 123, no. 1 (2008): 188–94, especially 190–91. One of the most interesting recent works on the politics of form has stressed the overlapping of the literary and the social: in both cases, form can be defined as "all shapes and configurations, all ordering principles, all patterns of repetition and difference." Caroline Levine, *Forms: Whole, Rhythm, Hierarchy, Network* (Princeton: Princeton University Press, 2015), 3. I find it enlivening to broaden "form" so that it connects literature to the social, and throughout this book I will look to explore such overlaps—for example, in how the ordering principle of the modern state both produces and polices the figure of the fanatic, and how the fanatic shatters and produces new poetic forms. Yet I also worry that if "form" can mean all this, we risk forgetting the specific, historically mediated repertoire of techniques that is available to poets. (This is not Levine's project, of course.) For my purposes, I narrow the term "form" to mean "poetic technique" in this study in hopes of being precise about the thinking that these poems undertake.

89. Simon Jarvis, "For a Poetics of Verse," *PMLA* 125, no. 4 (Oct. 2010): 931–32. For Jarvis's critique of how overbroad uses of "form" can become "conceptual governors" that obscure more than they reveal the minute techniques of thinking in verse, see Jarvis, "How to Do Things with Tunes," *ELH* 82, no. 2 (Summer 2015): 380. Umbrella terms can be useful, though, as

long as one is careful to be precise about the specific operations that fall under the category of "form." Jarvis has tended to use verse "technique" as a more general category instead of "form" in much of his work. My hope is that using "form" as a synonym for the narrower "technique" here will allow me to specify Spenser's, Donne's, and Milton's repertoires of poetic experimentation while still allowing my argument to speak more legibly to the variously emergent new formalisms. The analyses that follow do not exclusively focus on verse technique, but rather attempt to understand technique as a unique way of thinking about a problem—fanaticism—that is contested in a number of other domains under consideration here, as well.

90. *Works of John Milton*, 4:298.

91. Anthony Reed, *Freedom Time: The Poetics and Politics of Black Experimental Writing* (Baltimore: Johns Hopkins University Press, 2016), 8, 5; Colleen Ruth Rosenfeld, *Indecorous Thinking: Figures of Speech in Early Modern Poetics* (New York: Fordham University Press, 2018), 12. See also Rosenfeld's persuasive claim that conceptions of formal unity and diversity were by no means particular "to the New Criticism and its reworking of romanticism's conception of the organic whole," and that Renaissance poetic and rhetorical debates about form—and the way that figures of speech at once enabled and threatened normative conceptions of form—were central to the development of Renaissance English poetry itself (74–75).

92. John Carey, "A Work in Praise of Terrorism? September 11 and *Samson Agonistes*," *Times Literary Supplement* (September 6, 2002): 15–16; Mohamed, "Confronting Religious Violence: Milton's *Samson Agonistes*," *PMLA* 120, no. 2 (2005): 327–40. For a lucid—if brief—criticism of the fact that this debate took center stage in Milton studies only after September 11th, 2001, and in relation to the figure of the Muslim "terrorist," see Richard Halpern, *Eclipse of Action: Tragedy and Political Economy* (Chicago: University of Chicago Press, 2017), 292n17.

93. Mohamed, *Milton and the Post-Secular Present*, 115.

94. Mohamed, *Milton and the Post-Secular Present*, 32.

95. Mohamed, *Milton and the Post-Secular Present*, 23–27.

96. Mohamed, *Milton and the Post-Secular Present*, 124.

97. Gillian Rose, *The Broken Middle: Out of Our Ancient Society* (Oxford: Blackwell, 1992), 207.

## 1. ALLEGORICAL FANATICISM: SPENSER'S ORGANS

1. A key term for the poem, "ensample" is also central to Spenser's explanation of his poetic method in his "Letter to Raleigh," both in the sense of how his poem teaches and in how his poetic techniques are meant to imagine the world "such as might best be": "For this cause is Xenophon

preferred before Plato, for that the one in the exquisite depth of his iudgement, formed a Commune welth such as it should be, but the other in the person of Cyrus and the Persians fashioned a gouernment such as might best be: So much more profitable and gratious is doctrine by ensample, then by rule." Edmund Spenser, "Letter to Raleigh," *The Faerie Queene*, ed. A. C. Hamilton, with Hiroshi Yamashita, Toshiyuki Suzuki, and Shohachi Fukuda, 2nd ed. (London: Longman, 2007), 716. Unless otherwise noted, quotations from the poetry of *The Faerie Queene* are from this edition, and citations will be given parenthetically in the text by book, canto, and stanza. See Colleen Ruth Rosenfeld, *Indecorous Thinking: Figures of Speech in Early Modern Poetics* (New York: Fordham University Press, 2018), 97–119, on the significance of "such as might best be" for simile in *Faerie Queene*.

2. Edmund Spenser, *The Faerie Qveene* (London, 1590), A2.

3. See Jeff Dolven, *Scenes of Instruction in Renaissance Romance* (Chicago: University of Chicago Press, 2007), 141, on the scholarly tendency to understand a particular book of the poem to have achieved its goal when a character comes to stand as an exemplar for that book's virtue.

4. Spenser's "Letter to Raleigh" states that the "generall end therefore of all the booke is to fashion a gentleman or noble person in vertuous and gentle discipline" (713).

5. Hamilton's note calls attention to disagreements over how to read this pronominal ambiguity in John K. Hale, "Spenser's *Faerie Queene*, 1.11.52 and 53," *Explicator* 53, no. 1 (1994): 6–7, and John McDermott, "Spenser's *Faerie Queene*, 1.11.52 and 53," *Explicator* 54, no. 4 (1996): 198–99.

6. See Carol V. Kaske, *Spenser's Biblical Poetics* (Ithaca, N.Y.: Cornell University Press, 2000), 73. Drawing most canonically from Paul's comments in Ephesians 6:17 ("And take the helmet of Salvation, and the sword of the Spirit, which is the word of God") and from the description in Revelations 19:15 of Christ on a white horse during the apocalypse ("And out of his mouth went out a sharp sword, that with it he should smite the heathen: for he shall rule them with a rod of iron, for he it is that treadeth the winepress of the fierceness and wrath of Almighty God"), Spenser makes use of this iconography most explicitly in the prehistory in the "Letter to Raleigh" of the armor that "a faire Ladye" brings for Redcrosse, parenthetically glossed as "the armour of a Christian man specified by Saint Paul v. Ephes" (717). Spenser's gloss is relatively humble, given the text to which he alludes. The sword of the spirit, along with the rest of the armor that comes with it, is more than just the "armour of a Christian man"—it is the word of God itself (per Ephesians), but can as easily be recast to represent apocalyptic divine violence (per Revelations). This militaristic iconography was widespread during the Reformation. While Luther made selective use of biblical

representations of the sword of the spirit to realign the image of the sword with princely authority, other reformers, as David Norbrook has shown in *Poetry and Politics in the English Renaissance* (Oxford: Oxford University Press, 2002), took the sword as a favorite emblem, depicting the Bible "as a sword issuing out of Christ's mouth, an image conveying the sharpness and radical immediacy of the divine message in its vernacular form" (32). See Martin Luther, "On Secular Authority," in *Luther and Calvin on Secular Authority*, ed. and trans. Harro Höpfl (Cambridge: Cambridge University Press, 1991), 1–46. Spenser turns the sword of the spirit into a literalized figure for the unmediated violence of the Word that Redcrosse becomes as an organ of God's might, thus conflating the sword of the spirit of Ephesians (God's Word) with the sword of Revelations (divine violence).

7. We are introduced to Redcrosse in the first stanza as a knight whose arms bear the marks of many battles, only to learn at the start of that stanza's second quatrain that he is not as he appears: "Yet armes till that time did he neuer wield" (1.1.5).

8. Thomas Müntzer, *Schriften und Briefe: Kritische Gesamtausgabe*, ed. Günther Franz (Gütersloh, Ger.: Gütersloh Verlaghaus Gerd Mohn, 1968), 251 (my translation).

9. Compare Dolven's comment that "the incomplete success of Holiness (as a vertical, transcendent virtue that can be figured on earth, but not yet realized) propels the poem into experiment with Temperance (a horizontal, practical virtue that we might exercise here and now)." Dolven, "Panic's Castle," *Representations* 120, no. 1 (2012): 11. I would suggest that Redcrosse's transformation offers the possibility that holiness is, for an unverifiable moment, not only figured but also realized. The Palmer's elision of this possibility—or at least his reduction of holiness to Redcrosse's achievement—is that much more notable since he wishes that God will guide Guyon in Book II. It may be the unverifiability of whether Redcrosse has achieved an action or was mere organ that propels the poem into its experiment with Temperance. This muddling of action and passion will return to haunt Book II again in Guyon's destruction of the Bower of Bliss, to which I return later in this chapter.

10. Darryl Gless, *Interpretation and Theology in Spenser* (Cambridge: Cambridge University Press, 1994), 179; A. S. P. Woodhouse, "Nature and Grace in *The Faerie Queene*," *ELH* 16, no. 3 (1949): 131. See also Sean Kane, *Spenser's Moral Allegory* (Toronto: University of Toronto Press, 1989), 8.

11. David Landreth persuasively reads "goodwill" here as something external to Redcrosse—namely, as the force that "replaces his own control over what his hands accomplish with the agency of God. . . . Redcrosse's mental faculties of 'reason' and 'will' succeed by effacing themselves into a

holy instrumentality." Landreth, *The Face of Mammon: The Matter of Money in English Renaissance Literature* (Oxford: Oxford University Press, 2012), 88. Landreth's analysis is clarifying and compelling, but it sets aside the ambiguity of Redcrosse's transformation and the fact that the poem never finally authorizes Redcrosse's interpretation as the *right* corrective to the Palmer's emphasis on willful achievement.

12. Daniel Wegner, *The Illusion of Conscious Will* (Cambridge: MIT Press, 2002).

13. Gordon Teskey, *Allegory and Violence* (Ithaca, N.Y.: Cornell University Press, 1996).

14. Andrew Escobedo, *Nationalism and Historical Loss in the English Renaissance: Foxe, Dee, Spenser, Milton* (Ithaca, N.Y.: Cornell University Press, 2004), 122.

15. Angus Fletcher, *Allegory: The Theory of a Symbolic Mode* (Princeton: Princeton University Press, 2012).

16. Teskey, *Allegory and Violence*, 18. For criticisms of Teskey's account of allegorical capture, see Judith Anderson, "Review of Gordon Teskey, *Allegory and Violence*," *Arthuriana* 7 (1997), 125–28, which questions his rendering of narrative as "'the other' of 'allegorical meaning'" (126), and Escobedo, *Volition's Face: Personification and the Will in Renaissance Literature* (Notre Dame, Ind.: University of Notre Dame Press, 2017), which sees personification not only as "a kind of aggressive hylomorphism" but also as "channel[ing]" and "represent[ing] the energies passing back and forth between us and the landscape" (54).

17. Susanne Lindgren Wofford, *The Choice of Achilles: The Ideology of Figure in the Epic* (Stanford: Stanford University Press, 1992), 276–77.

18. Isabel Gamble MacCaffrey, *Spenser's Allegory: The Anatomy of Imagination* (Princeton: Princeton University Press, 1976), 37–38.

19. "Letter to Raleigh," 714.

20. See Dolven, "Panic's Castle," 11.

21. See Stephen Greenblatt, *Renaissance Self-Fashioning: From More to Shakespeare* (Chicago: University of Chicago Press, 1980), 189; Anthony Esolen, "Spenser's 'Alma Venus': Energy and Economics in the Bower of Bliss," *English Literary Renaissance* 23, no. 2 (Spring 1993): 270; Kenneth Gross, *Spenserian Poetics: Idolatry, Iconoclasm, and Magic* (Ithaca, N.Y.: Cornell University Press, 1985), 182; and Jennifer Summit, "Monuments and Ruins: Spenser and the Problem of the English Library," *ELH* 70, no. 1 (Spring 2003): 1–34.

22. See Harry Berger Jr., *The Allegorical Temper: Vision and Reality in Book II of Spenser's "Faerie Queene"* (New Haven, Conn.: Yale University Press, 1957), 67.

23. Critics have suggested possible causes of Guyon's spasmatic violence at this moment, of course, but the poem cannot be said to authorize any of them explicitly. Dolven, for instance, suggests the "most immediate provocation" might be jealousy, the flickering revelation of Guyon's desire for Verdant, "some shadow, *mutatis mutandis*, of the crisis of identity we now call homosexual panic." Dolven, "Panic's Castle," 7.

24. For a fuller analysis of the surprising parallel between Guyon and Talus, see Landreth, *Face of Mammon*, 93. There, Landreth intriguingly claims there that Guyon and Talus are both "insufficiently self-conscious instrument[s]."

25. Elsewhere, Spenser makes use of the image of a tempest to describe a collective of Irish rebels who, "like a sudden tempest," rebel in hopes of effacing all the colonizing work that the English undertake on their island. Spenser, *A View of the Present State of Ireland* (Oxford: Clarendon, 1970), 16.

26. Landreth has developed the fullest and most persuasive analysis of how this stanza's pronominal elision and meter perform the "evaporation" of Guyon's agency into an atmospheric condition. See Landreth, *Face of Mammon*, 92.

27. See Dolven, *Scenes of Instruction*, 164, on the "uneducat[ing]" of Guyon.

28. Greenblatt, *Renaissance Self-Fashioning*, 157–92, provides the most-canonical interpretation that insists on the poem's embrace of this violence for the colonial and subject-fashioning program to which he sees *The Faerie Queene* being overwhelmingly committed. For an interpretation that breaks with Greenblatt to assert that the poem offers "a critique of the overt politics of Guyon's destruction of the Bower of Bliss," see Wofford, *Choice of Achilles*, 271–72. For a recent account of Book II as a "critique of an ideology of temperance," see Joseph Campana, "Boy Toys and Liquid Joys: Pleasure and Power in the Bower of Bliss," *Modern Philology* 106, no. 3 (2009): 465–96, revised in Campana, *The Pain of Reformation: Spenser, Vulnerability, and the Ethics of Masculinity* (New York: Fordham University Press, 2012), Chapter 4.

29. Wofford draws a connection between Guyon's fury and the personification of Fury throughout Book II. See Wofford, *Choice of Achilles*, 271–72.

30. John Guillory, *Poetic Authority: Spenser, Milton, and Literary History* (New York: Columbia University Press, 1983), 23–45.

31. For an extended reading of this scene and its relationship to the Neoplatonic-influenced concept of love-melancholy, see Marion Wells, *The Secret Wound: Love-Melancholy and Early Modern Romance* (Stanford: Stanford University Press, 2007), 220–60.

32. On the poetics of rapture and the seizure of the will in *The Faerie Queene*, see Escobedo, *Volition's Face*, 173–207.

33. The other instance of unambiguously narrated inspiration—the story of Orgoglio's literally inspired birth in Book I—also shifts to a classical idiom, but in that case the poem is developing a dark parody of the Holy Spirit's inspiration of a believer. Orgoglio is conceived through a corrupt inspiration when Æolus's breath—which seems literally to be the breath of the wind "which through the world doth pas"—"secretly inspyre[s]" the Earth's "hollow womb." While Redcrosse, Guyon, and Britomart seem to be emptied of their own will so that the divine acts through them, Orgoglio, by contrast, is "puft up with emptie wynd, and fild with sinfull cryme" (1.7.9). Orgoglio, that is, is made perpetually prideful by the fact of his inspired conception, but what inspires him is entirely "emptie"; rather than God's overtaking his will, his inspiration fills him up with pride. Hobbes echoes this parody of inspiration almost exactly to deride the claims of fanatics to have divine spirit present within them, to which I return in Chapter 3. On pride in the Orgoglio episode as a failure to follow Christ's instructions to humble oneself (and thus as Orgoglio as a psychomachic manifestation of Redcrosse's own rebellion against God), see Vern Torgzon, "Spenser's Orgoglio and Despaire," *Texas Studies in Literature and Language* 3, no. 1 (1961): 123–28.

34. On the poem's more general tendency to represent female characters being "overtaken by a force greater than themselves as a rape" and "uniformly glossed as external aggression to be resisted," see Wofford, *Choice of Achilles*, 366; and Katherine Eggert, "Spenser's Ravishment: Rape and Rapture in *The Faerie Queene*," *Representations* 70 (Spring 2000): 1–26.

35. See Wofford, *Choice of Achilles*, 328–30, on the significance of the richness of Britomart's character development.

36. Dolven, "Panic's Castle."

37. See Étienne Balibar, "Spinoza, the Anti-Orwell: The Fear of the Masses," in *Masses, Classes, Ideas: Studies on Philosophy and Politics before and after Marx*, trans. James Swenson (New York: Routledge, 1994), 3–37; Warren Montag, *Bodies, Masses, Power: Spinoza and His Contemporaries* (London: Verso, 1999); Montag, "Who's Afraid of the Multitude? Between the Individual and the State," *South Atlantic Quarterly* 104, no. 4 (Fall 2005): 655–73.

38. On the context of Müntzer and Anabaptism, see David Loewenstein, *Treacherous Faith: The Specter of Heresy in Early Modern English Literature and Culture* (Oxford: Oxford University Press, 2013), 172–76; and Frederick M. Padelford, "Spenser's Arraignment of the Anabaptists," *Journal of English and Germanic Philology* 12, no. 3 (1913): 434–48. On this episode's evocation of "Gaelic 'extra-legal' appeals both to commonness and ancient custom," see Bradin Cormack, *A Power to Do Justice: Jurisdiction, English Literature, and the Rise of Common Law, 1509–1625* (Chicago: University of Chicago

Press, 2007), 167–68; and also Annabel Patterson, "The Egalitarian Giant: Representations of Justice in History/Literature," *Journal of British Studies* 31, no. 2 (1992), 116.

39. See note 64 in the Introduction for Luther's central texts on fanaticism. For a philological map of the passage of *Schwärmerei* to the English "fanaticism," via French, see Dominique Colas, *Civil Society and Fanaticism: Conjoined Histories*, trans. Amy Jacobs (Stanford: Stanford University Press, 1997).

40. Angus Fletcher, *The Prophetic Moment: An Essay on Spenser* (Chicago: University of Chicago Press, 1971), 52.

41. Fletcher, *Prophetic Moment*, 245.

42. See Greenblatt, "Murdering Peasants: Status, Genre, and the Representation of Rebellion," *Representations* 1 (1983): 21; Annabel Patterson, "The Egalitarian Giant: Representations of Justice in History/Literature," *Journal of British Studies* 31, no. 2 (1992): 97–132; Elizabeth Fowler, "The Failure of Moral Philosophy in the Work of Edmund Spenser," *Representations* 51 (1995): 47–76; and Anderson, *Words That Matter: Linguistic Perception in Renaissance England* (Stanford: Stanford University Press, 1996), 175. Cormack, in *Power to Do Justice*, persuasively claims that Artegall is "Spenser's and England's bureaucratic hero" (170), but reveals how manipulative Artegall's argumentative stratagems are. Cormack argues that Artegall effects "an institutional deformation of the debate he finds himself in: the historically relevant point is not that he mischaracterizes equity, but that he should redefine an ethical issue of distribution as one of judicial and statutory interpretation" (169) and thus makes a genuine debate impossible. That Artegall channels Theseus's self-aggrandizing "First Moevere" speech from Chaucer's "Knight's Tale" is further reason to cast a skeptical eye on this particular strategy of divinely authorized, allegorical power maintenance. See Geoffrey Chaucer, *The Riverside Chaucer*, 3rd ed., ed. Larry Benson (Boston: Houghton Mifflin, 1987), frag. 1, lines 2987–3093.

43. See James Stayer, *The German Peasants' War and Anabaptist Community of Goods* (Quebec: McGill-Queen's University Press, 1994), 107–23.

44. Admittedly, as I have already mentioned in passing, Spenser's egalitarian Giant does not make explicit a theory of mystical self-annihilation like the one we find in Müntzer. Nonetheless, the resonances between this episode in *The Faerie Queene* and the German Peasants' Revolt are sufficiently clear for me to suggest that this idea of self-emptying is in the background of the Giant's rebellious project for creating a new commons.

45. Jean-François Lyotard, *The Differend: Phrases in Dispute*, trans. Georges Van Den Abbeele (Manchester: Manchester University Press,

1988), xi; *Le Différend* (Paris: Les Éditions de Minuit, 1983), 9: "Qui ne pourrait pas être tranché équitablement faute d'une règle de jugement applicable aux deux argumentations."

46. See Dolven, *Scenes of Instruction*, 207–38, on allegory as punishment.

47. Julia Lupton has suggested to me that Luther's use of the swarm as a way to designate an absence of rationality in the collective seems retroactively ironic, given the fact that in systems analysis, swarms have become exempla of collective intelligence and self-organization. See for example Eric Bonabeau, Marco Dorigo, and Guy Theraulaz, *Swarm Intelligence: From Natural to Artificial Systems* (Oxford: Oxford University Press, 1999), which has influenced Michael Hardt and Antonio Negri's theory of the multitude. Hardt and Negri, *Multitude: War and Democracy in the Age of Empire* (New York: Penguin, 2004), 91–93. See also Page Dubois, "The Democratic Insect: Productive Swarms," *differences: A Journal of Feminist Cultural Studies* 20, nos. 2–3 (Summer/Fall 2009): 36–53. On the contemporary settler-colonial state's capacity to appropriate swarming as a military tactic, see Eyal Weizman's *Hollow Land: Israel's Architecture of Occupation* (New York: Verso, 2007), 190–92.

48. Peter Fenves, *Arresting Language: From Leibniz to Benjamin* (Stanford: Stanford University Press, 2002), 101. This destabilization of individual and collective identity is present at other moments of swarming in the poem—such as the "swarme of Gnats at euentide / Out of the fennes of Allan" that attack the House of Alma at the end of Book II in which, perhaps not coincidentally, every member of the swarm has a body that fades into substancelessness upon examination: "For though they bodies seeme, yet substaunce from them fades" (*Faerie Queene*, 2.9.15–16). As Rosenfeld has compellingly analyzed this episode, Spenser's swarms there "cast the excessive numbers of the group as a whole as a corporeal problem for each individual within the group, each part of that whole. . . . And *The Faerie Queene* suggests that they are deformities in body because their excessive numbers threaten to disform the poem itself." Rosenfeld, "The Artificial Life of Rhyme," *ELH* 83, no. 1 (Spring 2016): 78.

49. See John Milton, *Paradise Lost*, ed. Gordon Teskey (New York: Norton, 2004): "As bees / In spring time . . . / . . . so thick the airy crowd / Swarmed and were straitened" (1.768–76). See Geoffrey Hartman, "Milton's Counterplot," *ELH* 25, no. 1 (Mar. 1958): 1–12.

50. Campana, "The Bee and the Sovereign (II): Segments, Swarms, and the Shakespearean Multitude," in *The Return of Theory in Early Modern English Studies*, ed. Paul Cefalu, Gary Kuchar, and Bryan Reynolds, vol. 2 (New York: Palgrave Macmillan, 2014), 60. On Spenser's ability both to affirm and to question human sovereignty more generally through his representations of animals, see Campana, "Spenser's Inhumanity," *Spenser Studies* 30 (2015): 277–99.

51. This claim is influenced by Stephano Harney and Fred Moten, *The Undercommons: Fugitive Planning and Black Study* (New York: Autonomedia, 2013); for the importance of the idiom "in but not of" that I borrow, see Harney and Moten, *Undercommons*, 26.

52. See Wofford, *Choice of Achilles*, 228–29; Teskey, *Allegory and Violence*, 23; and Dolven, *Scenes of Instruction*, 136–37.

53. There is a vital critical tradition that takes the failure of the poem's allegories to be one of the main features that drives Spenser's poetic process. For one of the earliest analyses of Spenser's technique of dilating the instabilities of his allegorical images, see Berger, *Allegorical Temper*, 122–23.

54. Spenser, *The Yale Edition of the Shorter Poems of Edmund Spenser*, ed. William A. Oram, Einar Bjorvand, Ronald Bond, Thomas H. Cain, Alexander Dunlop, and Richard Schell (New Haven, Conn.: Yale University Press, 1989), 170.

55. See John Skelton, "A Replication against Certain Young Scholars Abjured of Late," in *The Complete English Poems*, ed. John Scattergood, rev. ed. (Liverpool: Liverpool University Press, 2015), 339, lines 380–85.

56. Spenser, *Shorter Poems*, 175, lines 100–1.

57. For a sociological account of the significance of English *furor poeticus* during the Renaissance, see John Huntington, "Furious Insolence: The Social Meaning of Poetic Inspiration in the 1590s," *Modern Philology* 94, no. 3 (1997): 305–26.

58. For an extended commentary on Plato's *Ion*, inspiration, and "divine sharing," see Jean-Luc Nancy, "Sharing Voices," in *Transforming the Hermeneutic Context: From Nietzsche to Nancy*, ed. Gayle L. Ormiston and Alan D. Schrift (Albany: State University of New York Press, 1990), 211–59.

## 2. LYRIC FANATICISM: DONNE'S ANNIHILATION

1. "The impulse to cancel out one's own existence, like the desire to deny God's existence, is finally inconceivable." Ramie Targoff, *John Donne, Body and Soul* (Chicago: University of Chicago Press, 2008), 122.

2. *The Complete Poems of John Donne*, ed. Robin Robbins (Harlow, Eng.: Longman, 2010), lines 15–16. Quotations of Donne's poems, except for the *Holy Sonnets*, are from this edition, cited by line number. *Holy Sonnets* are quoted from the Westmoreland sequence, in *The Variorum Edition of the Poetry of John Donne*, vol. 7, pt. 1, gen. ed. Gary A. Stringer (Bloomington: Indiana University Press, 2005), 11–20.

3. John Donne, *Devotions upon Emergent Occasions*, ed. Anthony Raspa (Oxford: Oxford University Press, 1987), 3. *Devotions* was originally published in 1624.

4. Donne, *Devotions*, 51.

5. For a contemporary example of this usage, with which Donne was likely familiar, see Benet of Canfield, *The rule of perfection contayning a breif and perspicuous abridgement of all the wholle spirituall life, reduced to this only point of the vvill of God* (Roan, Nor., 1609), 13.

6. *Oxford English Dictionary*, 2nd ed. (Oxford: Oxford University Press, 1989), s.v. exinanition, n.

7. Pierre de Béreulle, *Opuscules de piété* (Grenoble, Fr.: Jérôme Millon, 1997), 148, 226–28, 344–46. See also Béreulle's first published work, *Bref discours de l'abnégation intérieure* (1597), for the centrality of annihilation in his theology, in *Oeuvres complètes du Cardinal de Bérulle*, vol. 2 (Montsoult, Fr.: Maison d'Institution de l'Oratorie, 1960), 644–77.

8. Jean Yves Lacoste, *Encyclopedia of Christian Theology*, vol. 1 (New York: Routledge, 2001), 201.

9. Canfield, *Rule of perfection*, 166.

10. See Nigel Smith, "What's Inside? Donne, Interiority, and Independency," in *John Donne and Modernity*, ed. Robert Ellrodt (Nanterre, Fr.: Université Paris–X, 1995), 31.

11. Donne, *Biathanatos*, ed. Michael Rudick and M. Pabst Battin (New York: Garland, 1982), 171.

12. Donne, *Devotions*, 106.

13. Donne, *Devotions*, 181. Elsewhere in Donne's writing, "exinanition" and "annihilation" are synonymous.

14. Donne, *Sermons of John Donne*, ed. George R. Potter and Evelyn M. Simpson (Berkeley: University of California Press, 1953–62), 7:363.

15. *Sermons of John Donne*, 1:155.

16. *Sermons of John Donne*, 4:120.

17. For corroborating dictionary definitions, see, for example, the entry for "muto, mutas, mutare" in Thomas Cooper, *Thesaurus Linguae Romanae & Britannicae*, 4th ed. (London, 1584), in which "exchange" and "batter" are used as synonyms; and the entry on "clinch" in Henry Mainwaring, *Nomenclator Navalis* (1623), published in modern edition as *The Seaman's Dictionary*, in *The Life and Works of Sir Henry Mainwaring*, ed. George Ernest Manwaring and William Gordon Perrin, vol. 2, 69–260 (London: Naval Records Society, 1920–22), 127: "To Clinch is to batter or rivet a bolt's end upon a ring, or turn back the end of any nail so as to make it fast at the end which is driven through; we also call that part of the cable which is seized about the ring of the anchor the clinch of the cable."

18. "Batter" may hint at the preparation of food to be eaten as well, as though the speaker were asking for God to eat his heart (perhaps reminiscent of Dante's dream that Beatrice is forced to eat his "fiery" heart in *Vita Nuova* III)—which would further connect "Batter my hart" to the "fiery

Zeale" I have discussed from "I ame a litle World," which transforms the speaker by "eating" him.

19. For more on the significance of this dual rhyme scheme and its relationship to prosodic irregularity in the sonnet, see Jean Fuzier, "John Donne et la formalité de l'essence," in *John Donne*, ed. Jean-Marie Benoist (Évreux, Fr.: Hérissey, 1983), 39–49.

20. Targoff comments that Donne confronts in "Batter my hart" the self-annihilation that he so feared throughout much of his earlier poetry and prose, and she canvasses some of the different meanings that "nothing" takes on in Donne's prose. Targoff, *John Donne*, 121–22. Though I find Targoff's reading of this sonnet compelling, I disagree, as I suggested at the start of this chapter, that there is, in the end, no desire for annihilation in "Batter my hart"; the poem's intense fascination with divine violence exceeds a desire for what Targoff calls "the repair of what already exists" (122).

21. "Décréation" is Simone Weil's term for the process of emptying out the self—she calls the self a "false divinity"—modeled explicitly on Christ's *kenosis*: "Il s'est vidé de sa divinité. Nous devons nous vider de la fausse divinité avec laquelle nous sommes nés." Weil, *La Pesanteur et la grâce* (Paris: Plon, 1948), 38. See Anne Carson, *Decreation: Poetry, Essays, Opera* (New York: Alfred A. Knopf, 2005), for a searching exploration of the significance of Weil's term.

22. For a survey of valuable critical interpretations of this poem's depiction of sexual violence that focus on Donne's self-representation as feminized and/or queer, see Richard Rambuss, *Closet Devotions* (Durham, N.C.: Duke University Press, 1998), 50–54.

23. See Katherine Eggert, "Spenser's Ravishment: Rape and Rapture in *The Faerie Queene*," *Representations* 70 (Spring 2000): 8–9.

24. Gordon Teskey, *Allegory and Violence* (Ithaca, N.Y.: Cornell University Press, 1996), 18n24. Teskey cites Edgar Wind as the origin of this analysis of *rapere* as a translation of *harpazein* in *In Parmenidem* 5, col. 1033.27, in Proclus, *Procli philosophi Platonici opera inedita*, ed. Victor Cousin, 2nd ed. (Paris, 1864). See Wind, *Pagan Mysteries in the Renaissance* (New Haven, Conn.: Yale University Press, 1958), 48n1, 40nn4–5.

25. Teskey, *Allegory and Violence*, 18.

26. Linville writes, "The plea for a personal apocalypse or destruction of the old world of the self, and the summoning up of souls of Judgment Day, both entail annihilation of present temporal and spatial order, an annihilation which rhythm helps to reflect." Susan E. Linville, "Enjambment and the Dialectics of Line Form in Donne's 'Holy Sonnets,'" *Style* 18, no. 1 (Winter 1984), 68. See also Lisa Steinman's comment about "Batter my hart": "You could then also say that the predetermined metrical pattern of

the sonnet, into which the language tries to, but does not easily, fit echoes the theme of trying to submerge the ego or individual within a larger pattern, namely God's pattern." Steinman, *Invitation to Poetry: The Pleasures of Studying Poetry and Poetics* (Oxford: Blackwell, 2008), 98. I depart from Steinman's excellent insight here only by suggesting that the vocabulary of a submersion of self in God might be rendered more precise with reference to the process of self-annihilation and the transformation of self into an instrument of God that I bring to bear in my reading.

27. Compare Stanley Fish's claim that Herbert's poems "become the vehicle of their own abandonment" when we recognize that Christ is the substance of all things and the performer of all actions. Fish, *Self-Consuming Artifacts: The Experience of Seventeenth-Century Literature* (Berkeley: University of California Press, 1972), 157–58.

28. "A thought to Donne was an experience; it modified his sensibility. When a poet's mind is perfectly equipped for its work, it is constantly amalgamating disparate experience; the ordinary man's experience is chaotic, irregular, fragmentary. The latter falls in love, or reads Spinoza, and these two experiences have nothing to do with each other, or with the noise of the typewriter or the smell of cooking; in the mind of the poet these experiences are always forming new wholes. We may express the difference by the following theory: The poets of the seventeenth [Donne is Eliot's exemplar], the successors of the dramatists of the sixteenth, possessed a mechanism of sensibility which could devour any kind of experience." T. S. Eliot, "The Metaphysical Poets," in *Selected Essays* (London: Faber and Faber, 1934), 287.

29. Eggert suggests that in *The Faerie Queene*, "the narrative event of rape itself is a metaphoric maneuver, a substitute action foisted on the narrative in order to conceal or evade a rapturous mode of poetic operation." Eggert, "Spenser's Ravishment," 3. One could say something similar about "Batter my hart," but add that rape is foisted on the sonnet's narrative (insofar as it has one) in order to conceal or evade the *absence* of a rapturous mode of poetic operation.

30. James I, King of England, *King James VI and I: Political Writings*, ed. Johann P. Sommerville (Cambridge: Cambridge University Press, 1995), 86. Intriguingly, in the wake of the Gunpowder Plot, an act (anno 3, jac. 1, cap. 1: "An Act for a Publick Thanksgiving to Almighty God every Year on the Fifth Day of November") was issued, presumably with James's support, that required it be announced aloud in churches annually that James himself foiled the Gunpowder Plot thanks to divine inspiration: the Gunpowder Plot "would have turned to the utter ruin of this whole Kingdom, had it not pleased Almighty God, by inspiring the King's most Excellent Majesty with

a divine Spirit, to interpret some dark Phrases of a Letter shewed to His Majesty, above and beyond all ordinary Contraction, thereby miraculously discovering this hidden Treason not many Hours before the appointed Time for the Execution therof." See Church of England, *The Thirty-Nine Articles, and the Constitutions and Canons, of the Church of England; Together with Several Acts of Parliament and Proclamations Concerning Ecclesiastical Matters . . .* (London, 1773), 91.

31. "I have beene ever kept awake in a meditation of Martyrdome, by being derived from such a stocke and race, as, I beleeve, no family . . . hath endured and suffered more in their persons and fortunes, for obeying the Teachers of Romane Doctrine, then it hath done." Donne, *Pseudo-Martyr: Wherein out of certaine propositions and gradations, this conclusion is evicted. That those which are of the Romane religion in this Kingdome, may and ought to take the Oath of Allegiance,* ed. Anthony Raspa (Montreal: McGill-Queen's University Press, 1993), 8.

32. *Sermons of John Donne,* 8:312.

33. *Sermons of John Donne,* 8:313.

34. *Sermons of John Donne,* 8:320.

35. *Sermons of John Donne,* 8:327. For a brief but careful reading of Donne's analysis of grace and passivity in this sermon, see Brian Cummings, *The Literary Culture of the Reformation: Grammar and Grace* (Oxford: Oxford University Press, 2002), 416–17. Donne's phrase "meerely passive," according to Cummings, "expresses a grammatical, not a psychological, statement" (416), and I am indebted to his analysis of the significance of *metabalomenoi* as middle passive.

36. See Jonathan Goldberg, *James I and the Politics of Literature:* Jonson, *Shakespeare, Donne, and their Contemporaries* (Baltimore: Johns Hopkins University Press, 1983), 210–19; Annabel Patterson, *Censorship and Interpretation: The Conditions of Writing and Reading in Early Modern England* (Madison: University of Wisconsin Press, 1991), 100–13; Debora Shuger, *Habits of Thought in the English Renaissance: Religion, Politics and the Dominant Culture* (Toronto: University of Toronto Press, 1997), 159–217; and Jesse M. Lander, *Inventing Polemic: Religion, Print, and Literary Culture in Early Modern England* (Cambridge: Cambridge University Press, 2006), 145–79. Lander argues that in *Pseudo-Martyr,* Donne seeks to represent anyone who would not take the Oath of Allegiance (and thus potentially turn themselves into martyrs) as "fanatical extremists" (151). Though scholars have not explored the positive theory of martyrdom in Donne's writing that I outline in this chapter, some have analyzed Donne's contradictory feelings about James's need for obedience and his own investment in individual conscience. For example, Rebecca Lemon usefully studies how Donne agrees with and

departs from James's insistence on obedience, ultimately viewing Donne as conflicted: she insists on his skepticism toward martyrdom yet analyzes acutely how he articulates a right of conscience for Catholics and others. See Lemon, *Treason by Words: Literature, Law and Rebellion in Shakespeare's England* (Ithaca, N.Y.: Cornell University Press, 2006), 107–36. See also Nancy E. Wright, "The *Figura* of the Martyr in John Donne's Sermons," *ELH* 56, no. 2 (1989): 293–309. Wright emphasizes Donne's interest in recuperating a definition of martyr as "witness" while denying it to Catholics who were killed for their participation in the Gunpowder Plot. Olga Valbuena, "Casuistry, Martyrdom, and the Allegiance Controversy in Donne's 'Pseudo-Martyr,'" *Religion & Literature* 32, no. 2 (Summer 2000): 49–80, suggests that Donne can only endorse a "living martyrdom" that involves outward submission to sovereignty. Adam H. Kitzes, "Paradoxical Donne: *Biathanatos* and the Problems of Political Assimilation," *Prose Studies* 24, no. 3 (2001): 1–17, assiduously traces Donne's ambivalence toward martyrdom as an act that coincides with the natural inclination to suicide. Susannah Brietz Monta, *Martyrdom and Literature in Early Modern England* (Cambridge: Cambridge University Press, 2005), 131–50, argues that though Donne rejects martyrdom, he is still compelled by the idea that persecution and suffering are undeniable Christian virtues and difficult to disentangle from martyrdom. And James Kuzner, "Donne's *Biathanatos* and the Public Sphere's Vexing Freedom." *ELH* 81 (2014): 61–81, emphasizes how Donne implicitly questions any supposed demystification of the motives of martyrs by insisting on the opacity of conscience. For illuminating and important studies of Donne's commitment to freedom of conscience and skepticism toward all earthly power, see William Empson, "Donne the Spaceman," *Kenyon Review* 19, no. 3 (Summer 1957), 337–99; and Richard Strier, *Resistant Structures: Particularity, Radicalism, and Renaissance Texts* (Berkeley: University of California Press, 1995), 118–64.

37. Patterson, *Censorship and Interpretation*, 103.

38. Donne, *Pseudo-Martyr*, 8.

39. Donne, *Pseudo-Martyr*, 240.

40. Smith, "What's Inside?," 31.

41. Donne, *Biathanatos*, 46.

42. Donne, *Biathanatos*, 78. See the helpful commentary in the Introduction of Michael Rudick and M. Pabst Battin's edition of *Biathanatos* on Donne's radical departure from Aquinas's argument that "everything naturally keeps itself in being, and resists corruptions so far as it can (quaelibet res naturaliter conservat se in esse et corrumpentibus resistit quantum potest)" (l–li), though Donne will, perversely, cite Aquinas twice at just the moment when he defines the desire to be dissolved. Thomas

Aquinas, *Summa Theologiae, Secunda Secundae*, ed. John Mortensen and Enrique Alarcón, trans. Fr. Laurence Shapcote, O.P., 1–90 (Lander, Wyo.: The Aquinas Institute, 2012), q. 64, a. 5.

43. Donne, *Biathanatos*, 166–67. Donne returns to this phrase, *cupio dissolvi*, throughout his sermons; Katrin Ettenhuber has located a particularly large number of references in the sermons of 1625 and 1626. See Ettenhuber, *Donne's Augustine: Renaissance Cultures of Interpretation* (Oxford: Oxford University Press, 2011), 145n19. The phrase is a reference to the Vulgate translation of Philippians 1:23: "coartor autem e duobus desiderium habens dissolvi et cum Christo esse multo magis melius."

44. Donne, *Biathanatos*, 173.

45. Brad Gregory, *Salvation at Stake* (Cambridge: Harvard University Press, 2001), 8.

46. He will, for instance, sometimes shift quickly, even in a single passage, between valuing this passive, unexemplary theory of martyrdom and celebrating it as "an heroic act of fortitude" (Donne, *Biathanatos*, 173).

47. Donne *Biathanatos*, 187.

48. Donne *Biathanatos*, 182.

49. Donne *Biathanatos*, 181.

50. Donne *Biathanatos*, 181–82.

51. Kitzes, "Paradoxical Donne," 10–11.

52. In addition to Michael Heyd, *"Be Sober and Reasonable": The Critique of Enthusiasm in the Seventeenth and Early Eighteenth Centuries* (Leiden, Neth.: Brill, 1995), on the idea of enthusiastic madness in these writers, see Kinch Hoekstra, "Disarming the Prophets: Thomas Hobbes and Predictive Power," *Rivista di sotria della filosofia* 21, no. 1 (2004): 97–154.

53. Donne, *Biathanatos*, 77–78.

54. Donne, *Biathanatos*, 76.

55. Kitzes, "Paradoxical Donne," 10.

56. Donne, *Pseudo-Martyr*, 35.

57. On martyrdom's "uninterpretab[ility]" in *Pseudo-Martyr*, see also Cummings, *Literary Culture*, 375.

58. Martin Luther, "On Secular Authority," in *Luther and Calvin on Secular Authority*, ed. and trans. Harro Höpfl (Cambridge: Cambridge University Press, 1991), 22.

59. John Milton, *Milton: The Complete Shorter Poems*, ed. John Carey (Harlow: Pearson, 2007), lines 1709–10.

60. *Sermons of John Donne*, 10:241.

61. Kuzner has recently shown persuasively that Donne's account of suicide leads him to a general theory of public opacity that resonates with my analysis of the illegibility of Samson in Donne's account: "Donne insists

that the suicide's conscience is totally opaque to others; in this, Donne suggests an ethics that would never admit of public justification. . . . *Biathanatos* insists time and again on the opacity of conscience to all but oneself and God." Kuzner, "Donne's *Biathanatos*," 61–62, 66. Kuzner's important and persuasive argument seems to me just a little too quick to conclude that Donne "rejects the standard Augustinian reading that redeems Samson's self-inflicted death by attributing it to divine inspiration" (66). Once one puts into conversation Donne's comments on Samson in *Biathanatos*, *Pseudo-Martyr*, and select sermons, it becomes clear that Donne also renders the question of the judge's divine inspiration—not only what Kuzner refers to as his "conscience"—opaque. This specific opacity—the inability to determine if Samson was willful revenger or passive instrument of God—does more than question the "ethical standing" of Samson's death by making it impossible to know whether Samson undertook a willful suicide attack or was an instrument for God's action (67).

62. Alice Dailey, *The English Martyr from Reformation to Revolution* (Notre Dame, Ind.: Notre Dame University Press, 2012), 241. See also Dailey's claim that "the construction of martyrdom depends on the exteriorization and legibility—the public witness and testimony—of the heart of the victim, particularly in circumstances when an alternative text of the heart is being asserted, as in the injunction to behold the heart of a traitor" Dailey, *English Martyr*, 227. In Dailey's terms, Donne's model of martyrdom most closely resembles the illegibility and unverifiability of the conscience-based model of martyrdom she suggests Milton inaugurates.

63. For an account of the differences between these two traditions of imitation, see Richard Halpern, *The Poetics of Primitive Accumulation: English Renaissance Culture and the Genealogy of Capital* (Ithaca, N.Y.: Cornell University Press, 1991), 44–45. There, Halpern sees the crucial difference as follows: "The *imitatio cristi* always aimed—asymptotically, it is true—at the ideal of perfect imitation, so that the individual subject was ultimately absorbed and canceled by Christ as ideological model. Renaissance (or at least Erasmian) imitation, by contrast, posited and even encouraged an irreducible difference between model and copy, and thereby tended to redistribute some cultural authority to the latter." For Donne, the true imitation of Christ in martyrdom would not be willfully imitative—it would require that the subject who would imitate be annihilated and transformed into an instrument of the divine will. Donne's temporality of true martyrdom inverts Halpern's account of *imitatio Christi*: the canceling of the subject is not the ideal telos of imitation but that which makes imitation, understood as an intentional act, an impossible means of becoming a proper martyr.

64. Timothy Hampton, *Writing from History: The Rhetoric of Exemplarity in Renaissance Literature* (Ithaca, N.Y.: Cornell University Press, 1990), 4–5.

65. *Sermons of John Donne*, 9:278.

66. Bruce W. Young has shown that Hobbes was generally opposed to experimentation with poetic form, and one can only imagine that his worry over Spenser's, Donne's, and Milton's poetic experiments would be that much more acute given how those experiments emerge in part to cultivate a subtle engagement with fanaticism's epistemological and political ambiguities. See Young, "Thomas Hobbes versus the Poets: Form, Expression, and Metaphor in Early Seventeenth-Century Poetry," *Encyclia* 63: 151–62.

### 3. READERLY FANATICISM: HOBBES'S OUTWORKS

1. Thomas Hobbes, *Leviathan*, ed. Noel Malcolm (Oxford: Clarendon Press, 2012), Epistle Dedicatory, 6.

2. See Richard Tuck, "The 'Christian Atheism' of Thomas Hobbes," in *Atheism from the Reformation to the Enlightenment*, ed. Michael Cyril William Hunter and David Wootton (Oxford: Oxford University Press, 1992), 111–30; Peter Geach, "The Religion of Thomas Hobbes," *Religious Studies* 17, no. 4 (1981): 549–58; and Samuel L. Mintz, *The Hunting of Leviathan: Seventeenth-Century Reactions to the Materialism and Moral Philosophy of Thomas Hobbes* (Cambridge: Cambridge University Press, 1962). For an account that suggests that Hobbes's supposed atheism was interpreted at times during the Restoration, by a diverse group of theologians that included Samuel Parker and Ralph Cudworth, as a kind of (or enabling influence on) different kinds of "enthusiasm," see J. G. A. Pocock, "Thomas Hobbes: Atheist or Enthusiast? His Place in a Restoration Debate," *History of Political Thought* 11, no. 4 (1990): 737–49.

3. *The English Works of Thomas Hobbes of Malmesbury*, ed. Sir William Molesworth (London, 1839–45), 4:328.

4. Hobbes, *Leviathan*, chap. 8, p. 110.

5. Hobbes, *Leviathan*, Epistola Dedicatoria, 7.

6. I take Hobbes's "Enemy" first and foremost to be the fanatic, not least because Hobbes names the fanatic as the utmost threat. But it is true that this enemy takes many names in Hobbes's writing: fanatic, enthusiast, zealot, martyr, madman, and prophet, among others. Hobbes sometimes differentiates between these terms, though they are often conflated in his writing and strung together in a long list. For the purposes of this chapter, I propose that Hobbes generally defines fanatics as those who claim divine inspiration to justify disobeying the state and potentially even sacrificing their own lives.

7. Here, one senses in Hobbes's depiction of the state's vulnerability to fanaticism something along the lines of what Barbara Johnson has called "muteness envy": "Far from being the opposite of authority, victimhood would seem to be the most effective *model* for authority, particularly literary and cultural authority. It is not that the victim always gets to speak—far from it—but that the most highly valued speaker gets to claim victimhood." See Johnson, "Muteness Envy," in *The Barbara Johnson Reader: The Surprise of Otherness*, ed. Melissa Feuerstein, Bill Johnson González, Lili Porten, and Keja L. Valens (Durham, N.C.: Duke University Press, 2014), 215.

8. Hobbes dispatches with this blurring of inside and outside in the Latin edition: "quia loca illa Potestatem Civilem oppugnantibus, quasi Inimicorum." Hobbes, *Leviathan*, Epistola Dedicatoria, 7.

9. See, respectively, Tomaž Mastnak, "Behemoth: Democraticals and Religious Fanatics," *Filozofski vestnik* 24, no. 2 (2003): 139–68; and Kinch Hoekstra, "Disarming the Prophets: Thomas Hobbes and Predictive Power," *Rivista di sotria della filosofia* 21, no. 1 (2004): 97–154. Though our emphases are different, I have learned a great deal from Hoekstra's comprehensive account of Hobbes's skepticism toward claims of divine inspiration. The method of Hoekstra's perspicacious study requires that he accept uncritically Hobbes's argument that all claims to divine inspiration are false, and he seems to accept Hobbes's contention that "demonstrating their falsity destroys the belief, and obviates the effect. . . . By blunting the belief in prophecy, Hobbes disarms the prophet." Hoekstra, "Disarming the Prophets," 141, 151.

10. Victoria Kahn, *Wayward Contracts: The Crisis of Political Obligation in England, 1640–1674* (Princeton: Princeton University Press, 2004), 170.

11. See Hoekstra, "Disarming the Prophets," 137, on Hobbes's suggestion that belief in divine inspiration spreads like a contagious disease.

12. Leo Strauss, *Hobbes's Critique of Religion and Related Writings*, trans. Gabriel Bartlett and Svetoza Minkov (Chicago: University of Chicago Press, 2011); originally published in *Leo Strauss: Gesammelte Schriften*, vol. 3, *Hobbes' politische Wissenschagt und zugehoerige Schriften—Briefe*, ed. Heinrich Meier and Wibke Meier, 2nd rev. ed. (Stuttgart: J. B. Metzler, 2008).

13. Pocock, "Time, History and Eschatology in the Thought of Thomas Hobbes," in *Politics, Language, and Time: Essays on Political Thought and History* (New York: Atheneum, 1960), 166.

14. For the strategic reasons that Hobbes wishes to "block political historicism" and tie sovereignty to the ahistorical laws of logic as a way of eliminating the problem of the Conquest of England, see Michel Foucault, *Society Must Be Defended: Lectures at the Collège de France, 1975–1976*, ed. Mauro Bertani and Alessandro Fontana, trans. David Macey (New York: Picador, 2003), 97–111.

15. Hobbes, *Leviathan*, chap. 3, p. 46. See also chap. 34, pp. 610–33, in which Hobbes repeats this idea in order to achieve a materialist "constant Signification" of the words "spirit" and "inspiration," countering arguments that seek to prove the existence of incorporeal substances or bodies. Aryeh Botwinick has gone so far as to place this claim within the history of negative theology and James Martel follows him. See Botwinick, *Skepticism, Belief, and the Modern: Maimonides to Nietzsche* (Ithaca, N.Y.: Cornell University Press, 1997), 112–63; and Martel, *Subverting the Leviathan: Reading Thomas Hobbes as a Radical Democrat* (New York: Columbia University Press, 2007), 68–70, 79–106. Pocock has emphasized the Jewish influences in Hobbes's "radically nominalist theology," which entails "a God of whom nothing could be known except his existence and his infinite power," and dismisses the God of Greek and scholastic philosophy "in favour of a purely Hebrew I AM." Pocock, "Time, History and Eschatology," 193. I agree with Pocock that Hobbes's radical nominalism leads Hobbes to posit a God of whom nothing can be known, but Hobbes has no patience for the central concerns of negative theologians (e.g., divine names, theophany, apophatic language, and the annihilation of the soul). For a careful account of the relationship between nominalism and mysticism during the Reformation, see Steven Ozment, "Mysticism, Nominalism, and Dissent," in *The Pursuit of Holiness in Late Medieval and Renaissance Religion*, ed. Charles Trinkaus with Heiko Oberman (Leiden, Neth.: Brill, 1974), 67–92.

16. Hobbes, *Leviathan*, chap. 36, p. 664. Hobbes claims that the prophets generally received God's word through "the imaginations which they had in their sleep, or in an Extasie" (chap. 36, p. 666), except perhaps for Moses, who had a somewhat more familiar relationship with God, which I analyze later. Hobbes's thinking on the historically mediated condition of the Bible, and the Pentateuch in particular, is generally consistent throughout his career, but specific aspects do change, especially between *De cive* and *Leviathan*. Noel Malcolm shows convincingly that *Leviathan* inaugurates Hobbes's argument that Moses was not the author of the Pentateuch. See Malcolm, "Hobbes, Ezra, and the Bible: The History of a Subversive Idea," in *Aspects of Hobbes* (Oxford: Oxford University Press, 2002), 383–431.

17. Hobbes, *Leviathan*, chap. 32, p. 578. The text continues: "It is true, that if he be my Soveraign, he may oblige me to obedience, so, as not by act or word to declare I beleeve him not; but not to think any otherwise then my reason perswades me. But if one that hath not such authority over me, shall pretend the same, there is nothing that exacteth beleefe, or obedience" (578). I will return to this distinction between public profession and private belief later in this chapter.

18. Hobbes, *Leviathan*, chap. 32, p. 580.

19. Hoekstra, "Disarming the Prophets," 126–27. Hoekstra there argues that the only time Hobbes (ambivalently) approves of a pretended claim of divine inspiration is "when the pretender uses imposture to set up sovereign order where there was none, or to reinforce it where he is already sovereign" (127). He also claims that "Hobbes may equivocate about the idea of sovereign enthusiasm in the case of Moses" (129n141).

20. Hobbes, *Leviathan*, chap. 7, pp. 100–2.

21. Hobbes notes, somewhat cryptically, that when the Bible asserts that God is "speaking to men immediately," what it means by "speaking to men immediately" is "that way (whatsoever it be), by which God makes them understand his will: And the wayes whereby he doth this, are many; and to be sought onely in the Holy Scripture: where though many times it be said, that God spake to this, and that person, without declaring in what manner; yet there be again many places, that deliver also the signes by which they were to acknowledge his presence, and commandement; and by these may be understood, how he spake to many of the rest." Hobbes, *Leviathan*, chap. 36, p. 662.

22. John Calvin, *Institutio Christianae Religionis* (Paris, 1559); Calvin, *Institutes of the Christian Religion*, ed. John T. McNeill, trans. Ford Lewis Battles (Louisville: Westminster Press, 1960), 1.7.1. The first French and English editions were published in 1560 and 1561, respectively. For a helpful study of Reformation debates about the authority of the Bible, see Henk van den Belt, *The Authority of Scripture in Reformed Theology: Truth and Trust* (Leiden, Neth.: Brill, 2008).

23. Hobbes, *Leviathan*, chap. 40, p. 746.

24. Hobbes, *Leviathan*, chap. 36, p. 664.

25. Hobbes, *Leviathan*, chap. 36, pp. 664–66. On rabbinic claims about what Moses and the Jews heard at Sinai, and about Maimonides's suggestion that God spoke to Moses but that the Jews heard nothing or perhaps only a voice but not distinct words, see Daniel Heller-Roazen, "Speaking in Tongues," *Paragraph* 25, no. 2 (2002): 101–3.

26. Hobbes, *Leviathan*, chap. 36, p. 668.

27. Hobbes, *Leviathan*, chap. 33, p. 586. Malcolm argues that Hobbes's desire for ultimate authority and interpretative univocity of scripture resembles the rigidity of institutionalized Catholic hierarchies of scriptural interpretation. See Malcolm, "Leviathan, the Pentateuch, and the Origins of Modern Biblical Criticism," in *Leviathan after 350 Years*, ed. Tom Sorell and Luc Foisneau (Oxford: Clarendon Press, 2004), 256–57. Malcolm also claims that Hobbes's philology presupposes God as "unattainable and unknowable, and thus caus[es] the Scriptures to be essentially indistinguishable from any other human writing" (261). See also Arrigo Pacchi, "Hobbes and Biblical

Philology in the Service of the State," *Topoi* 7, no. 3 (1988): 233; and
C. B. Macpherson, *The Political Theory of Possessive Individualism: Hobbes to Locke*
(Oxford: Clarendon, 1962), 90–95. Strauss has shown lucidly but controver-
sially that this univocity of the sovereign's interpretation of scripture is
unique to *Leviathan*, contrasting sharply with *Elements of Law* and *De cive*, in
which Hobbes had defended the Episcopal constitution of the Church of
England and therefore the church's claim to be an interpreter of scripture in
potential competition with the sovereign. Strauss, *The Political Philosophy of
Hobbes: Its Basis and Its Genes*, trans. Elsa M. Sinclair (Chicago: University of
Chicago Press, 1952), 73.

28. Hobbes, *Leviathan*, chap. 21, p. 328. For an interpretation of this
passage in light of Lucian's fable of Hercules, see Quentin Skinner, *Hobbes
and Republican Liberty* (Cambridge: Cambridge University Press, 2008), 170.

29. Hobbes, *Leviathan*, chap. 32, p. 578.

30. Hobbes, *Leviathan*, chap. 32, p. 584. Compare Hobbes, *The Elements
of Law, Natural and Politic*, ed. Ferdinand Tönnies (London, 1889), 26.11.

31. See D. P. Walker, "The Cessation of Miracles," in *Hermeticisim and
the Renaissance: Intellectual History and the Occult in Early Modern Europe*, ed.
Ingrid Merkel and Allen G. Debus (Washington, D.C.: Folger Shakespeare
Library, 1988), 110–24.

32. See Hobbes, *Leviathan*, chap. 32, p. 585: "Cessantibus autem jam
pridem Miraculis, signum, quô Revelationem, aut Inspirationem hominis
cujusquam privati cognoscamus, aut ad Doctrinam ejus recipiendam
obligemur, habemus nullum, praeter Scripturas Sacras, quae à temore
Apostolorum miraculorum locum supplent, & Prophetiae cessationem satis
compensant."

33. See Colossians 2:9–10 (KJV): "For in him dwelleth all the fullness of
the Godhead bodily. And ye are complete in him, which is the head of all
principality and power." Vulgate: "quia in ipso inhabitat omnis plenitudo
divinitatis corporaliter et estis in illo repleti qui est caput omnis principatus
et potestatis." Greek Bible: "hoti en autō katoikei pan to plērōma tēs
Theotētos sōmatikōs, kai este en autō peplērōmenoi, hos estin hē kephalē
pasēs archēs kai exousias." Hobbes evacuates the meaning from "plērōma"
in a reading of Mark 1:15 as well, reducing the coming of Christ to a mere
announcement of "good news": "And our Saviour preached, saying, *The Time
is fulfilled, and the Kingdome of God is at hand, Repent and Beleeve the Evangile*
[Mark 1:15], that is, the Good news that the Christ was come. Therefore to
Repent, and to Beleeve that Jesus is the Christ, is all that is required to
Salvation." Hobbes, *Leviathan*, chap. 43, p. 950.

34. See Eric Nelson's *The Hebrew Republic: Jewish Sources and the Transformation of European Political Thought* (Cambridge: Harvard University Press,

2011), especially Chapters 1 and 2, on how interpretations of Hebrew biblical texts in seventeenth-century Europe "transformed the politics of the modern world" and cast monarchy itself as a sin (26). Nelson's focus is on republican exegetes who resist sovereignty, rather than on those more radical or millenarian sects of the English Revolution that claimed inspiration directly from God, though Hobbes tends to conflate all under the banner of "fanaticism."

35. My argument here is indebted to Pocock, who has developed the most persuasive analysis of Hobbes's commentary on the election of Saul. See Pocock, "Time, History and Eschatology," 170–71. See also Pacchi's argument that, according to Hobbes, "the civil nature of this divine sovereignty was emphasized by the fact that it ended at the point when the Jews passed from the rule of Priests to a true human monarchy, after the political crisis at the time of the Judges." Pacchi, "Hobbes and Biblical Philology," 237.

36. This is the KJV (1611) of excerpts from verses 5 and 7. In the Vulgate, the term God uses to describe God's rejection by the Jews in their demand for an earthly king is *abiecerunt*, from *abicio*, meaning "to throw or hurl down violently." The Hebrew, *ma'asu*, comes from the root *ma'ac*, meaning "to abhor."

37. Hobbes's peculiar views on prophecy are discussed in the previous section of this chapter.

38. Hobbes, *Leviathan*, chap. 35, p. 640.

39. Hobbes, *Leviathan*, chap. 35, p. 640.

40. See also Pocock: "It would on the whole appear that a kingdom of men legitimized by nature exists only in an interlude of sin and rebellion against God. The king reigns in God's absence, but that absence is caused by the king's election." Pocock, "Time, History and Eschatology," 172n40. Whereas Pocock argues that Hobbes believes this history of rebellion and the origins of kingship, I claim that his account is part of a strategy to create a vision of eschatology that undermines religion's ability to authorize the disobeying of sovereign civil power. Admittedly, this is a different kind of rebellion from the one Hobbes worries about in his own age; whereas the rebellion against God is meant to institute a king as sovereign, the kinds of rebellion that Hobbes battled were meant to get rid of kingship altogether.

41. Nelson, *Hebrew Republic*, 25. Nelson claims that the utterly new readings of 1 Samuel 8 became possible for one reason: "The reading in question derives from a tradition of rabbinic commentary on Deuteronomy and 1 Samuel that became available to the Christian West only during the Hebrew revival of the late sixteenth and early seventeenth centuries" (26). It

is perhaps not surprising, as Nelson also shows, that Hobbes's exegesis of 1 Samuel 8 was met with more hostility from Hobbes's contemporaries than was just about any other passage in *Leviathan*.

42. Hobbes, *Leviathan*, chap. 40, p. 756.

43. See Christopher Hill, *The World Turned Upside Down: Radical Ideas during the English Revolution* (New York: Penguin, 1984).

44. Hobbes, *Leviathan*, chap. 41, p. 768. This typology also informs Hobbes's bold recasting of the Trinity as a relationship of Moses, Jesus, and Apostles rather than as Father, Son, and Holy Ghost; see Hobbes, *Leviathan*, chap. 42, p. 776: "Here wee have the Person of God born now the third time. For as Moses, and the High Priests, were Gods Representative in the Old Testament; and our Savior himselfe as Man, during his abode on earth: So the Holy Ghost, that is to say, the Apostles, and their successors, in the office of Preaching, and Teaching, that had received the Holy Spirit, have Represented him ever since. But a Person, (as I have shewn before, chapt. 13.) is he that is Represented; and therefore God, who has been Represented (that is, Personated) thrice, may properly enough be said to be three Persons." On Hobbes's antitrinitarianism in Chapter 42 of the English *Leviathan* as a form of "modalisme juridique" that denies the distinctions between the persons of God, see Alexandre Matheron, "Hobbes, la Trinité et les caprices de la représentation," in *Thomas Hobbes: Philosophie première, théorie de la science et politique*, ed. Yves Charles Zarka and Jean Bernhardt (Paris: Presses universitaires de France, 1990), 381–90. For a defense of Hobbes as sincere Trinitarian, see A. P. Martinich, *The Two Gods of Leviathan* (Cambridge: Cambridge University Press, 2003), 203–8. For Hobbes's attempt to unearth a pre-Boethian definition of *persona* in Cicero (person not as substance but as someone acting on behalf of another who would justify) as a method of justifying his ideas about the Trinity, see Mónica Brito Vieira, *The Elements of Representation in Hobbes: Aesthetics, Theatre, Law and Theology in the Construction of Hobbes's Theory of the State* (Leiden, Neth.: Brill, 2009), 209–34.

45. Hobbes, *Leviathan*, chap. 41, p. 764.

46. Hobbes, *Leviathan*, chap. 35, p. 642. The radical nature of this claim that the Lord's Prayer is superfluous should not be underestimated. For an argument for the essential nature of this prayer ("Thy kingdom come"), see Calvin, *Institutes of the Christian Religion*, 2.20.43.

47. Hobbes, *Leviathan*, chap. 38, pp. 698–725.

48. Hobbes, *Leviathan*, chap. 46, p. 1084.

49. Hobbes, *Leviathan*, chap. 41, p. 762.

50. See Nigel Smith, *Perfection Proclaimed: Language and Literature in English Radical Religion, 1640–1660* (Oxford: Oxford University Press, 1989);

and Crawford Gribben, *The Puritan Millennium: Literature and Theology, 1550–1682* (Eugene, Ore.: Wipf and Stock, 2008). On Fifth Monarchists' particular attachment to millenarianism, see Bernard Capp, *The Fifth Monarchy Men: A Study in Seventeenth-Century English Millenarianism* (London: Faber, 1972).

51. Hobbes, *English Works*, 4:327.

52. Hobbes, *Behemoth, or The Long Parliament*, ed. Paul Seaward (Oxford: Clarendon Press, 2010), 291.

53. Hobbes, *Leviathan*, chap. 43, pp. 949–50.

54. For example, Gerrard Winstanley's discussion of false saviors in "A New Year's Gift for the Parliament and Army," in *Winstanley: "The Law of Freedom" and other Writings*, edited by Christopher Hill (Cambridge: Cambridge University Press, 1983), 194: "Then next the art of buying and selling promises to save the creation and bring it into peace; but this is a hypocritical false cheating Christ too. For hereby covetous self-love with his flattering tongue cheats honest-hearted ones and casts them under tyranny, and gets the fulness of the earth into his hands, and lock[s] it up in chests and barns from others, and saith this is righteous and God gave it him. But thou cheater, thou liest; God the King of righteousness gave it thee not, he bids thee sell all that thou hast and give to the poor. . . . Now all these saviours . . . set up self and particular power, and so to save but part of the creation, for every one are destroyers of universal love." Sometimes this passage from Luke was conflated with Acts 4:32, as in the famous passage from Winstanley, "The True Levellers Standard Advanced: or, The State of Community Opened, and Presented to the Sons of Men": "And when the Son of Man, was gone from the apostles, his spirit descended upon the apostles and brethren, as they were waiting at Jerusalem; and rich men sold their possessions, and gave part to the poor; and no man said that ought that he possessed was his own, for they had all things Common, Acts 4.32" (88).

55. More recently, unorthodox readings have suggested that Hobbes is undercutting the very grounds of sovereignty after Saul. Martel, to take a radical and intriguing case, makes the surprising argument that between Saul and the Second Coming, no proper sovereignty is possible, only poor imitations of Moses's real sovereignty—power-hungry idolaters "simply asserting themselves without any foundational substance." Martel, *Subverting the Leviathan*, 74.

56. Hobbes, *Leviathan*, chap. 12, pp. 164–66.

57. Hobbes, *Leviathan*, chap. 12, pp. 164–66.

58. Hobbes, *Leviathan*, chap. 36, p. 680.

59. John Locke, *A Letter Concerning Toleration*, ed. James Tully (New York: Hackett, 1983), 33. On the privatization of religion as a tool of

depoliticization, see Wendy Brown, *Regulating Aversion: Tolerance in the Age of Identity and Empire* (Princeton: Princeton University Press, 2008), 1–47. For a Foucauldian critique of the privatization of belief in the history of liberalism that calls into question its definition of and prioritization of freedom as subjective agency, see Saba Mahmood, *The Politics of Piety: The Islamic Revival and the Feminist Subject* (Princeton: Princeton University Press, 2004).

60. Carl Schmitt, *The Leviathan in the State Theory of Thomas Hobbes: Meaning and Failure of a Political Symbol*, trans. George Schwab and Erna Hilfstein (Chicago: University of Chicago Press, 2008), 57. On conscience as the most dangerous metaphor for Hobbes, see Karen S. Feldman, "Conscience and the Concealments of Metaphor in Hobbes's *Leviathan*," *Philosophy and Rhetoric* 34, no. 1 (2001): 21–37. See also Alan Ryan, "Hobbes, Toleration, and the Inner Life," in *The Nature of Political Theory*, ed. David Miller and Larry Siedentop (Oxford: Clarendon Press, 1983); and Tuck, "Hobbes and Locke on Toleration," in *Thomas Hobbes and Political Theory*, ed. Mary Dietz (Lawrence: University Press of Kansas, 1990), 153–71.

61. Hobbes, *Leviathan*, chap. 37, p. 696.

62. Hobbes's original discussion of conscience in *Elements of Law* is very different; there he reduces conscience to mere opinion, opinion that is only settled insofar as it is determined by the public will of the sovereign: "For the conscience being nothing else but a man's settled judgment and opinion, when he hath once transferred his right of judging to another, that which shall be commanded, is no less his judgment, than the judgment of that other; so that in obedience to laws, a man doth still according to his conscience, but not his private conscience" (2.6.12). For a reading of this passage that claims that there is no internal conscience in Hobbes that is not already a function of sovereign judgment, see Tuck, "Hobbes and Democracy," in *Rethinking the Foundations of Modern Political Thought* (Cambridge: Cambridge University Press, 2007), especially 174–75.

63. Michael Walzer, *The Revolution of the Saints: A Study in the Origins of Radical Politics* (Cambridge: Harvard University Press, 1982), 42.

64. Hobbes, *Leviathan*, Introduction, 18.

65. Hobbes's translation was almost certainly intentional, since there is no lack of evidence to demonstrate his tremendous ability to translate classical Latin and Greek. "Know thyself" was the standard translation of *nosce teipsum* in Hobbes's time. Interestingly, the contemporary texts that dispute Hobbes's understanding of the Delphic maxim in *Leviathan* (and which were usually critical of his idea that it should apply to discovering the similitude of the thoughts or passions of others) sometimes use Hobbes's vocabulary of "reading" and sometimes translate it into the terms of knowing.

For an example of the former, see Edward Hyde, Earl of Clarendon, *A Brief View and Survey of the Dangerous and Pernicious Errors to Church and State, in M. Hobbes's Book, entitled Leviathan* (Oxford, 1676), 11–15; for the latter, see James Lowde, *A Discourse Concerning the Nature of Man, Both in his Natural and Political Capacity: Both as he is a Rational Creature and Member of a Civil Society. With an Examination of Some of Mr. Hobbs's Opinions relating hereunto* (London, 1694), 2–3.

66. See Hobbes, *Elements of Law*, 1.5.14.

67. See Kahn, *Wayward Contracts*, Chapter 6, especially 149–50, where she writes, "In the Introduction to *Leviathan* as well, political contract depends on our subscribing to a linguistic contract. . . . A precondition of this stipulation is the contract to redescribe the potentially dangerous social construction of the passions as a matter of 'fixed similitude.' . . . Crucial to this contract is a clarification of the relation of passions to the imagination—a clarification, that is, regarding mimetic desire. Contract in the Introduction then is a metaphor for both the Hobbesian commonwealth and the process of analogical reasoning that checks the errant activity of the imagination. . . . To shore up this perception of likeness in the Introduction, Hobbes eliminates the diverse objects of the passions and, while recommending comparison, he also eliminates other human subjects, as though in tacit recognition that mimetic desire feeds on the imagination and perception of others, and generates not only rivalry but dissimulation."

68. Hobbes, *Leviathan*, chap. 16, p. 248.

69. On representation in Hobbes, see Hanna Pitkin, *The Concept of Representation* (Berkeley: University of California Press, 1972); and Skinner, "Hobbes on Representation," *European Journal of Philosophy* 13, no. 2 (2005): 155–84, especially 170: "It is true that, once the individual members of the multitude agree to submit to a sovereign, this finally has the effect of converting them from a mere throng into one Person. This is because they now have a single will and voice—that of their sovereign representative—which counts as the voice of them all."

70. Hobbes, *Leviathan*, chap. 8, pp. 110–14.

71. I do not claim that Hobbes's "may" is meant to be at all tentative here; more likely, it is meant to be an invitation to assurance. But the equivocation of the term allows us to see "may" in contrast with the certainty of "is," even if that is not at all the intention we might logically project behind this sentence.

72. On madmen (along with children as fools) as incapable of being authors of their own actions, and therefore not fulfilling a necessary feature of Hobbes's definition of the human person, see Hobbes, *Leviathan*, chap. 16, p. 248.

73. Hobbes, *English Works*, 4:328. Hobbes also claims Bramhall misunderstands what "inspiration" is: while, according to Hobbes, Bramhall "understands it properly of God's breathing into a man, or pouring into him the Divine substance, or Divine graces," Hobbes claims that inspiration is only a metaphor for pedagogy, "for God's guidance of our minds to truth and piety." Hobbes, *English Works*, 4:327–28. I analyze Hobbes's redefinition of inspiration in more detail at the start of Chapter 4.

74. Hobbes, *English Works*, 4:328.

75. See Karl Gerhard Steck, *Luther und die Schwärmer* (Zurich: Evangelischer Verlag, 1955); Niklaus Largier, "Mysticism, Modernity, and the Invention of Aesthetic Experience," *Representations* 105 (2009): 37–60; and Ozment, *Mysticism and Dissent*. For the evolution of understanding madness in seventeenth-century England, see Michael MacDonald, *Mystical Bedlam: Madness, Anxiety, and Healing in Seventeenth-Century England* (Cambridge: Cambridge University Press, 1983).

76. Hobbes, *English Works*, 4:327. Hobbes claims that he and Bramhall are in agreement about the great danger of fanaticism: "I think his Lordship was of my opinion; for he called those men, which in the late civil war pretended the spirit, and new light, and to be the only faithful men, fanatics; for he called them in his book, and did call them in his life-time, fanatics." Hobbes, *English Works*, 4:328.

77. On Hobbes's fear of the multitude and his attempt to reduce the right of resistance to solitary individuals that should never become part of such a collective roar, see Warren Montag, *Bodies, Masses, Power: Spinoza and His Contemporaries* (London: Verso, 1999), 119.

78. Hobbes, *De cive: The English Version*, ed. Howard Warrender (Oxford: Clarendon Press, 1983); Hobbes, *De cive: The Latin Version*, ed. Howard Warrender (Oxford: Clarendon Press, 1983), 18.13.

79. Hobbes, *Leviathan*, chap. 42, pp. 786–88.

80. Hobbes, *Leviathan*, chap. 42, p. 788.

81. Hobbes, *Leviathan*, chap. 42, p. 788.

82. Hobbes, *Leviathan*, chap. 14, p. 214.

83. For a brief survey of early modern accounts of whether or not Jesus's death counts as sacrifice, see Jonathan Sheehan, "Sacrifice before the Secular," *Representations* 105 (Winter 2009): 12–36. The Socinian counterargument would be that Jesus's death is not actually a sacrifice necessary for salvation (Jesus's forgiveness is sufficient) but the sign of his benevolent nature.

84. See Hobbes, *De cive*, 6.13.

85. See Susanne Sreedhar, *Hobbes on Resistance: Defying the Leviathan* (Cambridge: Cambridge University Press, 2010), 77–78, on the fact that this

is the single example of Hobbes putting a dishonorable command in a sovereign's mouth. She suggests that it is, in fact, so dishonorable that obeying it would actually undercut the purpose of sovereignty, since it would require the son to "live in infamy and loathing."

86. Hobbes, *Leviathan*, chap. 14, p. 198. For a reading of how all primary, formal appetites (those innate appetites such as hunger) relate to the Law of Nature and thus encompass the forbidding of self-destruction in Hobbes's philosophy, see Ioannis D. Evrigens, *Fear of Enemies and Collective Action* (Cambridge: Cambridge University Press, 2008), 106–7.

87. See *The Judgment and Decree of the University of Oxford* (Oxford, 1683), 3–4. On this burning of Hobbes's books, see Christopher Warren, "When Self-Preservation Bids: Approaching Milton, Hobbes and Dissent," *English Literary Renaissance* 37 (2007): 134–35, in which Warren explains that one reason that Hobbes's books were burned was that his argument about self-preservation had been appropriated by dissenters' arguments during the Restoration. The Earl of Clarendon was worried early on about the centrality of Hobbes's doctrine of self-preservation, especially because of the kinds of self-defense it might license. See Clarendon, *Brief View and Survey*, 138–43.

88. In *Leviathan*, the one possible exception remaining to Hobbes's insistence on self-preservation is his declaration, in the Review and Conclusion, that military defense of the state is necessary:

> To the Laws of Nature, declared in the 15. Chapter, I would have this added, That every man is bound by Nature, as much as in him lieth, to protect in Warre, the Authority, by which he is himself protected in time of Peace. For he that pretendeth a Right of Nature to preserve his owne body, cannot pretend a Right of Nature to destroy him, by whose strength he is preserved: It is a manifest contradiction of himselfe. And though this Law may bee drawn by consequence, from some of those that are there already mentioned; yet the Times require to have it inculcated, and remembered. (Hobbes, *Leviathan*, Review and Conclusion, 1133)

This exception—if it is one—does not contradict my argument, since Hobbes only declares that the possible self-sacrifice inherent in being a soldier in war is necessary insofar as one is protecting the sovereign who protects the soldier's life in a time of peace. Though it sounds like a paradox to risk one's life to protect the sovereign's protection of it, Hobbes claims that it would actually be a "contradiction of himself" if one did not fight to preserve the authority that protects oneself. This particular form of self-sacrifice is acceptable for Hobbes only because it protects the sovereign. See also Deborah Baumgold, "Soldiers and Subjects: Hobbes on

Military Service," *History of Political Thought* 4, no. 1 (1983): 43–63. Compare the following passage: "And whereas he saith the law of nature is a law without our assent, it is absurd; for the law of nature is the assent itself that all men give to the means of their own preservation." Hobbes, *English Works*, 5:180.

89. Hobbes, *Elements of Law*, 1.14.6.

90. Hobbes, *De cive*, 1.7. I have silently altered the 1651 English translation for clarity.

91. See Strauss, *Hobbes's Critique of Religion*, 91.

92. Hobbes, *Elements of Law*, 1.1.8 (my emphasis).

93. On the importance of this annihilation of the world experiment for Hobbes, see Strauss, *Hobbes's Critique of Religion*, 92–105, in which he analyzes this fundamental human resistance to the possibility of self-annihilation. Strauss writes, "If being is fundamentally resistibility, being must be radically understood from the most fundamental instance of resistance. But the most fundamental resistance is the resistance on the part of other men that threatens my life. Therefore, fear of violent death not only is the principle of right and of the state, but is at the same time the principle of *all* reasonable conduct, of all enlightenment, of all awakening to the understanding of being" (*Hobbes's Critique of Religion*, 104n277). See also Yves Charles Zarka, "*L'Annihilatio Mundi*," in *La décision metaphysique de Hobbes: Conditions de la politique* (Paris: Librairie Philosophique J. Vrin, 1987), 36–58.

94. See Matthew 26:53–54 (KJV): "Thinkest thou that I cannot now pray to my Father, and he shall presently give me more than twelve legions of angels? But how then shall the scriptures be fulfilled, that thus it must be?" This passage describes how Jesus's renunciation of resistance at the moment of his arrest by agents of Roman sovereignty is precisely this *fulfillment*— again the term *plērōthōsin* is from *plērōma*—of the law, with the law here being figured as scriptures, *graphe*.

95. See Zarka, "The Political Subject," in *Leviathan after 350 Years*, ed. Tom Sorell and Luc Foisneau (Oxford: Clarendon, 2004), 167–82, especially 180. Whereas Zarka claims that Hobbes's "right of resistance defines, from now on, the proper sphere on which the political power cannot encroach" (180), the figure of the fanatic, inseparable from self-annihilation, offers the outlines of an inverted model of resistance, one that locates resistance in a sacrifice of the natural law of self-preservation. For fuller accounts of active resistance in Hobbes, see Glenn Burgess, "On Hobbesian Resistance Theory," *Political Studies* 42, no. 1 (1994): 62–83; Sreedhar, *Hobbes on Resistance*; and Eleanor Curran, *Reclaiming the Rights of the Hobbesian Subject* (Houndmills, Eng.: Palgrave Macmillan, 2007).

96. Debora Shuger, *The Renaissance Bible: Scholarship, Sacrifice, and Subjectivity* (Berkeley: University of California Press, 1994), 72n57. Shuger cites Hugo Grotius, *Defensio fidei catholicae de satisfactione Christi adversus Faustum Socinum*, in *Opera omnia theologica in tres tomos divisa*, ed. Theodore Hillensberg (Amsterdam: Blaeu, 1679), vol. 4, p. 315.

97. Hobbes, *Leviathan*, chap. 36, p. 668.

98. On Hobbes's denial of the divinity of Jesus despite his occasional reference to him as God and Man, see Strauss, *Hobbes's Critique of Religion*, 71. This was also a charge that was made against Hobbes a number of times in his life: see for example Bramhall's claim, which Hobbes quotes in his posthumously published final rebuttal, that Hobbes "knoweth no difference between one who is mere man, and one who is both God and man; between a Levitical sacrifice, and the all-sufficient sacrifice of the cross; between the blood of a calf, and the precious blood of the Son of God." Hobbes's response is characteristically dismissive: "Yes, I know there is a difference between blood and blood, but not any such as can make a difference in the case here questioned. Our Saviour's blood was most precious, but still it was human blood; and I hope his Lordship did never think otherwise, or that it was not accepted by his Father for our redemption." Hobbes, *English Works*, 4:324. See Jeffrey Collins, *The Allegiance of Thomas Hobbes* (Oxford: Oxford University Press, 2008), for an assessment of the evolution of the debate over whether Hobbes truly denied Jesus's divinity or maintained a true trinitarianism.

99. This is the KJV translation (1611).

100. Hobbes, *De cive*, 15.15. "The one who fashions the sacred images from gold or marble does not make the Gods; he who prays makes them." Martial, *Epigrams*, vol. 2, Loeb Classical Library (Cambridge: Harvard University Press, 1993), 8.24.5–6.

101. On the sovereign as "Mortall God," see Hobbes, *Leviathan*, chap. 17, p. 260. Recent research on the origins of Hobbes's reference to "Mortall God" relates it, somewhat surprisingly, to the Hermetic text reproduced in the Renaissance called *Asclepius*. See Horst Bredekamp, *Thomas Hobbes. Der Leviathan: Das Urbild des modernen Staates und seine Gegenbilder: 1651–2001* (Berlin: Akademie Verlag), 56–71; and Gianni Paganini, "Hobbes's 'Mortal God' and Renaissance Hermeticism," *Hobbes Studies* 23 (2010): 7–28.

## 4. TRAGIC FANATICISM: MILTON'S MOTIONS

1. I leave aside here the larger question of how Hobbes's determinism recasts the question of passion and action in his own philosophy. Suffice it to say that an action is not the expression of a free will for Hobbes; it emerges from a chain of causation that cannot be chosen. For more on Hobbes's

conception of the will, see Jürgen Overhoff, *Hobbes's Theory of the Will: Ideological Reasons and Historical Circumstances* (Lanham, Md.: Rowman and Littlefield, 2000).

2. Thomas Hobbes, *Leviathan*, ed. Noel Malcolm (Oxford: Clarendon Press, 2012), chap. 34, p. 616.

3. Since Hobbes refers to zeal and courage as "extraordinary affections" in the marginal heading, he never takes the time to define affections precisely in this section, though elsewhere in his writing he usually assumes that "affections" is a synonym for "passions"; the passions are defined at length in Chapter 6 of *Leviathan*, titled "Of the Interiour Beginnings of Voluntary Motions; commonly called the PASSIONS. And the Speeches by which they are expressed." See *Leviathan*, chap. 6, pp. 78–97. Courage is included among Hobbes's list of the passions there; zeal is not. It is noteworthy that Hobbes might be said to define "affections" as such in *Leviathan* only when he declares the contingent and disputable nature of all moral evaluations (including, presumably, his own moral evaluations of fanaticism, though he also claims to make supposedly discrete ontological claims about fanaticism, too). In "Of Speech," in *Leviathan*, during his discussion of "the names of such things as affect us," Hobbes defines "affections" as "conceptions," which are invariably colored by our passions: "For seeing all names are imposed to signifie our conceptions; and all our affections are but conceptions; when we conceive the same things differently, we can hardly avoyd different naming of them. For though the nature of that we conceive, be the same; yet the diversity of our reception of it, in respect of different constitutions of body, and prejudices of opinion, gives every thing a tincture of our different passions." *Leviathan*, chap. 4, p. 62.

4. For an overview of Renaissance interpretations of Samson and whether his zealous violence had a divine origin, see Joseph Wittreich, *Interpreting* Samson Agonistes (Princeton: Princeton University Press, 1986), chap. 4.

5. My comparison of *Leviathan* and *Samson Agonistes* implies that I assume the latter to have been conceived primarily during the Restoration. For a useful overview of the controversies over dating the composition of *Samson Agonistes*, see the headnote in the Longman edition of John Milton, *Complete Shorter Poems*, 2nd ed., ed. John Carey (London: Longman, 1997), 349–50. Unless otherwise noted, quotations of Milton's poetry are from this volume, hereinafter cited parenthetically by line number. For the most influential reading of the differences between Milton's and Hobbes's monisms, see Stephen Fallon, *Milton among the Philosophers: Poetry and Materialism in Seventeenth-Century England* (Ithaca, N.Y.: Cornell University Press, 1991), especially 194–222.

6. For a suggestive argument that Milton, in his dramatic depiction of Samson, was likely influenced by Donne's commentary on Samson in *Biathanatos*, see George F. Butler, "Donne's *Biathanatos* and *Samson Agonistes*: Ambivalence and Ambiguity," *Milton Studies* 34 (1996): 199–219.

7. Note that in Milton's version of the Samson story, unlike in Judges 16:30, Samson kills the Philistine leaders ("Lords, ladies, captains, counsellors, or priests" [1653]), while the general population escapes unharmed ("The vulgar only scap'd who stood without" [1659]).

8. For extended engagements with Milton's opposition to Hobbes in *Samson Agonistes*, see Ashraf H. Rushdy, *The Empty Garden: The Subject of Late Milton* (Pittsburgh: University of Pittsburgh Press, 1992), 399–437; and Catherine Gimelli Martin, "The Phoenix and the Crocodile: Milton's Natural Law Debate with Hobbes Retried in the Tragic Forum of *Samson Agonistes*," in *The English Civil Wars in the Literary Imagination*, ed. Claude J. Summers and Ted-Larry Pebworth (Columbia: University of Missouri Press, 1999), 242–70. For an argument that claims in fascinating ways that there is an analogy between Hobbes's state of nature and Samson's experience of imprisonment, and that suggests Hobbes's and Milton's surprisingly similar investments in self-preservation during the Restoration, see Christopher Warren, "When Self-Preservation Bids: Approaching Milton, Hobbes and Dissent," *English Literary Renaissance* 37 (2007): 118–50. The premise and historical evidence for Warren's general argument is compelling. But his specific claim, at the end of the essay, that Milton's Samson should be understood as a "sovereign subject" akin to "a liberal democratic 'citizen'" (149) seems to me to sidestep the question of whether Samson at the end of the play can properly be called a "subject" or even a self. Rather than exploring the ambiguous possibility of Samson's self-emptying and inspiration, Warren proposes that "Samson's submission to God and the Philistines is ultimately a submission to God's 'nature within [him]'—that is, to himself" (149). But why "himself"? By this, Warren does not mean the possibility of the unmaking of the difference between God and Samson, the annihilation of Samson as a subject and the immanence in him of God's action; instead, he proposes a vertical model that assumes a transcendent God who bestows his grace on a human agent who, in turn, submits only to himself. Even when Warren's argument leads him to claim that Samson's self-preserving sovereignty and his "ecstatic submission" to God are one and the same (148), "submission" presupposes a willful subject, which begs the question.

9. *The Works of John Milton*, ed. Frank Allen Patterson (New York: Columbia University Press, 1931–38), 7:218 (translation altered).

10. Aristotle, *Ethicorum ad Nicomachum Libri Decem* (London, 1581).

11. These passages from Aristotle are quoted and analyzed in Bradin Cormack, "On Will: Time and Voluntary Action in *Coriolanus* and the Sonnets," *Shakespeare* 5, no. 3 (2009): 255. He also discusses Aristotle's category of mixed action, which is both voluntary (the cause originates in the subject) and involuntary (external circumstances make it seem necessary). On Milton's interest in this Aristotelian category of mixed action, see Joshua Scodel, "Edenic Freedoms," *Milton Studies* 56 (2015): 188.

12. Tobias Gregory, "The Political Messages of *Samson Agonistes*," *Studies in English Literature, 1500–1900* 50, no. 1 (Winter 2010): 176. A recent exception to this trend is Drew Daniel, *The Melancholy Assemblage: Affect and Epistemology in the English Renaissance* (New York: Fordham University Press, 2013), 200–27.

13. Feisal Mohamed, *Milton and the Post-Secular Present: Ethics, Politics, Terrorism* (Stanford: Stanford University Press, 2011), 114.

14. Mohamed, *Milton and the Post-Secular Present*, 115.

15. Victoria Kahn, *Wayward Contracts: The Crisis of Political Obligation in England, 1640–1674* (Princeton: Princeton University Press, 2004), 275; Helen Lynch, *Milton and the Politics of Public Speech* (New York: Routledge, 2015), 166.

16. Mohamed, *Milton and the Post-Secular Present*, 124. Even if I also view my own work on fanaticism as unsettling assumptions within what Mohamed labels broadly as "Western liberal humanism" and its assumptions about religious violence, I nevertheless find that his analysis inadvertently depends on some of those assumptions insofar as it takes a polemical term such as "terrorism" as a descriptor of "barbarisms." Mohamed, *Milton and the Post-Secular Present*, 126.

17. Mohamed is aware of this concern when discussing the work of Talal Asad, whose meditations on the opaque motivations of the suicide bomber lead Mohamed to conclude that "the self-immolation of the suicide bomber creates an aporia that narrative conventions of cause and effect can supplement but never fill." Mohamed, *Milton and the Post-Secular Present*, 108. This conclusion is not applied in his reading of *Samson Agonistes*.

18. This claim radicalizes and historicizes Brendan Quigley's compelling Kierkegaardian analysis of the irreducibly "secret" relationship of Milton's Samson to God—a relationship that is secret to the author, to readers, and to Samson himself. Quigley, "The Distant Hero of *Samson Agonistes*," *ELH* 72, no. 3 (2005): 529–51.

19. *Works of John Milton*, 3:5. On the relevance of the Protestant understanding of "calling" for *Samson Agonistes*, see Kahn, *Wayward Contracts*, 260; and John Guillory, "The Father's House: *Samson Agonistes* in its Historical Moment," in *In Re-membering Milton: Essays on the Texts and Traditions*,

ed. Mary Nyquist and Margaret W. Ferguson (New York: Muthuen, 1987), 148–76. For parallels between Samson's labor and that of contemporary dissenters, see Blair Hoxby, *Mammon's Music: Literature and Economics in the Age of Milton* (New Haven, Conn.: Yale, 2002), 205–32.

20. Stanley Fish, *How Milton Works* (Cambridge: Harvard University Press, 2003), 391–473. Fish has provided us with one of the best accounts of the "absence of intelligibility" at the heart of *Samson Agonistes* (472). Nonetheless, his conclusion that "the only wisdom to be carried away from the play is that there is no wisdom to be carried away" (473) makes illegibility paralytic, which seems to me to betray the play's emphasis on witness and the necessity of cultivating responsiveness to unknowing. Moreover, though Fish briefly discusses the "difficulty of distinguishing between inspiration and inclination" in the play (430; see also 453–54), his concerns are ultimately with Samson's "reading of divine will" (426), "his desire to conform to that will" (426), the "purity of his intentions" (428), and our inability to find any other standard from which to evaluate the commitment that arises from Samson's reading. Fish's resolution to describe Samson's violence as "virtuous action" settles on it as an achievement of will (426), which actually tends to lessen the unintelligibility around which the play is structured.

21. Milton himself notes that the German Calvinist Daniel Paraeus had analyzed the Book of Revelation "as a tragedy" in the Preface. Milton, *Complete Shorter Poems*, 355.

22. For explicit attempts to come to terms with how Milton in the Preface to *Samson Agonistes* is working with the terms Aristotle uses to define tragedy, see Paul Sellin, "Sources of Milton's Catharsis: A Reconsideration," *Journal of English and Germanic Philology* 60, no. 4 (1961): 712–30; and Martin Mueller, "Sixteenth-Century Italian Criticism and Milton's Theory of Catharsis," *Studies in English Literature, 1500–1900* 6, no. 1 (1966): 139–50. While the former holds that Milton's translation of Aristotle and his theory of tragedy more generally draw most deeply from the Renaissance Dutch scholar Daniel Heinsius (in particular his *De tragoediae constitutione*, first published in 1611), the latter argues that Milton's theory of tragedy here is mediated through sixteenth-century Italian thinkers such as Pietro Vettori and Lorenzo Giacomini and decidedly not through Heinsius. For a thorough analysis of the import of Milton's translation of Aristotle and his debts to Heinsius and Gerardus Joannes Vossius especially, see Russ Leo, "Milton's Aristotelian Experiments: Tragedy, *Lustratio*, and Secret Refreshings in *Samson Agonistes* (1671)," *Milton Studies* 52 (2011): 221–52. See also Kahn's comments on Milton's theory of tragedy as a kind of Brechtian epic theater *avant la lettre*, in which aesthetics becomes critique and refuses the two tendencies of Renaissance commentators on Aristotle's theory of

tragedy, commentators who "can be divided into those who moralize catharsis as a vehicle of the ethical and political dimension of tragedy and those who emphasize the pleasure we derive from artistry of imitation (Minturno on the one hand and Castelvetro on the other)." Kahn, *Wayward Contracts*, 276.

23. See the title page of *Samson Agonistes* in Milton, *Paradise Regain'd. A Poem in IV Books. To which is added Samson Agonistes* (London, 1671). See Aristotle, *Poetics* 1449b24, in Aristotle, Longinus, and Demetrius, *Aristotle: Poetics; Longinus: On the Sublime; Demetrius: On Style*, ed. Donald Russell, trans. Stephen Halliwell, W. H. Fyfe, Doreen C. Innes, and W. Rhys Roberts (Cambridge: Harvard University Press, 1995). The Greek translates in this way: "Tragedy is the imitation of a serious action, etc." Milton keeps the Greek script for his truncated quotation, which I transliterate here.

24. Title page of *Samson Agonistes* in Milton, *Paradise Regain'd*. Milton's Latin translates: "Tragedy is the imitation of a serious action, etc., by pity and fear perfecting the lustration of such affects."

25. Milton, *Complete Shorter Poems*, 355.

26. On the subtle distinctions between Aristotle's terms for action in the *Poetics*, see Elizabeth Belfiore, "Aristotle's Concept of *Praxis* in the *Poetics*," *Classical Journal* 79, no. 2 (Dec. 1983–Jan. 1984): 110–24.

27. Elizabeth D. Harvey, "*Samson Agonistes* and Milton's Sensible Ethics," in *The Oxford Handbook of Milton*, ed. Nicholas McDowell and Nigel Smith (Oxford: Oxford University Press, 2009), 653. Harvey continues: "Suffering or passion thus encodes an economy of subject and object, a reciprocal ligature of agency and reception, a subordination of the object to the force exerted upon it." For an illuminating philological account of the equivocation of *passio* between passivity and activity—its movement in classical, stoical, and Christian sources from suffering to mystical identification with Christ's wounds, and to an activity of the emotions in the early modern period—see Erich Auerbach, "*Passio* als Leidenschaft," in *Gesammelte Aufsätze zur romanischen Philologie* (Bern, Ger.: Francke Verlag, 1967), 161–75.

28. Kahn, *Wayward Contracts*, 272 (original emphasis).

29. For a reading of a similar dialectic in Spenser, see Andrew Escobedo, *Volition's Face: Personification and the Will in Renaissance Literature* (Notre Dame, Ind.: University of Notre Dame Press, 2017), 184–200.

30. Aristotle, *Poetics*, 1449b24. Milton's translation of Aristotle's *teleias* is *perficiens*. *Perficiens* is also a translation in Jerome's Latin Vulgate of the *telias* that famously appears in the passage from 2 Corinthians 12:9, a passage that Milton took as a kind of self-applied motto: "And he said unto me, My grace

is sufficient for thee: for my strength is made perfect [teleitai/perficitur] in weakness [en astheneia/in infirmitate]." Beza's Latin translation (1585), from which Milton often quotes, gives a different emphasis: "Sufficit tibi gratia mea; nam potentia mea per infirmitatem ad finem suum adducitur." Theodoro Beza, *Testamenti veteris Biblia sacra sive libri canonici, priscae Iudaeorum Ecclesiae a Deo traditi* . . . (London: Guliel Norton, 1585).

31. English is from the King James Version. *Katharizetai* was rendered as "mundatur" in the Vulgate, and "purificantur" in Beza's Latin translation. For a useful elaboration of the different resonances of "catharsis" in Aristotle, see Jonathan Lear, "Katharsis," *Phronesis* 33, no. 3 (1988): 297–326.

32. For a compelling account of the importance of *lustratio*—a translation of Aristotle that may have been unique to Milton—see Leo, "Milton's Aristotelian Experiments," 248–52.

33. Debora Shuger, *The Renaissance Bible: Scholarship, Sacrifice, and Subjectivity* (Berkeley: University of California Press, 1994), 130. Shuger also aptly brings together the realms of tragedy and sacrifice in a reference to Walter Burkert's genealogy of tragedy: "Burkert's argument that 'tragedy' derives from the 'trugos' or goat sacrificed to Dionysius during ancient religious festival corresponds to the etymology preserved in all Renaissance discussions of tragedy" (132). See Burkert's influential study, *Homo Necans: The Anthropology of Ancient Greek Sacrificial Ritual and Myth*, trans. Peter Bing (Berkeley: University of California Press, 1983).

34. For these definitions of "lustratio," see *A Latin Dictionary*, ed. Charleton T. Lewis and Charles Short (Oxford: Clarendon Press, 1879), s.v. "lustratio"; and *The Oxford Latin Dictionary*, ed. P. G. W. Glare (Oxford: Oxford University Press, 1968), s.vv. "lustrātiō," "lustrō."

35. See Jason P. Rosenblatt, *Renaissance England's Chief Rabbi: John Selden* (Oxford: Oxford University Press, 2006), in which Rosenblatt insists on how a "Hebraic monist" reading of *Samson Agonistes* would insist on "the harmony between Judaic law and the spirit" (105). I am in agreement with Rosenblatt that a dualist reading of the play that views its "Hebraism" as an element structurally overcome by Samson's turn to a more Pauline model of grace is misguided. In my reading, however, Milton is fundamentally interested in the ambiguity or undecidability of the relationship between law and grace (or, to use a more Miltonic idiom, divine dispensation)—how the priority of their relation to salvation or to the political is ultimately illegible and requires not a decision but rather a maintenance of their mutually determining, anamorphic character.

36. See Aryeh Kosman, "Acting: Drama as the Mimesis of Praxis," in *Essays on Aristotle's Poetics*, ed. Amélie Oksenberg Rorty (Princeton: Princeton University Press), 51–72 in which Kosman compellingly argues that the

proliferation of meanings to which I am alluding already exists in the term "catharsis":

> Despite (or perhaps because of) the intense and voluminous discussion it has received, the exact sense of *catharsis* in its cameo appearance in [Aristotle's] *Poetics* may well continue to elude us. But much of the controversy, and in particular the familiar opposition between lustrative and purgative interpretations, may be unnecessary; to stress the lustrative sense of *catharsis* is not per se to deny its purgative sense, for lustration is a purging of the purified object from its impurities and pollutions. It is certainly this lustrative sense that we find prominent in Plato (a fact which may help to balance the antilustrative weight characteristically given the single discussion of catharsis in the *Politics*). (67)

Kosman also helpfully demonstrates how Aristotle's mention of *catharsis* in the *Politics* (1341b32) became important in late-antique Christian meditations on Christ's passion and mimetic representations of it.

37. Milton, *Complete Shorter Poems*, 355.

38. Jay P. Green, *The Interlinear Hebrew-Greek-English Bible* (Peabody, Mass.: Hendrickson Publishers, 2005), Numbers 6.

39. For a useful reading of touch and the attempt to expel femininity in the play, see Stevie Davies, "Words Bereft of Touch or Trust," in *Milton* (New York: Harvester Wheatsheaf, 1991), 179–205.

40. Fish argues that Samson's first marriage to the woman of Timna occurs because he believes he is moved by "intimate impulse," and his second marriage to Dalila is merely an act of desire, "which he reinterpreted as inspiration." Fish, *How Milton Works*, 399.

41. Judges 13:25. In this instance, Milton's unspecified genitive— "motioned was of God"—also echoes Judges 14:4 in the King James Version: "But his father and his mother knew not that it was of the Lord, that he sought an occasion against the Philistines."

42. For an analysis of strength infused into the gathering of Samson's hair as suggestive of a political allegory of "diffusion of power across a multitude," see Joanna Picciotto, "The Public Person and the Play of Fact," *Representations* 105 (2009): 102.

43. "The light of the body is the eye: if therefore thine eye be single, thy whole body shall be full of light." John Rogers calls attention to this and other biblical allusions to light and sight in Samson. Rogers, "The Secret of *Samson Agonistes*," *Milton Studies* 33 (1996): 111–32.

44. In Augustine's meditations on the simplicity of the soul in *De Trinitate*, he claims that the soul is not diffused over a determined amount of space but is, in each body, whole in the whole body, and whole in every one

of its parts: "Nam ideo simplicior est corpore, quia non mole diffunditur per spatium loci, sed in unoquoque corpore, et in toto tota est et in qualibet eius parte tota est." Augustine, *De Trinitate*, 6.6.8, in J.-P. Migne, ed. *Patrologiae cursus, completus, series Latina* (Paris, 1849–64), vol. 42, col. 929.

45. See Rogers, "Secret of *Samson Agonistes*."

46. As a theory of substance, monism may not be as appropriate as Rogers suggests for considering which organs perform specific functions for an individual character.

47. Picciotto, "Public Person," 111, 130n123.

48. See Leo, "Milton's Aristotelian Experiments," 251–52: "Milton invokes Aristotle here, in his monist experiment. Where the introduction of a god or device obscures the constitution of the elements in the tragedy, Milton, with Aristotle and Heinsius, pursues this to the opposite extreme: the slippery possessive pronouns"—specifically, the possessive subject "His" in lines 1754 and 1755, carried over from 1749—"invite us to consider that all is God here, at the end of *Samson Agonistes*, and this is precisely the object of expiation. God is the subject (or object) that has 'all passion spent.'"

49. See Guillory, "Father's House," especially 206–9, for a careful analysis of Milton's use of election, calling, and "special vocation" in *De Doctrina*.

50. See for example Ephesians 3:2, which refers to the "oikonomian tēs charitos tou Theou" (in Vulgate: "dispensationem gratae Dei"). Beza translates this as "dispensationem" as well.

51. Milton, *Complete Shorter Poems*, 358.

52. Hobbes, *Leviathan*, chap. 6, p. 78.

53. Adam Littleton, *Linguae Latinae Liber Dictionarius Quadripartitus. A Latin Dictionary in Four Parts. I. An English-Latine. II. A Latine-Classical. III. A Latine-Proper. IV. A Latine-Barbarous. Wherein the Latine and English are adjusted, with what care might be, both as to Stock of Words and Proprieties of Speech* (London, 1678), s.v. "mōtus, a, um." See also Daniel's study of Samson (Chapter 6 of *Melancholy Assemblage*) for the ambiguities of "motion" in Aristotelian, Stoic, and Galenic contexts. I have found particularly suggestive Daniel's claim that the Galenic science of melancholy has a relationship to "the epistemological structure of aporia within early modernity" in general and to Samson in particular as "a radical and complete unknown for the 'others' who blindly surround him" (223).

54. *Institutio Oratoria of Quintilian*, ed. H. E. Butler, Loeb Classical Library (Cambridge: Harvard University Press, 1976), 9.1.

55. See, for example, the following passage from Aquinas: "Sicut motus naturalis est ab aliquo principio intrinseco, ita motus voluntaries est ab aliquo intrinseco. Igitur si actus caritatis esset totaliter ab exteriori movente, non esset voluntaries. . . . Igitur est aliquis talis habitus creatus in nobis [Just

as a natural movement arises from some intrinsic beginning, so a motion of will arises from something intrinsic. And so, if the act of charity should arise completely from an exterior movement, it would not be voluntary. . . . Therefore there is some such disposition created in us]." Thomas Aquinas, *De caritate*, q. 1, a.1, resp. J, in *Quaestiones disputatae S. Thomae Aquinatis*, ed. P. Bazzi (Turin: Marietti, 1953); quoted in D. Vance Smith, *The Book of the Incipit: Beginnings in the Fourteenth Century* (Minneapolis: University of Minnesota Press, 2001), 181–82.

56. See *Works of John Milton*, 15:92–94: "Ordinaria, qua Deus constantem illum causarum ordinem qui ab ipso constitutus in principio est, retinet ac servat . . . Haec vulgo et nimis etiam frequenter Natura dicitur . . . Providentia Dei extraordinaria est, qua Deus quicquam extra solitum rerum ordinem producit . . . Miraculum dicitur."

57. Rogers, "Secret of *Samson Agonistes*," 126.

58. *Works of John Milton*, 7:144–45: "quis nescit non privati solùm, sed etiam servi personam ideò sumpsisse, ut nos liberi essemus. Neque hoc de interna tantùm libertate intelligendum est, non de civili." See also the beginning *Of Reformation* (*Works of John Milton*, 3.1:5), in which Milton describes martyrs as wielding the "unresistable *might* of *Weakness*."

59. See *George Buchanan Tragedies*, ed. P. Sharratt and P. G. Walsh (Edinburgh: Scottish Academic Press, 1983), especially lines 1093–104, where Buchanan's John the Baptist says, "So my spirit is eager to fly free from the unbarred prison of the body to where the whole world will sooner or later pass. In my view a long life is nothing but lingering slavery in a grim prison. O death, alone the respite from harsh toil: death, harbor from grief and repose from evil, benefit which few appreciate, a source of fear for the debased but an aspiration by the good." See also John Dryden, *Tyrannick Love: A Royal Martyr*, vol. 10 of *The Works of John Dryden*, ed. Maximillian E. Nozak and George R. Guffey (Berkeley: University of California Press, 1970), first performed in 1669, two years before the publication of *Samson Agonistes*, for the discussion between Catherine, Porphyrius, and Bernie about the conflicted loving life despite maintaining a resolution to die, and Catherine's ultimate commitment to die in Act V:

> To beg your life—
> Is not to ask a grace of *Maximin*:
> It is a silent bargain for a sin.
> Could we live always, life were worth our cost;
> But now we keep with care what must be lost.
> Here we stand shiv'ring on the Bank, and cry,
> When we should plunge into Eternity.

One moment ends our pain;
And yet the shock of death we dare not stand,
By thought scarce measur'd, and too swift for sand:
'Tis but because the Living death ne'er knew,
They fear to prove it as a thing that's new.
Let me th' Experiment before you try,
I'le show you first how easie 'tis to dye. (5.228–41)

60. "In Samson vas erat, in Spiritu plenitudo erat. Vas impleri et exinaniri potest. Omne autem vas aliunde habet complementum" (In Samson we have a vessel, in the Spirit, what fills it. A vessel can be filled and emptied. Every vessel, however, has what fills it from elsewhere). Augustine, Sermon 364, in *Patrologiae cursus, completus, series Latina*, ed. Migne, vol. 39, col. 1639.

61. John Calvin, *Institutio Christianae Religionis* (Paris, 1559), 3.20.15. There, Calvin reads Samson as a vengeful hero but still maintains that God fulfills his prayer, maintaining that Samson has been "seized" by a fervor if not of God's annihilating will: "Talis etiam feruor Samsonen rapuit." See also Mohamed, *Milton and the Post-Secular Present*, 114, where Mohamed interprets Calvin's analysis of Samson to show that Samson's prayer in Judges need not exclude his return to a heroic narrative of vengeance.

62. A number of critics have commented on the parallel of this moment both to Eve's consumption of the apple in *Paradise Lost* (9.781: "She plucked, she eat") and Jesus's defeat of Satan in *Paradise Regained* (4.561: "He said and stood").

63. "To invoke the phrase 'of my own accord' or 'of his own accord', then, is to align oneself with the discourse of God, who, more than anyone else in Scriptures, acts of his own accord (by himself) and customarily in the context of swearing an oath." Michael Lieb, "'Our Living Dread': The God of *Samson Agonistes*," *Milton Studies* 33 (1996): 16. For Lieb, Samson becomes in this moment "that *tremendum* through which 'our living Dread' is made manifest," which is sharply different from his early idolatrous self-identification as a "petty god" (line 529), since it is something more akin to a mystical annihilation of self that precipitates divine instrumentalization.

64. For an elaboration of the dramatic representation of prophets and early modern Hebraicist debates over whether or not the behaviors of the prophet were part of their prophet gifts, see Nigel Smith, *Perfection Proclaimed: Language and Literature in English Radical Religion, 1640–1660* (Oxford: Oxford University Press, 1989), 30–31.

65. On the "meaninglessness" of Samson's milling, see Richard Halpern, *Eclipse of Action: Tragedy and Political Economy* (Chicago: University of Chicago Press, 2017), 168. On the related "meaninglessness" of Samson's

final violence, Halpern writes that "the meaninglessness of the event, its inability to escape from the circularity of the mill, is enforced by the failure of the nation to heed Samson's call" (177). Halpern's ingenious claim that Samson's final act may be a continuation of the mill's colonization of his body and mind is quite different from mine, but it is instructive that Halpern admits that the play leaves uncertain whether Samson has become an instrument of some other power (the mill's or God's) or whether he acts on his own will at the end of the play. Though Halpern ultimately argues that Samson merges with the mill, he also suggests that the issue is as unknowable as the source of the "rousing motions" Samson feels: "It may be that the echo is meant to signal how Samson's final act transcends and negates his productive activity, but it may also reduce his final act to a mere continuation of it" (167).

66. Hobbes, in language Samson himself uses in lines 1206–7 ("force with force / Is well ejected when the conquer'd can"), writes: "A Covenant not to defend my selfe from force, by force, is always voyd." No man, according to Hobbes, can transfer or otherwise abnegate the right to defend himself physically "from Death, Wounds, and Imprisonment." Hobbes, *Leviathan*, chap. 14, p. 214.

67. Fish makes a similar point in "Spectacle and Evidence in *Samson Agonistes*," *Critical Inquiry* 15, no. 3 (1989): 563.

68. It is an intriguing question whether Samson, at these earlier moments, was trying to block the process of monumentalization in general or, in a more specific sense, wished to unmake the kind of monument that the Philistines were in the process of fashioning him into. I tend to read Samson—at least at his more self-reflective moments—as resistant to even positive monumentalization, having learned that it participates in the same fantasies that made him think of himself as a "petty god." But one could also interpret Manoa's specific monumentalizing desires as being oriented toward continuing the project that Judges 13:5 states Samson was only ever supposed to begin: "And he shall begin [Hebrew Bible: yā ḥêl; Vulgate: incipiet] to deliver Israel out of the hand of the Philistines." In either case, I agree with Alice Dailey's assessment that Milton's works tend to undercut the generic function of martyr literature, which she describes as "reorganiz[ing] sites of horror into sites of beauty—[reconstituting] dismembered burned, and opened bodies into closed and perfected hermeneutic systems." Dailey, *The English Martyr from Reformation to Revolution* (Notre Dame, Ind.: Notre Dame University Press, 2012), 250. I do not, however, think that such a skepticism toward monumentalization equals a skepticism toward a poetics or aesthetics of martyrdom for Milton—at least not in the case of *Samson Agonistes*.

69. Judith Butler, *Frames of War: When Is Life Grievable?* (London: Verso, 2009), 41. Butler is drawing on Talal Asad, *On Suicide Bombing* (New York: Columbia University Press, 2007).

70. For an analysis of the use of "amaze" in the play, see Dennis Kezar, "Samson's Death by Theater and Milton's Art of Dying," *ELH* 66, no. 2 (1999): 323–24.

71. Asad, *On Suicide Bombing*, 75–76. I find Asad's definition of horror as "the result of [the] deliberate transgression of boundaries that separate the human from the inhuman, the creature from the Creator" useful for considering the horror that Samson provokes in Milton's play (78).

Achinstein, Sharon. *Literature and Dissent in Milton's England*. Cambridge: Cambridge University Press, 2003.

Adorno, Theodor. *Aesthetic Theory*. Translated by Robert Hullot-Kentor. Minneapolis: University of Minnesota Press, 1997.

———. *Ästhetische Theorie*. Frankfurt am Main: Suhrkamp, 1970.

Aers, David. "A Whisper in the Ear of Early Modernists; or, Reflections on Literary Critics Writing the 'History of the Subject.'" In *Culture and History, 1350–1600: Essays on English Communities, Identities, and Writing*, edited by David Aers, 177–203. Detroit: Wayne State University Press, 1992.

Agamben, Giorgio. *The End of the Poem: Studies in Poetics*. Translated by Daniel Heller-Roazen. Stanford: Stanford University Press, 1999.

Allewaert, Monique. *Ariel's Ecology: Plantations, Personhood, and Colonialism in the American Tropics*. Minneapolis: University of Minnesota Press, 2013.

Anderson, Judith. "Review of Gordon Teskey, *Allegory and Violence*." *Arthuriana* 7 (1997): 125–28.

———. *Words That Matter: Linguistic Perception in Renaissance England*. Stanford: Stanford University Press, 1996.

Andrewes, Lancelot. *The Works of Lancelot Andrewes, Sometime Bishop of Winchester*. Vol. 3. Edited by J. P. Wilson and James Bliss. Oxford: J. H. Parker, 1841.

Appelbaum, Robert. *Terrorism before the Letter: Mythography and Political Violence in England, Scotland, and France 1559–1642*. Oxford: Oxford University Press, 2016.

Aquinas, Thomas. *Quaestiones disputatae S. Thomae Aquinatis*. Edited by P. Bazzi. Turin: Marietti, 1953.

———. *Summa Theologiae, Secunda Secundae*. Edited by John Mortensen and Enrique Alarcón. Translated by Fr. Laurence Shapcote, O.P., 1–90. Lander, Wyo.: The Aquinas Institute, 2012.

Aristotle. *Ethicorum ad Nicomachum Libri Decem*. London, 1581.

Aristotle, Longinus, and Demetrius. *Aristotle: Poetics; Longinus: On the Sublime; Demetrius: On Style*. Edited by Donald Russell. Translated by

Stephen Halliwell, W. H. Fyfe, Doreen C. Innes, and W. Rhys Roberts. Cambridge: Harvard University Press, 1995.

Asad, Talal. *On Suicide Bombing.* New York: Columbia University Press, 2007.

Auerbach, Erich. "Excursus: *Gloria Passionis.*" In *Literary Language and Its Public in Late Latin Antiquity and in the Middle Ages,* translated by Ralph Manheim, 67–82. Princeton: Princeton University Press, 1993.

———. "*Passio* als Leidenschaft." In *Gesammelte Aufsätze zur romanischen Philologie,* 161–75. Bern, Ger.: Francke Verlag, 1967.

Badiou, Alain. *Saint Paul: La foundation de l'universalisme.* Paris: Presses Universitaires de France, 1997.

Balibar, Étienne. *Identity and Difference: John Locke and the Invention of Consciousness.* Translated by Warren Montag. New York: Verso, 2013.

———. "Spinoza, the Anti-Orwell: The Fear of the Masses." In *Masses, Classes, Ideas: Studies on Philosophy and Politics before and after Marx,* translated by James Swenson, 3–37. New York: Routledge, 1994.

Baumgold, Deborah. "Soldiers and Subjects: Hobbes on Military Service." *History of Political Thought* 4, no. 1 (1983): 43–63.

Belfiore, Elizabeth. "Aristotle's Concept of *Praxis* in the *Poetics.*" *Classical Journal* 79, no. 2 (Dec. 1983–Jan. 1984): 110–24.

Belt, Henk van den. *The Authority of Scripture in Reformed Theology: Truth and Trust.* Leiden, Neth.: Brill, 2008.

Benjamin, Walter. "Zur Kritik der Gewalt." In Vol. 2.1 of *Gesammelte Schriften,* edited by Rolf Tiedemann and Hermann Schweppenhäuser, 179–203. Frankfurt am Main: Suhrkamp, 1999.

Béreulle, Pierre de. *Bref discours de l'abnégation intérieure.* In *Oeuvres complètes du Cardinal de Bérulle,* vol. 2, 644–77. Montsoult, Fr.: Maison d'Institution de l'Oratorie, 1960.

———. *Opuscules de piété.* Grenoble, Fr.: Jérôme Millon, 1997.

Berger, Harry, Jr. *The Allegorical Temper: Vision and Reality in Book II of Spenser's "Faerie Queene."* New Haven, Conn.: Yale University Press, 1957.

Bersani, Leo. "Is the Rectum a Grave?" *October* 43 (Winter 1987): 197–222.

Beza, Theodoro. *Testamenti veteris Biblia sacra sive libri canonici, priscae Iudaeorum Ecclesiae a Deo traditi . . .* London, 1585.

Bloch, Ernst. *Thomas Münzer als Theologe der Revolution.* Frankfurt am Main: Suhrkamp, 1960.

Bonabeau, Eric, Marco Dorigo, and Guy Theraulaz. *Swarm Intelligence: From Natural to Artificial Systems.* Oxford: Oxford University Press, 1999.

Botwinick, Aryeh. *Skepticism, Belief, and the Modern: Maimonides to Nietzsche.* Ithaca, N.Y.: Cornell University Press, 1997.

Bredekamp, Horst. *Thomas Hobbes. Der Leviathan: Das Urbild des modernen Staates und seine Gegenbilder: 1651–2001*. Berlin: Akademie Verlag, 2012.

Brown, Jericho. "The Burning Bush." In *Please*, 42. Kalamazoo, Mich.: New Issues Poetry & Prose, 2008.

Brown, Wendy. *Regulating Aversion: Tolerance in the Age of Identity and Empire*. Princeton: Princeton University Press, 2008.

Buchanan, George. *George Buchanan Tragedies*. Edited by P. Sharratt and P. G. Walsh. Edinburgh: Scottish Academic Press, 1983.

Burgess, Glenn. "On Hobbesian Resistance Theory." *Political Studies* 42, no. 1 (1994): 62–83.

Burkert, Walter. *Homo Necans: The Anthropology of Ancient Greek Sacrificial Ritual and Myth*. Translated by Peter Bing. Berkeley: University of California Press, 1983.

Burton, Ben, and Elizabeth Scott-Baumann, eds. *The Work of Form: Poetics and Materiality in Early Modern Culture*. Oxford: Oxford University Press, 2014.

Butler, George F. "Donne's *Biathanatos* and *Samson Agonistes*: Ambivalence and Ambiguity." *Milton Studies* 34 (1996): 199–219.

Butler, Judith. *Frames of War: When Is Life Grievable?* London: Verso, 2009.

Calvin, John. *Institutes of the Christian Religion*. Edited by John T. McNeill. Translated by Ford Lewis Battles. 2 vols. Louisville: Westminster Press, 1960.

———. *Institutio Christianae Religionis*. Paris, 1559.

Campana, Joseph. "The Bee and the Sovereign (II): Segments, Swarms, and the Shakespearean Multitude." In *The Return of Theory in Early Modern English Studies*, edited by Paul Cefalu, Gary Kuchar, and Bryan Reynolds, 59–78. Vol. 2. New York: Palgrave Macmillan, 2014.

———. "Boy Toys and Liquid Joys: Pleasure and Power in the Bower of Bliss." *Modern Philology* 106, no. 3 (2009): 465–96.

———. *The Pain of Reformation: Spenser, Vulnerability, and the Ethics of Masculinity*. New York: Fordham University Press, 2012.

———. "Spenser's Inhumanity." *Spenser Studies* 30 (2015): 277–99.

Canfield, Benet of. *The rule of perfection contayning a breif and perspicuous abridgement of all the wholle spirituall life, reduced to this only point of the vvill of God*. Roan, Nor., 1609.

Capp, Bernard. *The Fifth Monarchy Men: A Study in Seventeenth-Century English Millenarianism*. London: Faber, 1972.

Carey, John. "A Work in Praise of Terrorism? September 11 and *Samson Agonistes*." *Times Literary Supplement*, September 6, 2002: 15–16.

Carson, Anne. *Decreation: Poetry, Essays, Opera*. New York: Alfred A. Knopf, 2005.

Cavanaugh, William. "The Invention of Fanaticism." *Modern Theology* 27, no. 2 (2011): 226–37.

———. *The Myth of Religious Violence: Secular Ideology and the Roots of Modern Conflict*. Oxford: Oxford University Press, 2009.

Chakrabarty, Dipesh. "Minority Histories, Subaltern Pasts." In *Provincializing Europe: Postcolonial Thought and Historical Difference*, 97–113. Princeton: Princeton University Press, 2000.

Chaucer, Geoffrey. *The Riverside Chaucer*. 3rd ed. Edited by Larry Benson. Boston: Houghton Mifflin, 1987.

Church of England. *The Thirty-Nine Articles, and the Constitutions and Canons, of the Church of England; Together with Several Acts of Parliament and Proclamations Concerning Ecclesiastical Matters*. London, 1773.

Clarendon, Earl of (Edward Hyde). *A Brief View and Survey of the Dangerous and Pernicious Errors to Church and State, in M. Hobbes's Book, entitled Leviathan*. Oxford, 1676.

Cicero. *On Old Age, On Friendship, On Divination*. Translated by W. A. Falconer. Loeb Classical Library, no. 154. Cambridge: Harvard University Press, 1923.

Colas, Dominique. *Civil Society and Fanaticism: Conjoined Histories*. Translated by Amy Jacobs. Stanford: Stanford University Press, 1997.

———. *Le Glaive et le Fléau: Généalogie du fanatisme et de la société civile*. Paris: B. Grasset, 1992.

Coleridge, Samuel Taylor. *Notes on English Divines*. Edited by Derwent Coleridge. London: Edward Moxon, 1853.

Collins, Jeffrey. *The Allegiance of Thomas Hobbes*. Oxford: Oxford University Press, 2008.

Coogan, Michael, Marc Z. Brettler, Carol Newsom, and Pheme Perkins, eds. *The New Oxford Annotated Bible*. 4th ed. New revised standard version. Oxford: Oxford University Press, 2001.

Cooper, Thomas. *Thesaurus Linguae Romanae & Britannicae*. 4th ed. London, 1584.

Cormack, Bradin. "On Will: Time and Voluntary Action in *Coriolanus* and the Sonnets." *Shakespeare* 5, no. 3 (2009): 253–70.

———. *A Power to Do Justice: Jurisdiction, English Literature, and the Rise of Common Law, 1509–1625*. Chicago: Chicago University Press, 2007.

Cudworth, Ralph. *The True Intellectual System of the Universe*. Vol. 1. 1845. Reprint, Bristol: Thoemmes, 1995.

Cummings, Brian. *The Literary Culture of the Reformation: Grammar and Grace*. Oxford: Oxford University Press, 2002.

Cummings, Brian, and Freya Sierhuis, eds. *Passions and Subjectivity in Early Modern Culture*. London: Ashgate, 2013.

Curran, Eleanor. *Reclaiming the Rights of the Hobbesian Subject*. Houndmills, Eng.: Palgrave Macmillan, 2007.

Dailey, Alice. *The English Martyr from Reformation to Revolution*. Notre Dame, Ind.: Notre Dame University Press, 2012.

Daniel, Drew. *The Melancholy Assemblage: Affect and Epistemology in the English Renaissance*. New York: Fordham University Press, 2013.

Davies, Stevie. "Words Bereft of Touch or Trust." In *Milton*, 179–205. New York: Harvester Wheatsheaf, 1991.

Dean, Tim, Hal Foster, Kaja Silverman, and Leo Bersani. "A Conversation with Leo Bersani." *October* 82 (Autumn 1997): 3–16.

Descartes, René. *The Philosophical Writings of Descartes*. Vol. 1. Translated by John Cottingham, Robert Stoothoff, and Dugald Murdoch. Cambridge: Cambridge University Press, 1985.

Dolven, Jeff. "Panic's Castle." *Representations* 120, no. 1 (2012): 1–16.

———. *Scenes of Instruction in Renaissance Romance*. Chicago: University of Chicago Press, 2007.

Donne, John. *Biathanatos*. Edited by Michael Rudick and M. Pabst Battin. New York: Garland, 1982.

———. *The Complete Poems of John Donne*. Edited by Robin Robbins. Harlow, Eng.: Longman, 2010.

———. *Devotions upon Emergent Occasions*. Edited by Anthony Raspa. Oxford: Oxford University Press, 1987.

———. *Pseudo-Martyr: Wherein out of certaine propositions and gradations, this conclusion is evicted. That those which are of the Romane religion in this Kingdome, may and ought to take the Oath of Allegiance*. Edited by Anthony Raspa. Montreal: McGill-Queen's University Press, 1993.

———. *Sermons of John Donne*. Edited by George R. Potter and Evelyn M. Simpson. 10 vols. Berkeley: University of California Press, 1953–62.

———. *The Variorum Edition of the Poetry of John Donne*. Edited by Gary A. Stringer. Vol. 7, pt. 1, *The Holy Sonnets*, edited by Gary A. Stringer and Paul A. Parrish. Bloomington: Indiana University Press, 2005.

Dryden, John. *Tyrannick Love: A Royal Martyr*. Vol. 10 of *The Works of John Dryden*, edited by Maximillian E. Nozak and George R. Guffey. Berkeley: University of California Press, 1970.

Dubilet, Alex. *The Self-Emptying Subject: Kenosis and Immanence, Medieval to Modern*. New York: Fordham University Press, 2018.

Dubois, Page. "The Democratic Insect: Productive Swarms." *differences: A Journal of Feminist Cultural Studies* 20, nos. 2–3 (Summer/Fall 2009): 36–53.

Dubrow, Heather. *The Challenges of Orpheus: Lyric Poetry and Early Modern England*. Baltimore: Johns Hopkins University Press, 2008.

———. "Guess Who's Coming to Dinner? Reinterpreting Formalism and the Country House Poem." *MLQ* 61, no. 1 (2000): 59–77.

Edwards, Brent Hayes. "Specters of Interdisciplinarity." *PMLA* 123, no. 1 (2008): 188–94.

Eggert, Katherine. "Spenser's Ravishment: Rape and Rapture in *The Faerie Queene*." *Representations* 70 (Spring 2000): 1–26.

Eliot, T. S. "The Metaphysical Poets." In *Selected Essays*, 281–91. London: Faber and Faber, 1934.

Empson, William. "Donne the Spaceman." *Kenyon Review* 19, no. 3 (Summer 1957): 337–99.

Engels, Friedrich. *Der deutsche Bauernkrieg*. Berlin: Neuer Weg, 1945.

Escobedo, Andrew. *Nationalism and Historical Loss in the English Renaissance: Foxe, Dee, Spenser, Milton*. Ithaca, N.Y.: Cornell University Press, 2004.

———. *Volition's Face: Personification and the Will in Renaissance Literature*. Notre Dame, Ind.: University of Notre Dame Press, 2017.

Esolen, Anthony. "Spenser's 'Alma Venus': Energy and Economics in the Bower of Bliss." *English Literary Renaissance* 23, no. 2 (Spring 1993): 267–86.

Ettenhuber, Katrin. *Donne's Augustine: Renaissance Cultures of Interpretation*. Oxford: Oxford University Press, 2011.

Evrigens, Ioannis D. *Fear of Enemies and Collective Action*. Cambridge: Cambridge University Press, 2008.

Fallon, Stephen. *Milton among the Philosophers: Poetry and Materialism in Seventeenth-Century England*. Ithaca, N.Y.: Cornell University Press, 1991.

Feldman, Karen S. "Conscience and the Concealments of Metaphor in Hobbes's *Leviathan*." *Philosophy and Rhetoric* 34, no. 1 (2001): 21–37.

Fenves, Peter. *Arresting Language: From Leibniz to Benjamin*. Stanford: Stanford University Press, 2002.

Ferrell, Lori Anne. *Government by Polemic: James I, the King's Preachers, and the Rhetorics of Conformity*. Stanford: Stanford University Press, 1998.

Fish, Stanley. *How Milton Works*. Cambridge: Harvard University Press, 2003.

———. *Self-Consuming Artifacts: The Experience of Seventeenth-Century Literature*. Berkeley: University of California Press, 1972.

———. "Spectacle and Evidence in *Samson Agonistes*." *Critical Inquiry* 15, no. 3 (1989): 556–86.

Flasch, Kurt. "Meister Eckhart und die 'Deutsche Mystik'—Zur Kritik eines historiographischen Schemas." In *Die Philosophie im 14 und 15 Jahrhundert*, edited by Olaf Pluta, 439–63. Amsterdam: B. R. Grüner, 1988.

Fletcher, Angus. *Allegory: The Theory of a Symbolic Mode*. Princeton: Princeton University Press, 2012.

———. *The Prophetic Moment: An Essay on Spenser*. Chicago: University of Chicago Press, 1971.

Font, Carme. *Women's Prophetic Writing in Seventeenth-Century Britain*. New York: Routledge, 2017.

Foucault, Michel. "How an Experience-Book Is Born." In *Remarks on Marx: Conversations with Duccio Trombadori*, translated by R. James Goldstein and James Cascaito, 25–42. New York: Semiotext(e), 1991.

———. *Society Must Be Defended: Lectures at the Collège de France, 1975–1976*. Edited by Mauro Bertani and Alessandro Fontana. Translated by David Macey. New York: Picador, 2003.

Fowler, Elizabeth. "The Failure of Moral Philosophy in the Work of Edmund Spenser." *Representations* 51 (1995): 47–76.

Fox, George A. *A Distinction between the Phanatick Spirit, and the Spirit of God*. London, 1660.

François, Anne-Lise. "'The feel of not to feel it,' or the Pleasures of Enduring Form." In *A Companion to Romantic Poetry*, edited by Charles Mahoney, 445–66. Oxford: Wiley-Blackwell, 2011.

Fuzier, Jean. "John Donne et la formalité de l'essence." In *John Donne*, edited by Jean-Marie Benoist. Évreux, Fr.: Hérissey, 1983: 39–49.

Geach, Peter. "The Religion of Thomas Hobbes." *Religious Studies* 17, no. 4 (1981): 549–58.

Glare, P. G. W., ed. *The Oxford Latin Dictionary*. Oxford: Oxford University Press, 1968.

Gless, Darryl. *Interpretation and Theology in Spenser*. Cambridge: Cambridge University Press, 1994.

Goldberg, Jonathan. *James I and the Politics of Literature: Jonson, Shakespeare, Donne, and their Contemporaries*. Baltimore: Johns Hopkins University Press, 1983.

Goldsmith, Steven. *Blake's Agitation: Criticism and the Emotions*. Baltimore: Johns Hopkins University Press, 2013.

Grazia, Margreta de, Maureen Quilligan, and Peter Stallybrass, eds. *Subject and Object in Renaissance Culture*. Cambridge: Cambridge University Press, 1999.

Green, Jay P., ed. *The Interlinear Hebrew-Greek-English Bible*. Peabody, Mass.: Hendrickson Publishers, 2005.

Greenblatt, Stephen. "Murdering Peasants: Status, Genre, and the Representation of Rebellion." *Representations* 1 (1983): 1–29.

———. *Renaissance Self-Fashioning: From More to Shakespeare*. Chicago: University of Chicago Press, 1980.

Gregory, Brad. *Salvation at Stake: Christian Martyrdom in Early Modern Europe*. Cambridge: Harvard University Press, 2001.

Gregory, Tobias. "The Political Messages of *Samson Agonistes*." *Studies in English Literature, 1500–1900* 50, no. 1 (Winter 2010): 175–203.

Gribben, Crawford. *The Puritan Millennium: Literature and Theology, 1550–1682*. Eugene, Ore.: Wipf and Stock, 2008.

Gritsch, Eric. *Thomas Müntzer: A Tragedy of Errors*. Minneapolis: Fortress, 1989.

Gross, Kenneth. *Spenserian Poetics: Idolatry, Iconoclasm, and Magic*. Ithaca, N.Y.: Cornell University Press, 1985.

Grotius, Hugo. *Defensio fidei catholicae de satisfactione Christi adversus Faustum Socinum*. Vol. 4 of *Opera omnia theologica in tres tomos divisa*, edited by Theodore Hillensberg, 293–348. Amsterdam: Blaeu, 1679.

Guha, Ranajit. *Elementary Aspects of Peasant Insurgency in Colonial India*. Delhi: Oxford University Press, 1983.

———. "The Prose of Counterinsurgency." In *Selected Subaltern Studies*, edited by Ranajit Guha and Gayatri Chakravorty Spivak, 45–86. New York: Oxford University Press, 1988.

Guha, Ranajit, and Gayatri Chakravorty Spivak, eds. *Selected Subaltern Studies*. New York: Oxford University Press, 1988.

Guillory, John. "The Father's House: *Samson Agonistes* in Its Historical Moment." In *Re-membering Milton: Essays on the Texts and Traditions*, edited by Mary Nyquist and Margaret W. Ferguson, 148–76. New York: Muthuen, 1987.

———. *Poetic Authority: Spenser, Milton, and Literary History*. New York: Columbia University Press, 1983.

Hale, John K. "Spenser's *Faerie Queene*, 1.11.52 and 53." *Explicator* 53, no. 1 (1994): 6–7.

Halpern, Richard. *Eclipse of Action: Tragedy and Political Economy*. Chicago: University of Chicago Press, 2017.

———. *The Poetics of Primitive Accumulation: English Renaissance Culture and the Genealogy of Capital*. Ithaca, N.Y.: Cornell University Press, 1991.

Hampton, Timothy. *Writing from History: The Rhetoric of Exemplarity in Renaissance Literature*. Ithaca, N.Y.: Cornell University Press, 1990.

Hanson, Elizabeth. *Discovering the Subject in Renaissance England*. Cambridge: Cambridge University Press, 1998.

Hardt, Michael, and Antonio Negri. *Multitude: War and Democracy in the Age of Empire*. New York: Penguin, 2004.

Harney, Stefano, and Fred Moten. *The Undercommons: Fugitive Planning and Black Study*. New York: Autonomedia, 2013.

Hartman, Geoffrey. "Milton's Counterplot." *ELH* 25, no. 1 (Mar. 1958): 1–12.

Harvey, Elizabeth D. "*Samson Agonistes* and Milton's Sensible Ethics." In *The Oxford Handbook of Milton*, edited by Nicholas McDowell and Nigel Smith, 649–66. Oxford: Oxford University Press, 2009.

Hegel, G. W. F. "Glauben und Wissen." In *Werke 2: Jenaer Schriften 1801–1807*, edited by Eva Moldenhauer and Karl Markus Michel, 287–433. Berlin: Suhrkamp, 1986.

Heller-Roazen, Daniel. "Speaking in Tongues." *Paragraph* 25, no. 2 (2002): 92–115.

Heyd, Michael. *"Be Sober and Reasonable": The Critique of Enthusiasm in the Seventeenth and Early Eighteenth Centuries*. Leiden, Neth.: Brill, 1995.

Hill, Christopher, ed. *Winstanley: "The Law of Freedom" and Other Writings*. Cambridge: Cambridge University Press, 1983.

———. *The World Turned Upside Down: Radical Ideas during the English Revolution*. New York: Penguin, 1984.

Hobbes, Thomas. *Behemoth; Or the Long Parliament*. Edited by Paul Seaward. Oxford: Clarendon Press, 2010.

———. *De cive: The English Version*. Edited by Howard Warrender. Oxford: Clarendon Press, 1983.

———. *De cive: The Latin Version*. Edited by Howard Warrender. Oxford: Clarendon Press, 1983.

———. *The Elements of Law, Natural and Politic*. Edited by Ferdinand Tönnies. London, 1889.

———. *The English Works of Thomas Hobbes of Malmesbury*. Edited by Sir William Molesworth. 11 vols. London, 1839–45.

———. *Leviathan*. Edited by Noel Malcolm. 3 vols. Oxford: Clarendon Press, 2012).

Hoekstra, Kinch. "Disarming the Prophets: Thomas Hobbes and Predictive Power." *Rivista di sotria della filosofia* 21, no. 1 (2004): 97–154.

Hollywood, Amy. *Acute Melancholia and Other Essays: Mysticism, History, and the Study of Religion*. New York: Columbia University Press, 2016.

———. *Sensible Ecstasy: Mysticism, Sexual Difference, and the Demands of History*. Chicago: University of Chicago Press, 2001.

Hoxby, Blair. *Mammon's Music: Literature and Economics in the Age of Milton*. New Haven, Conn.: Yale University Press, 2002.

Huntington, John. "Furious Insolence: The Social Meaning of Poetic Inspiration in the 1590s." *Modern Philology* 94, no. 3 (1997): 305–26.

James I, King of England. *King James VI and I: Political Writings*. Edited by Johann P. Sommerville. Cambridge: Cambridge University Press, 1995.

Jarvis, Simon. "For a Poetics of Verse." *PMLA* 125, no. 4 (Oct. 2010): 931–35.

———. "How to Do Things with Tunes." *ELH* 82, no. 2 (Summer 2015): 365–83.

Johnson, Barbara. "Muteness Envy." In *The Barbara Johnson Reader: The Surprise of Otherness*, edited by Melissa Feuerstein, Bill Johnson González, Lili Porten, and Keja L. Valens, 200–16. Durham, N.C.: Duke University Press, 2004.

*The Judgment and Decree of the University of Oxford*. Oxford, 1683.

Kahn, Victoria. *The Future of Illusion: Political Theology and Early Modern Texts*. Chicago: University of Chicago Press, 2014.

———. *Wayward Contracts: The Crisis of Political Obligation in England, 1640–1674*. Princeton: Princeton University Press, 2004.

Kane, Sean. *Spenser's Moral Allegory*. Toronto: University of Toronto Press, 1989.

Kaplan, Benjamin J. *Divided by Faith: Religious Conflict and the Practice of Toleration in Early Modern Europe*. Cambridge: Harvard University Press, 2010.

Kaske, Carol V. *Spenser's Biblical Poetics*. Ithaca, N.Y.: Cornell University Press, 2000.

Keller, Mary. *The Hammer and the Flute: Women, Power, and Spirit Possession*. Baltimore: Johns Hopkins University Press, 2005.

Kezar, Dennis. "Samson's Death by Theater and Milton's Art of Dying." *ELH* 66, no. 2 (1999): 295–336.

Kitzes, Adam H. "Paradoxical Donne: *Biathanatos* and the Problems of Political Assimilation." *Prose Studies* 24, no. 3 (2001): 1–17.

Kosman, Aryeh. "Acting: Drama as the Mimesis of Praxis." *Essays on Aristotle's Poetics*, edited by Amélie Oksenberg Rorty, 51–72. Princeton: Princeton University Press, 1992.

Kramnick, Jonathan, and Anahid Nersessian. "Form and Explanation." *Critical Inquiry* 43 (Spring 2017): 650–69.

Kuzner, James. "Donne's *Biathanatos* and the Public Sphere's Vexing Freedom." *ELH* 81 (2014): 61–81.

Lacoste, Jean Yves. *Encyclopedia of Christian Theology*. Vol. 1. New York: Routledge, 2001.

Lander, Jesse M. *Inventing Polemic: Religion, Print, and Literary Culture in Early Modern England*. Cambridge: Cambridge University Press, 2006.

Landreth, David. *The Face of Mammon: The Matter of Money in English Renaissance Literature*. Oxford: Oxford University Press, 2012.

Largier, Niklaus. "Mysticism, Modernity, and the Invention of Aesthetic Experience." *Representations* 105 (2009): 37–60.

Lear, Jonathan. "Katharsis." *Phronesis* 33, no. 3 (1988): 297–326.

Lemon, Rebecca. *Addiction and Devotion in Early Modern England*. Philadelphia: University of Pennsylvania Press, 2018.

————. *Treason by Words: Literature, Law and Rebellion in Shakespeare's England*. Ithaca, N.Y.: Cornell University Press, 2006.

Leo, Russ. "Milton's Aristotelian Experiments: Tragedy, *Lustratio*, and Secret Refreshings in *Samson Agonistes* (1671)." *Milton Studies* 52 (2011): 221–52.

Levine, Caroline. *Forms: Whole, Rhythm, Hierarchy, Network*. Princeton: Princeton University Press, 2015.

Levinson, Marjorie. "What Is New Formalism?" *PMLA* 122, no. 2 (Mar. 2007): 558–69.

Lewis, Charleton T., and Charles Short. *A Latin Dictionary*. Oxford: Clarendon Press, 1879.

Libera, Alain de. "L'Un ou la trinité? Sur un aspect trop connu de la théologie eckhartienne." *Revue des sciences religieuses* 70, no. 1 (1996): 31–47.

Lieb, Michael. "'Our Living Dread': The God of *Samson Agonistes*." *Milton Studies* 33 (1996): 3–25.

Linville, Susan E. "Enjambment and the Dialectics of Line Form in Donne's 'Holy Sonnets.'" *Style* 18, no. 1 (Winter 1984), 64–82.

Littleton, Adam. *Linguae Latinae Liber Dictionarius Quadripartitus. A Latin Dictionary in Four Parts. I. An English-Latine. II. A Latine-Classical. III. A Latine-Proper. IV. A Latine-Barbarous. Wherein the Latine and English are adjusted, with what care might be, both as to Stock of Words and Proprieties of Speech*. London, 1678.

Locke, John. *An Essay Concerning Human Understanding*. Oxford: Clarendon Press, 1975.

————. *A Letter Concerning Toleration*. Edited by James Tully. New York: Hackett, 1983.

Loewenstein, David. *Treacherous Faith: The Specter of Heresy in Early Modern English Literature and Culture*. Oxford: Oxford University Press, 2013.

Lowde, James. *A Discourse Concerning the Nature of Man, Both in his Natural and Political Capacity: Both as he is a Rational Creature and Member of a Civil Society. With an Examination of Some of Mr. Hobbs's Opinions relating hereunto*. London, 1694.

Lupton, Julia Reinhard. *Citizen-Saints: Shakespeare and Political Theology*. Chicago: University of Chicago Press, 2005.

Lupton, Julia Reinhard, and Graham Hammill, eds. *Political Theology and Early Modernity*. Chicago: University of Chicago Press, 2012.

Luther, Martin. *D. Martin Luthers Werke: Kritische Gesammtausgabe*. 73 vols. Edited by J. K. F. Knaake, et al. Weimar: H. Böhlau, 1883–2009.

————. *Luther's Works*. 54 vols. Edited by Jaroslav Pelican and Helmut T. Lehmann. St. Louis: Concordia, 1955–.

———. "On Secular Authority." In *Luther and Calvin on Secular Authority*, edited and translated by Harro Höpfl, 1–46. Cambridge: Cambridge University Press, 1991.

Lynch, Helen. *Milton and the Politics of Public Speech*. New York: Routledge, 2015.

Lyotard, Jean-François. *Le Différend*. Paris: Les Éditions de Minuit, 1983.

———. *The Differend: Phrases in Dispute*. Translated by Georges Van Den Abbeele. Manchester: Manchester University Press, 1988.

MacCaffrey, Isabel Gamble. *Spenser's Allegory: The Anatomy of Imagination*. Princeton: Princeton University Press, 1976.

MacDonald, Michael. *Mystical Bedlam: Madness, Anxiety, and Healing in Seventeenth-Century England*. Cambridge: Cambridge University Press, 1983.

Macpherson, C. B. *The Political Theory of Possessive Individualism: Hobbes to Locke*. Oxford: Clarendon, 1962.

Mack, Phyllis. *Visionary Women: Ecstatic Prophecy in Seventeenth-Century England*. Berkeley: University of California Press, 1992.

Mahmood, Saba. *The Politics of Piety: The Islamic Revival and the Feminist Subject*. Princeton: Princeton University Press, 2004.

Mainwaring, Henry. *The Seaman's Dictionary*. In *The Life and Works of Sir Henry Mainwaring*, edited by George Ernest Manwaring and William Gordon Perrin, vol. 2, 69–260. London: Naval Records Society, 1920–22.

Malcolm, Noel. "Hobbes, Ezra, and the Bible: The History of a Subversive Idea." In *Aspects of Hobbes*, 383–431. Oxford: Oxford University Press, 2002.

———. "Leviathan, the Pentateuch, and the Origins of Modern Biblical Criticism." In *Leviathan after 350 Years*, edited by Tom Sorell and Luc Foisneau, 241–64. Oxford: Clarendon Press, 2004.

Marno, David. *Death Be Not Proud: The Art of Holy Attention*. Chicago: University of Chicago Press, 2016.

Marshall, Cynthia. *The Shattering of the Self: Violence, Subjectivity, and Early Modern Texts*. Baltimore: Johns Hopkins University Press, 2002.

Martel, James. *Subverting the Leviathan: Reading Thomas Hobbes as a Radical Democrat*. New York: Columbia University Press, 2007.

Martial. *Epigrams*. Vol. 2, bks. 6–10. Loeb Classical Library. Cambridge: Harvard University Press, 1993.

Martin, Catherine Gimelli. "The Phoenix and the Crocodile: Milton's Natural Law Debate with Hobbes Retried in the Tragic Forum of *Samson Agonistes*." In *The English Civil Wars in the Literary Imagination*, edited by Claude J. Summers and Ted-Larry Pebworth, 242–70. Columbia: University of Missouri Press, 1999.

Martinich, A. P. *The Two Gods of Leviathan*. Cambridge: Cambridge University Press, 2003.

Martz, Louis. *The Poetry of Meditation: A Study in English Religious Literature of the Seventeenth Century*. New Haven, Conn.: Yale University Press, 1976.

Marx, Karl. *Zur Kritik der Hegelschen Rechtsphilosophie*. In *Marx-Engels-Werke*, vol. 1, by Karl Marx and Friedrich Engels, 378–91. Berlin: Dietz Verlag, 1976.

Mastnak, Tomaž. "Behemoth: Democraticals and Religious Fanatics." *Filozofski vestnik* 24, no. 2 (2003): 139–68.

Matheron, Alexandre. "Hobbes, la Trinité et les caprices de la représentation." In *Thomas Hobbes: Philosophie première, théorie de la science et politique*, edited by Yves Charles Zarka and Jean Bernhardt, 381–90. Paris: Presses universitaires de France, 1990.

McDermott, John. "Spenser's *Faerie Queene*, 1.11.52 and 53." *Explicator* 54, no. 4 (1996): 198–99.

Miernowski, Jan. "Can a Human Bomb Be Human? Humanist and Antihumanist Perspectives on War and Terrorism." In *Early Modern Humanism and Postmodern Antihumanism in Dialogue*, edited by Jan Miernowski, 139–71. London: Palgrave, 2016.

Migne, J.-P., ed., *Patrologiae cursus, completus, series Latina*. 221 vols. Paris: 1844–64.

Milton, John. *Complete Shorter Poems*, 2nd ed. Edited by John Carey. London: Longman, 1997.

———. *Paradise Lost*. Edited by Gordon Teskey. New York, Norton: 2004.

———. *Paradise Regain'd. A Poem in IV Books. To which is added Samson Agonistes*. London, 1671.

———. *The Works of John Milton*. Edited by Frank Allen Patterson. 18 vols. New York: Columbia University Press, 1931–38.

Mintz, Samuel L. *The Hunting of Leviathan: Seventeenth-Century Reactions to the Materialism and Moral Philosophy of Thomas Hobbes*. Cambridge: Cambridge University Press, 1962.

Mitchell, Timothy. "Nobody Listens to a Poor Man." In *Rule of Experts: Egypt, Techno-Politics, Modernity*, 153–78. Berkeley: University of California Press, 2002.

Mohamed, Feisal. "Confronting Religious Violence: Milton's *Samson Agonistes*." *PMLA* 120, no. 2 (2005): 327–40.

———. *Milton and the Post-Secular Present: Ethics, Politics, Terrorism*. Stanford: Stanford University Press, 2011.

Monta, Susannah Brietz. *Martyrdom and Literature in Early Modern England*. Cambridge: Cambridge University Press, 2005.

Montag, Warren. *Bodies, Masses, Power: Spinoza and His Contemporaries.* London: Verso, 1999.

———. "Commanding the Body: The Language of Subjection in *Ethics* III, P2S." In *Resistance and Power in Ethics.* Vol. 1 of *Spinoza's Authority*, edited by A. Kiarina Kordela and Dimitris Vardoulakis, 147–72. New York: Bloomsbury, 2017.

———. "A Parallelism of Consciousness and Property: Balibar's Reading of Locke." In *Balibar and the Citizen Subject*, edited by Warren Montag and Hanan Elsayed, 157–81. Edinburgh: Edinburgh University Press, 2017.

———. "Who's Afraid of the Multitude? Between the Individual and the State." *South Atlantic Quarterly* 104, no. 4 (Fall 2005): 655–73.

Morgan, Edmund S. *Visible Saints: The History of a Puritan Idea.* Ithaca, N.Y.: Cornell University Press, 1965.

Mueller, Martin. "Sixteenth-Century Italian Criticism and Milton's Theory of Catharsis." *Studies in English Literature, 1500–1900* 6, no. 1 (1966): 139–50.

Munro, Ian. *The Figure of the Crowd in Early Modern London: The City and Its Double.* New York: Palgrave Macmillan, 2005.

Müntzer, Thomas. *Schriften und Briefe: Kritische Gesamtausgabe.* Edited by Günther Franz. Gütersloh, Ger.: Gütersloh Verlaghaus Gerd Mohn, 1968.

Nancy, Jean-Luc. "Sharing Voices." In *Transforming the Hermeneutic Context: From Nietzsche to Nancy*, edited by Gayle L. Ormiston and Alan D. Schrift, 211–59. Albany: State University of New York Press, 1990.

Nelson, Eric. *The Hebrew Republic: Jewish Sources and the Transformation of European Political Thought.* Cambridge: Harvard University Press, 2011.

Norbrook, David. *Poetry and Politics in the English Renaissance.* Oxford: Oxford University Press, 2002.

Nuttall, Geoffrey F. *Visible Saints: The Congregational Way, 1640–1660.* Oxford: Blackwell, 1957.

Overhoff, Jürgen. *Hobbes's Theory of the Will: Ideological Reasons and Historical Circumstances.* Lanham, Md.: Rowman and Littlefield, 2000.

Owen, John. [*Pneumatologia*]: *A Discourse Concerning the Holy Spirit.* London, 1674.

Ozment, Steven. *The Age of Reform, 1250–1550: An Intellectual and Religious History of Late Medieval and Reformation Europe.* New Haven, Conn.: Yale University Press, 1980.

———. "Eckhart and Luther: German Mysticism and Protestantism." *Thomist* 42, no. 2 (1978): 259–80.

———. *Mysticism and Dissent: Religious Ideology and Social Protest in the Sixteenth Century.* New Haven, Conn.: Yale University Press, 1973.

———. "Mysticism, Nominalism, and Dissent." In *The Pursuit of Holiness in Late Medieval and Renaissance Religion*, edited by Charles Trinkaus with Heiko Oberman, 67–92. Leiden, Neth.: Brill, 1974.

Pacchi, Arrigo. "Hobbes and Biblical Philology in the Service of the State." *Topoi* 7, no. 3 (1988): 231–39.

Padelford, Frederick M. "Spenser's Arraignment of the Anabaptists." *Journal of English and Germanic Philology* 12, no. 3 (1913): 434–48.

Paganini, Gianni. "Hobbes's 'Mortal God' and Renaissance Hermeticism." *Hobbes Studies* 23 (2010): 7–28.

Patterson, Annabel. *Censorship and Interpretation: The Conditions of Writing and Reading in Early Modern England.* Madison: University of Wisconsin Press, 1991.

———. "The Egalitarian Giant: Representations of Justice in History/ Literature." *Journal of British Studies* 31, no. 2 (1992): 97–132.

Picciotto, Joanna. "The Public Person and the Play of Fact." *Representations* 105 (2009): 85–132.

Pitkin, Hanna. *The Concept of Representation.* Berkeley: University of California Press, 1972.

Plato. *Ion.* In *Plato: The Complete Works*, edited by John M. Cooper, 937–49. Indianapolis: Hackett, 1997.

Pocock, J. G. A. "Enthusiasm: The Antiself of Enlightenment." *Huntington Library Quarterly* 60, nos. 1/2 (1997): 7–28.

———. "Thomas Hobbes: Atheist or Enthusiast? His Place in a Restoration Debate." *History of Political Thought* 11, no. 4 (1990): 737–49.

———. "Time, History and Eschatology in the Thought of Thomas Hobbes." In *Politics, Language, and Time: Essays on Political Thought and History*, 148–200. New York: Atheneum, 1960.

Proclus. *Procli philosophi Platonici opera inedita.* Edited by Victor Cousin. 2nd ed. Paris, 1864.

Quigley, Brendan. "The Distant Hero of *Samson Agonistes*." *ELH* 72, no. 3 (2005): 529–51.

Quintilian. *Institutio Oratoria of Quintilian.* Edited by H. E. Butler. Bks. 7–9. Loeb Classical Library. Cambridge: Harvard University Press, 1976.

Rambuss, Richard. *Closet Devotions.* Durham, N.C.: Duke University Press, 1998.

Reed, Anthony. *Freedom Time: The Poetics and Politics of Black Experimental Writing.* Baltimore: Johns Hopkins University Press, 2016.

Reiss, Timothy. *Mirages of the Selfe: Patterns of Personhood in Ancient and Early Modern Europe.* Stanford: Stanford University Press, 2002.

Rivett, Sarah. *The Science of the Soul in Colonial New England.* Chapel Hill: University of North Carolina Press, 2011.

Rogers, John. "The Secret of *Samson Agonistes.*" *Milton Studies* 33 (1996): 111–32.

Rose, Gillian. *The Broken Middle: Out of Our Ancient Society.* Oxford: Blackwell, 1992.

Rosenberg, Jordana. *Critical Enthusiasm: Capital Accumulation and the Transformation of Religious Passion.* Oxford: Oxford University Press, 2011.

Rosenblatt, Jason P. *Renaissance England's Chief Rabbi: John Selden.* Oxford: Oxford University Press, 2006.

Rosenfeld, Colleen Ruth. "The Artificial Life of Rhyme." *ELH* 83, no. 1 (Spring 2016): 71–99.

———. *Indecorous Thinking: Figures of Speech in Early Modern Poetics.* New York: Fordham University Press, 2018.

Rushdy, Ashraf H. *The Empty Garden: The Subject of Late Milton.* Pittsburgh: University of Pittsburgh Press, 1992.

Ryan, Alan. "Hobbes, Toleration, and the Inner Life." In *The Nature of Political Theory*, edited by David Miller and Larry Siedentop. Oxford: Clarendon Press, 1983.

Schmitt, Carl. *The Leviathan in the State Theory of Thomas Hobbes: Meaning and Failure of a Political Symbol.* Translated by George Schwab and Erna Hilfstein. Chicago: University of Chicago Press, 2008.

———. *The* Nomos *of the Earth in the International Law of the* Jus Publicum Europaeum. Translated by G. L. Ulman. New York: Telos, 2003.

Schoenberger, Cynthia Grant. "Luther and the Justifiability of Resistance to Legitimate Authority." *Journal of the History of Ideas* 40, no. 1 (1979): 3–20.

Scodel, Joshua. "Edenic Freedoms." *Milton Studies* 56 (2015): 153–200.

Sellin, Paul. "Sources of Milton's Catharsis: A Reconsideration." *Journal of English and Germanic Philology* 60, no. 4 (1961): 712–30.

Sells, Michael. *Mystical Languages of Unsaying.* Chicago: Chicago University Press, 1994.

Shagan, Ethan H. *The Rule of Moderation: Violence, Religion, and the Politics of Restraint in Early Modern England.* Cambridge: Cambridge University Press, 2011.

Sheehan, Jonathan. "Sacrifice before the Secular." *Representations* 105 (Winter 2009): 12–36.

Shelley, Percy Bysshe. "A Defence of Poetry." In *Shelley's Poetry and Prose*, edited by Donald H. Reiman and Sharon B. Powers, 510–35. New York: Norton, 1977.

Shuger, Debora. *Habits of Thought in the English Renaissance: Religion, Politics and the Dominant Culture.* Toronto: University of Toronto Press, 1997.

———. *The Renaissance Bible: Scholarship, Sacrifice, and Subjectivity.* Berkeley: University of California Press, 1994.

Simpson, James. *Burning to Read: English Fundamentalism and Its Reformation Opponents.* Cambridge: Belknap, 2010.

Skelton, John. "A Replication against Certain Young Scholars Abjured of Late." In *The Complete English Poems*, edited by John Scattergood, 328–40. Liverpool: Liverpool University Press, 2015.

Skinner, Quentin. *Hobbes and Republican Liberty.* Cambridge: Cambridge University Press, 2008.

———. "Hobbes on Representation." *European Journal of Philosophy* 13, no. 2 (2005): 155–84.

Smith, D. Vance. *The Book of the Incipit: Beginnings in the Fourteenth Century.* Minneapolis: University of Minnesota Press, 2001.

Smith, Nigel. *Perfection Proclaimed: Language and Literature in English Radical Religion, 1640–1660.* Oxford: Oxford University Press, 1989.

———. "What's Inside? Donne, Interiority, and Independency." In *John Donne and Modernity*, edited by Robert Ellrodt. Nanterre, Fr.: Université Paris–X, 1995.

Spanheim, Friedrich. *Disputationum Anti-Anabaptisticarum Decima Sexta . . . De Enthusiasmo.* Leiden, Neth., 1646.

———. *Englands VVarning by Germanies Woe.* London, 1646.

Spenser, Edmund. *The Faerie Queene.* Edited by A. C. Hamilton, with Hiroshi Yamashita, Toshiyuki Suzuki, and Shohachi Fukuda. 2nd ed. London: Longman, 2007.

———. *The Faerie Qveene.* London, 1590.

———. "Letter to Raleigh." In Spenser, *Faerie Queene*, 714–18.

———. *A View of the Present State of Ireland.* Oxford: Clarendon, 1970.

———. *The Yale Edition of the Shorter Poems of Edmund Spenser.* Edited by William A. Oram, Einar Bjorvand, Ronald Bond, Thomas H. Cain, Alexander Dunlop, and Richard Schell. New Haven, Conn.: Yale University Press, 1989.

Sreedhar, Susanne. *Hobbes on Resistance: Defying the Leviathan.* Cambridge: Cambridge University Press, 2010.

Stampfer, Judah. *John Donne and the Metaphysical Gesture.* New York: Funk and Wagnalls, 1970.

Stayer, James. *The German Peasants' War and Anabaptist Community of Goods.* Quebec: McGill-Queen's University Press, 1994.

Steck, Karl Gerhard. *Luther und die Schwärmer.* Zurich: Evangelischer Verlag, 1955.

Steinman, Lisa. *Invitation to Poetry: The Pleasures of Studying Poetry and Poetics.* Oxford: Blackwell, 2008.

Stephanus, H. [Henri Estienne]. *Thesaurus Graecae linguae*, rev. ed. 10 vols. London, 1816–1828.

Strauss, Leo. *Hobbes's Critique of Religion and Related Writings.* Translated by
    Gabriel Bartlett and Svetoza Minkov. Chicago: University of Chicago
    Press, 2011.
———. *Leo Strauss: Gesammelte Schriften.* Edited by Heinrich Meier. Vol. 3.
    2nd rev. ed. Stuttgart: J. B. Metzler, 2008.
———. *The Political Philosophy of Hobbes: Its Basis and Its Genes.* Translated by
    Elsa M. Sinclair. Chicago: University of Chicago Press, 1952.
Strier, Richard. "How Formalism Became a Dirty Word, and Why We
    Can't Do without It." In *Renaissance Literature and Its Formal Engagements,*
    edited by Mark David Rasmussen, 207–15. New York: Palgrave, 2002.
———. *Resistant Structures: Particularity, Radicalism, and Renaissance Texts.*
    Berkeley: University of California Press, 1995.
Summit, Jennifer. "Monuments and Ruins: Spenser and the Problem of the
    English Library." *ELH* 70, no. 1 (Spring 2003): 1–34.
Targoff, Ramie. *John Donne, Body and Soul.* Chicago: Chicago University
    Press, 2008.
Taubes, Jacob. *Occidental Eschatology.* Translated by David Ratmoko. Stan-
    ford: Stanford University Press, 2009.
Teskey, Gordon. *Allegory and Violence.* Ithaca, N.Y.: Cornell University
    Press, 1996.
———. "The Ethics of Inspiration." In *Reading Renaissance Ethics,* edited by
    Marshall Grossman, 193–205. New York: Routledge, 2007.
Thiel, Udo. *The Early Modern Subject: Self-Consciousness and Personal Identity
    from Descartes to Hume.* Oxford: Oxford University Press, 2011.
Tilly, Charles. "Terror, Terrorism, Terrorists." *Sociological Theory* 22, no. 1
    (May 2014): 5–13.
Tilmouth, Christopher. *Passion's Triumph over Reason: A History of the Moral
    Imagination from Spenser to Rochester.* Oxford: Oxford University Press,
    2007.
Torgzon, Vern. "Spenser's Orgoglio and Despaire." *Texas Studies in Litera-
    ture and Language* 3, no. 1 (1961): 123–28.
Toscano, Alberto. *Fanaticism: On the Uses of an Idea.* New York: Verso, 2010.
Tuck, Richard. "The 'Christian Atheism' of Thomas Hobbes." In *Atheism
    from the Reformation to the Enlightenment,* edited by Michael Cyril
    William Hunter and David Wootton, 111–30. Oxford: Oxford University
    Press, 1992.
———. "Hobbes and Democracy." In *Rethinking the Foundations of Modern
    Political Thought,* 171–90. Cambridge: Cambridge University Press, 2007.
———. "Hobbes and Locke on Toleration." In *Thomas Hobbes and Political
    Theory,* edited by Mary Dietz, 153–71. Lawrence: University Press of
    Kansas, 1990.

Turner, Henry. "Lessons from Literature for the Historian of Science (and Vice Versa): Reflections on 'Form.'" *Isis* 101 (2010): 578–89.

Valbuena, Olga. "Casuistry, Martyrdom, and the Allegiance Controversy in Donne's 'Pseudo-Martyr.'" *Religion & Literature* 32, no. 2 (Summer 2000): 49–80.

Vieira, Mónica Brito. *The Elements of Representation in Hobbes: Aesthetics, Theatre, Law and Theology in the Construction of Hobbes's Theory of the State.* Leiden, Neth.: Brill, 2009.

Virgil. *Aeneid.* Bks. 7–12, *Appendix Vergiliana.* Edited by G. P. Goold. Translated by H. R. Fairclough. Loeb Classical Library. Cambridge: Harvard University Press, 2001.

Walker, D. P. "The Cessation of Miracles." In *Hermeticism and the Renaissance: Intellectual History and the Occult in Early Modern Europe*, edited by Ingrid Merkel and Allen G. Debus. Washington, D.C.: Folger Shakespeare Library, 1988.

Walzer, Michael. *The Revolution of the Saints: A Study in the Origins of Radical Politics.* Cambridge: Harvard University Press, 1982.

Warren, Christopher. "When Self-Preservation Bids: Approaching Milton, Hobbes and Dissent." *English Literary Renaissance* 37 (2007): 118–50.

Watt, David Harrington. *Antifundamentalism in Modern America.* Ithaca, N.Y.: Cornell University Press, 2017.

Watt, Diane. *Secretaries of God: Women Prophets in Late Medieval and Early Modern England.* Suffolk, Eng.: D. S. Brewer, 1997.

Weber, Max. "Politik als Beruf." In *Gesammelte politische Schriften*, 396–450. Munich: Drei Masken, 1921.

Wegner, Daniel. *The Illusion of Conscious Will.* Cambridge: MIT Press, 2002.

Weil, Simone. *Œuvres completes.* Bk. 6, vol. 2, *Cahiers* (September 1941–February 1942). Paris: Gallimard, 1997.

———. *La Pesanteur et la grâce.* Paris: Plon, 1948.

Weizman, Eyal. *Hollow Land: Israel's Architecture of Occupation.* New York: Verso, 2007.

Wells, Marion. *The Secret Wound: Love-Melancholy and Early Modern Romance.* Stanford: Stanford University Press, 2007.

Wind, Edgar. *Pagan Mysteries in the Renaissance.* New Haven, Conn.: Yale University Press, 1958.

Winstanley, Gerrard. "A New Year's Gift for the Parliament and Army." In Hill, *Winstanley*, 159–210.

———. "The True Levellers Standard Advanced: or, The State of Community Opened, and Presented to the Sons of Men." In Hill, *Winstanley*, 75–96.

Wittreich, Joseph. *Interpreting* Samson Agonistes. Princeton: Princeton
     University Press, 1986.
Wofford, Susanne Lindgren. *The Choice of Achilles: The Ideology of Figure in
     the Epic.* Stanford: Stanford University Press, 1992.
Wolfson, Susan. "Reading for Form." *MLQ* 61 (2000): 1–17.
Woodhouse, A. S. P. "Nature and Grace in *The Faerie Queene.*" *ELH* 16,
     no. 3 (1949): 194–228.
Wright, Nancy E. "The *Figura* of the Martyr in John Donne's Sermons."
     *ELH* 56, no. 2 (1989): 293–309.
Young, Bruce W. "Thomas Hobbes versus the Poets: Form, Expression, and
     Metaphor in Early Seventeenth-Century Poetry." *Encyclia* 63: 151–62.
Zarka, Yves Charles. "*L'Annihilatio Mundi.*" In *La décision metaphysique de
     Hobbes: Conditions de la politique,* 36–58. Paris: Libraire Philosophique J.
     Vrin, 1987.
———. "The Political Subject." In *Leviathan after 350 Years,* edited by
     Tom Sorell and Luc Foisneau, 167–82. Oxford: Clarendon, 2004.

**Ross Lerner** is Assistant Professor of English at Occidental College.

CPSIA information can be obtained
at www.ICGtesting.com
Printed in the USA
LVHW090245040519
616662LV00001B/126/P